The Parks, Gardens, Etc., of London and Its Suburbs, Described and Illustrated, for the Guidance of Strangers

403.

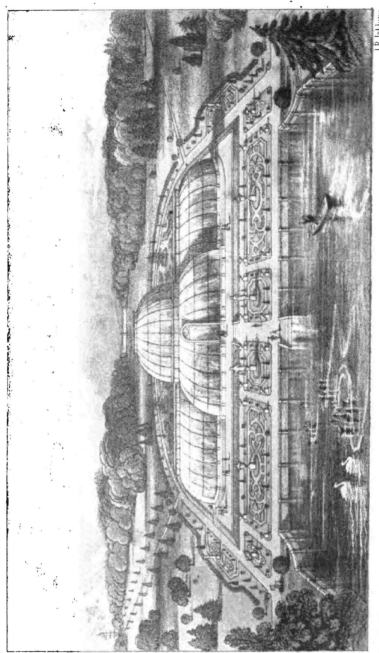

THE

PARKS, GARDENS,

ETC.,

OF

LONDON AND ITS SUBURBS

𝔇𝔢𝔰𝔠𝔯𝔦𝔟𝔢𝔡 𝔞𝔫𝔡 𝔌𝔩𝔩𝔲𝔰𝔱𝔯𝔞𝔱𝔢𝔡,

FOR

THE GUIDANCE OF STRANGERS.

BY

EDWARD KEMP,

LANDSCAPE GARDENER, BIRKENHEAD PARK.

LONDON:
JOHN WEALE, 59, HIGH HOLBORN.

MDCCCLI.

LONDON:

GEORGE WOODFALL AND SON,

ANGEL COURT, SKINNER STREET.

ADVERTISEMENT.

In the autumn of last year the writer of the following sketches was called upon to contribute some account of London Gardening for insertion in a general Guide Book to the Metropolis*. Finding, however, that the subject was too large to be satisfactorily dealt with in the narrow compass necessarily devoted to it in that volume, it was determined that the present fuller and more detailed description should be prepared, and issued separately; the Editor of the larger work condensing into its pages a portion of the materials comprised in this.

No other book of the kind here attempted being yet in existence, it has been thought that the numerous admirers of gardening who visit the metropolis would be glad to possess a manual like the present, which professes to indicate what is most worth seeing around London in the way of landscape features, horticulture, and the various useful and ornamental structures which fall within the province of the garden architect. The whole of the information now conveyed is drawn either from actual observation, or from the most authentic sources. And the author wishes gratefully to acknowledge the liberality with which he has, in every case, been permitted to inspect the gardens described. The necessity for preventing a book of this sort from becoming too voluminous has alone deterred him from noticing many other places with which he is familiar, and from giving a wider range to his researches.

Whatever may be the omissions of the book, and the brevity with which some of the places are referred to, it is hoped that it will present a tolerably correct and comprehensive view of the gardening of the present day, in all its more remarkable characteristics. To do full justice to such a theme would of course demand a work almost equal in bulk to a modern cyclopædia.

BIRKENHEAD PARK,
  March 15, 1851.

* *London and its Vicinity exhibited in* 1851 :—WEALE, High Holborn.

CONTENTS.

GARDENS,

CONSERVATORIES, AND PARKS,

OF

LONDON AND ITS VICINITY.

IT is an observation so common as almost to have become trite, that whatever distinctive peculiarities may be found in any of the different provincial towns of England, something exceedingly like them will be discovered in one unnoticed corner or other of the vast metropolis. There are, it is assumed, types or examples in some part of London of everything that is thought to have only a local character in a great number of country towns. But whatever amount of truth there may be in this opinion, the state of gardening around the metropolis is usually and perhaps justly regarded as embodying all that is known of excellence throughout the country, and as affording a fair criterion by which the progress of horticulture may be judged. And though there will doubtless be places, in rural districts, where local advantages, or superior means, or unusual skill, may carry some particular branch of gardening to a higher point than is commonly attained around London, yet, in general, gardening practice, within a radius of twenty miles all round St. Paul's, will be in advance, or at least comprehend all the excellence, of what is done throughout the rest of the country.

A description of metropolitan gardening, or a tour of observation through the London gardens, ought, therefore, if these premises be correct, to include specimens of whatever is really meritorious all over England. Possibly, however, the rule will hold good more extensively in reference to practical matters than as regards questions of taste; difference of climate and other local features often developing peculiar local beauties.

In describing what is worth seeing by the man of taste or the practical gardener who visits London, there may, perhaps, be many places inadvertently omitted; while, from the impossibility of including every garden that happens to deserve notice, such only are selected as have acquired a general reputation, or which are tolerably well known. The whole of the places described were visited in the autumn of 1850, and many of them have long been familiar. Our endeavour, then, will be to present the distinctive features of each place to the reader, and rather to point out what we conceive to be merits, or worthy of examination, than to take a critical survey; although we may occasionally

B

having some rather extensive open tracts of country and gentlemen's seats in its neighbourhood. From various parts of these hills, the views of London are extremely good; and the prospects into Hertfordshire, towards Barnet, as well as more westward, are exceedingly rich and varied. Farther from London, and a little more to the west, the comparatively isolated hill of Harrow, with its broad mass of trees, and the beautiful church spire before alluded to, makes a fine picture from a multitude of points on the south and west sides of the town. And one of the greatest beauties belonging to the hills thus spoken of is, that, being on the north-west side of London, they are often thrown out in strong and striking relief against a clear sky towards sunset, and for some time after.

Between Hampstead and Kensal Green there are other inferior hills, which occasionally rise into swells, and are continued towards the west, presenting broad masses of trees and glades of grass, with admirable sites for villas. Farther westward, on the Surrey side of the Thames, Richmond Hill, and the high ground on which the Park is situated, stands up conspicuously, with its ample crown of trees; and this range extends back to Roehampton, and Putney Heath, and Wandsworth; affording numberless positions for villas, and being splendidly furnished with woods. There are probably some of the finest villas round London in this direction. Wimbledon Hill, which is almost on a level with Putney Heath, is yet in part detached by the low ground in Wimbledon Park, and, from a great many points around the parks of Mrs. Marryatt, Mr. Peach, and that formerly belonging to Earl Spencer, displays the most charming diversity of lawn and trees. By a road which nearly takes the circuit of this hill, the whole country, for an immense distance around, is spread before the eye in extraordinary beauty. The hills of Streatham and Norwood (the latter of which was once covered with forest, of which some of the remains yet exist on the east side) possess great interest and variety; and from one of the Norwood hills, near Beulah, a large part of Kent expands to view, with all the country which the Surrey hills inclose on the south, and which Windsor Hill terminates on the west. Some of the Norwood hills are 389 feet above the level of the sea. From the neighbourhood between Streatham and Norwood, several of the noblest views of London are obtained, and we think this is decidedly the best side from which to get an agreeable distant picture of the metropolis. The hill of Greenwich Park, and Shooter's Hill beyond, bring the range again to the margin of the river.

At a greater distance, Addington Hills, near Croydon, with Banstead and Epsom Downs, from being comparatively bare and covered with heather, add a new feature to the scenery. Banstead Downs are 576 feet above the sea. Still further off, the Surrey hills are thrown up, like wave behind wave, in endless undulation and change. The highest of them (and the highest of any in this part of the country) is Leith Hill, a few miles below Dorking. This attains the unusual height of 993 feet above the sea, and from its summit, but from no other eminence in England, it is alleged that the sea and St. Paul's Cathedral are both distinctly visible in favourable weather. Box Hill, famed alike for its picturesque beauty, for the prospects which can be had from it, and for the extensive thickets of box by which it is crowned, is another eminence, between Dorking and Epsom, too striking and romantic to be passed over in silence. Even if the neighbourhood were not rich in gentlemen's seats, which the traveller in search of gardening beauties should by all means see, we should certainly recommend a journey to Box Hill, on account of the great beauty of the district, and because this is the only place in which natural thickets of box—almost deserving the title of a small forest—are to be found. Gilpin, with that eye for the picturesque which has rendered his works so much esteemed, in speaking of the box in this neighbourhood, says,—"Box has a mellower, a more varied, and a more accommodating tint than any evergreen. One other circumstance of advantage attends it. Almost every species of shrub in a few years outgrows its beauty. If the knife be not freely and frequently used, it becomes bare at the bottom, its branches dispart, and it rambles into a form too diffuse for its station. But box-wood long preserves its shape ; and in the wild state in which we found it here, is far from regular ; though its branches, which are never large, are close and compact." Entering some of the paths by which these coppices of box are intersected, the visitor will be astonished to find himself in an impenetrable thicket of box, with the stems growing athwart each other in all directions, and the branches interwoven above into a canopy of "thickest shade." But the best impression of the beauty of these box thickets will be gained by skirting the summit of the hill, a short distance from the outside trees. The face of Box Hill, with its mixture of shivering chalky surface and swells of verdure, is very beautiful ; and from the top, the valley of the Mole, the winding vale towards Dorking, and the more expansive plain on the south-east, with a great variety of pleasing eminences, are seen in many different aspects, and all good ones. The alders, by which the brink of the Mole is adorned, will be perceived to be the best possible adjuncts of so quiet and sluggish a stream.

It seems abundantly evident that the box-woods here are really natural, and of spontaneous growth ; for Gilpin observes in regard to a common tradition of the district that these woods were planted by an Earl of Arundel, that "it is certainly fabulous; for there are court rolls still existing which mention *the box-wood on the hill,* before any such artificial plantation could have taken place." Writing in 1798, he adds that, "insignificant as this shrub appears, it has been to its owner, Sir Henry Mildmay, a source of considerable profit. It is used chiefly in turning [and extensively for woodcut engraving]. But the ships from the Levant brought such quantities of it in ballast, that the wood on the hill could not find a purchaser, and, not having been cut in sixty-five years, was growing in many parts cankered. But the war having diminished the influx of it from the Mediterranean, several purchasers began to offer ; and in the year 1795, Sir Henry put it up to auction ; and sold it for the enormous sum of 12,000*l.* Box attains its full growth in about fifty years ; in which time, if the soil be good, it will rise fifteen feet, and form a stem of the thickness of a man's thigh."

We have just glanced at all these matters, because the hills are such important objects in the scenery of the suburbs, and, from the softness of their outline, the luxuriance of their woody clothing, the pleasing intermixture of villas on their slopes, and the boundless variety of prospect which they afford from their sides or their summits, rank among the greatest and most delightful ornaments of the district. Those who would study the landscape that comes within the province of the garden artist, especially in its broader scenes, will find an untiring fund of interest in the hills around London, whether regarded as objects themselves, or simply as points of observation. They must, of course, lay their account with finding some deformities; but they will also, if diligent, and possessed of the true feeling of art, be rewarded with the discovery of an infinite number of interesting combinations.

As regards minor features in the landscape, one of the most prominent is the common English Elm, which is more abundant for twenty miles round London, and attains greater perfection than in any other part of Britain. It is, in fact, the favourite tree of the London suburbs, and is always a good object, whether in avenues, or plantations, or in groups, or as single specimens in a park. Even in hedgerows, when not pruned up too much to a bare stem, it gives an excellent relief to a flat country, and enters into beautiful combinations there when a great breadth of such land is viewed from an eminence. It has, however, the reputation of being a gross feeder, and of spreading its roots far and wide in every direction, to the great injury of shrubs or of crops. It also throws up innumerable small suckers from the roots; and appears to be very liable to disease and the attacks of insects when growing in footpaths by the sides of roads, where there is not room or soil for its roots to extend into. Still, it has the high merit of retaining its deep verdure better than almost any other tree in dry seasons; and when most common trees had their foliage shrivelled or even stripped off, near London, in the early part of September, 1850, the elm remained, for the most part, entirely unaffected. It likewise retains its foliage a long time in the autumn, and, when it gets old, becomes exceedingly picturesque in October, by having the whole of the leaves, on here and there one of its branches, changed to pure yellow, while the rest continue green. For gardens or shrubberies, then, or for hedgerows, the abundance of its roots, and the manner in which it impoverishes the soil, render it in some measure unsuitable; but as a park tree, whether in avenues, or groups, or standing singly, it is admirable. Good specimens of it may be met with almost anywhere; but there are some particularly fine ones in Hampton Court Park, and one, which is as magnificent a tree as can be seen, is situated on the common between Tooting and Streatham, near Streatham Park. The circumference of this noble tree, at the base, is little short of thirty-four feet, and twenty-nine feet at a yard from the ground; and though the trunk is becoming hollow, the head is yet ample and flourishing. At twelve or fifteen feet high it is fully as large as at the base, and then divides into four large branches, which tower up into a splendid head. It has evidently, we think, at some period had the leading shoot or stem cut off.

Cedars of Lebanon, of great age and size, constitute a peculiar and very observable feature in the landscape of the suburbs, and are unusually numerous on the west and south-west sides. As the adjuncts of stately mansions or elegant villas, along the valley of the Thames, they are remarkably telling; and the traveller can scarcely pass a hundred yards down portions of the western roads, without coming upon fresh specimens or groups of them. It is scarcely necessary to add that they communicate a very marked and aristocratic character to the district. And they are as beautiful in a young state as they are venerable and majestic when old. They are here met with in avenues, and standing opposite each other near a house, or on a lawn, or as single trees, or parts of a mixed plantation. But very rarely are they found grouped together in masses of three, four, or more on lawns or in parks. Those at Holland House are a distinguished exception, but they are unfortunately now so shattered as to have lost their principal beauty. No tree, perhaps, if we may judge from the imperfect examples we have

seen, and the more·satisfactory representations of those still existing on
Lebanon, is better adapted to unite into a splendid group for a lawn, or
for the slope of a park, or especially for a swell or knoll in either a
park or garden, where they would be sufficiently sheltered. As trees for
detached grouping, with their own species alone, both this and the
Deodar have, we are convinced, yet to develop a new and most uncommon character in the southern counties of England.

Lombardy Poplars, again, are very freely (not often very judiciously)
introduced into the scenery around London ; and, from their towering
nature, show themselves most distinctly in every direction. They are
common, too, in many parts, in long rows ; sometimes placed in the hedges.
And in this way they generally form the greatest possible eyesores.
It is but seldom that this tree will bear to stand alone, or even in groups
of its own species, without support from other trees ; and still .more
rarely will it look well when planted in lines. Along the sides of a
straight flat road or on an embankment, where plantations are employed
to shut either of these in, the Lombardy poplar, at pretty regular intervals, may show itself favourably as viewed from the *road itself*. But
whenever such a line comes to be seen laterally, the poplar must be
much more irregularly placed, and thrown more into groups, to become
anything but a blemish. From the thin spiry habit of this tree, it
almost invariably demands the help of more spreading and round-headed
species to give it its legitimate effect. And when it is seen rising from
near the centre (not exactly from the middle) of a mass of oaks, elms, or
other similar kinds, or from a mixed group in which a few tall evergreens exist, it becomes a superlatively fine object. It seems to have
suffered greatly from the drought of last summer ; and, though a fast-
growing, appears by no means a very long-lived tree. We have seen a
group of three of these poplars, planted about ten feet apart, and of a
large size, which produced a cone of rather a handsome form. An
extensive weeding out of the Lombardy poplars round London is
much demanded. Those which were left would then have tenfold more
effect.

Beeches do not appear at home anywhere along the flat grounds near
the Thames ; but at Burnham, a little below Slough, there are some
celebrated ones, growing on a thin, light, gravelly soil, and Windsor Park
contains some superb specimens. In the neighbourhood of Sevenoaks,
Kent, also, the beeches at Knowle Park are of the finest order, while those
in the Marquess of Camden's park, adjoining, are superlatively beautiful,
being planted on the slope of a hill, and spreading down their branches
on the grass in the most graceful and natural fringe imaginable. On
the top of a hill not far from this, but nearer London, are the famous
Knockholt Beeches, which, standing alone in a large tuft, make a conspicuous landmark which can be seen for thirty miles around.

Of Spanish Chestnuts, we shall have some prodigious specimens to
notice on a property of the Duke of Devonshire, near Chiswick. In
Kensington Gardens, Greenwich Park, and other places, there are some
very fine ones, which we shall also describe. It is a first-rate park tree
for the low sheltered tract by the sides of the Thames ; and is hardly
enough esteemed. The extraordinary avenue of horse-chestnuts in
Bushy Park will be referred to in the proper place.

The Occidental Plane is evidently one of the best and most serviceable
of London trees, as may be seen in the various parks and square gardens.
The fine healthy tree, likewise, near the corner of Wood Street, Cheap-

side, which is ordinarily described as an elm, is of this kind, and usually has a crow's nest in it every year.

A little below Croydon and Epsom, where the Surrey hills commence, and a chalky substratum begins to appear, the common Juniper grows spontaneously, and is thickly scattered over the parks or through the woods, producing much novelty of character, and with the yews, which are also found wherever there is a chalky soil, contrasting finely in winter, when straggling along the margins of chalk pits, with the glaring whiteness of the chalk itself. In the same district, and also on the Hertfordshire side of the town, the hedgerows are often most picturesquely mantled with the common Clematis (*C. vitalba*), which, scrambling wildly about, exhibits, when laden with its pretty white flowers, or still whiter bearded fruit, a great deal of beauty, and forms itself into the most elegant garlands.

Weeping Willows, especially in the Surrey suburbs, are much used in some of the smaller villa gardens; and though more commonly reserved for the margins of water in larger places, or for overshadowing tombs in cemeteries (for both which latter purposes they are, perhaps, *most* characteristic and suitable), they yet look very well when planted to overshadow a gateway to a small garden, or to overhang the corner pillar of a wall or fence, or, indeed, to jut out at the point of a shrubbery plantation. And their leaves appear so early, and continue throughout of such a tender green, that they produce considerable variety, and have always a clean and lively appearance in the smoky atmosphere of town suburbs. For much the same reasons, the *Rhus typhinus* and *coriaria*, which are extensively planted along the western roads, and the *Ailanthus glandulosus*, Hickory, and common *Robinia*, all which are common around London, are most valuable in securing variety by their pale-green and large pinnated foliage; while the leaves of the two first-mentioned likewise fade away to rich reddish purple and yellow in the autumn.

Those who visit the neighbourhood of London in the autumn, will be much pleased by the appearance of the Virginian creeper, which abounds on houses, cottages, walls, gateways, &c. The mixture of red and yellow and a purplish tint in its foliage at that season imparts a great richness to its appearance. It is most cultivated on the western side of the town.

As a trifling feature, but one that is by no means insignificant, we may allude to the extraordinary commonness of the Tom Thumb Pelargonium in the gardens of the suburbs last season. There was scarcely a cottage or villa garden in which flowers were at all cultivated, or a tavern garden, or one of the highest pretensions, in which this most showy flower was not visible, either in beds, or borders, or pots, or vases. The gaiety it occasioned was most remarkable; and, supported as it was in a number of the smallest gardens, with such (till very lately) uncommon summer plants as Verbenas of different colours, Fuchsias, and even Calceolarias and Petunias, it supplied a startling and delightful evidence of the rapidity with which a taste for such comparative luxuries is spreading itself downwards to the great industrial classes.

One of the very best kinds of park or large garden fences, which are wanted to be close and to harmonize well with trees, is in general use around London, at a little distance from it, and is composed of split oak. It is made from five to six feet high, and has a framework of oak posts, placed about nine feet apart, with three somewhat triangular rails between them to support the paling, and sometimes a strong oak plank, nine inches wide, or a brick wall nine inches or a foot high, placed at the bottom, between the posts, to keep the paling off the ground. The individual pales are about four or five inches wide, and a quarter of an inch thick at one edge, being feathered off to nothing at the other. They are put up with the thick edge to overlap the thin one; and are sometimes plain at the top, but look better when placed so as to produce a battlemented form. It is most usual to have two higher pales and then three lower ones, which has a better appearance than keeping two higher and two lower ones uniformly throughout. Occasionally, these higher pales and the posts stand up a few inches more than usual, and are surmounted by a thin flat rail, which may or may not be covered with spikes. Where a rural appearance, and security against the public gaze or trespass, are desired, nothing can be more suitable than such a fence, which, from not requiring paint, soon acquires the greenish or grayish tint of mosses and age, and harmonizes perfectly with sylvan or general country scenery.

Having thus hurriedly glanced at the chief landscape peculiarities of the metropolitan suburbs, we shall proceed to give some account, in due order, of the public parks, public gardens, and the principal private gardens, nurseries, florists' gardens, and forcing gardens of the neighbourhood, embodying in this a summary view of the actual condition of London gardening in the present day.

PUBLIC PARKS.—London, like most other large and populous towns, has gradually spread itself so completely over the open spaces which formerly surrounded it, that it is now, as respects the number of its inhabitants, by no means liberally supplied with breathing places, or the means of open-air recreation. And this encroachment on its suburbs has been effected with such comparative slowness, and so silently, that it is only by the occurrence of modern epidemics, producing that attention to sanitary matters which forms such a prominent feature of the present age, that the necessity for good public parks has been duly recognised, and the insufficiency of those already existing properly felt. Attention having, however, been awakened to the matter, the evil has already been in part remedied, and further provision for meeting the public wants is in process of being made. There are also many open commons in the vicinity of the metropolis, which, as we shall afterwards show, answer all the purposes of parks.

St. James's Park, being one of the oldest, and nearest to London, we shall first describe. It contains about eighty-seven acres, but must originally have been much larger; what is now Pall Mall having formerly been within the inclosure. First formed by Henry VIII., it was rearranged and planted in the reign of Charles II. by Le Notre, the great French architect, by whom the gardens at Versailles were designed. At this period, a chain of small ponds was converted into a lake. Very recently, in the time of George IV., the whole was again remodelled, the lake greatly enlarged, and a number of new plantations added, as at present existing. This park is conspicuous for its fine sheet of water, which is kept full and pure by a supply from several waterworks, and is much enlivened by an extensive collection of aquatic birds, belonging to the Ornithological Society, which are a source of constant interest and amusement to the public. The eastern end of the lake is tolerably well masked by a long island, which is, however, almost entirely clothed with willows, and there is here a pretty Swiss Cottage belonging to the Ornithological Society, and used as the residence of their keeper. There is a fountain at the western end, opposite Buckingham Palace. The margin of the water, on the northern side, adjoins a gravel walk for some distance, and being unprotected against the action of winds, forms a hard and disagreeable line. As a rule, vegetable forms only are at all adapted for uniting with water along its margins, when these are tame and flattish; and grass, relieved by specimens or masses of shrubs and trees, is in such cases by far the most appropriate. Where the banks are steeper and bolder, rocks or roots, sprinkled irregularly over the surface, and accompanied with more ragged and wilder plants, will be exceedingly desirable.

But smooth gravel margins—although we are aware that the authority of the late Mr. Loudon is in favour of their introduction—are excessively harsh and disagreeable in an artificial scene, and are only to be tolerated —not admired—on the shores of natural lakes or rivers, when the water has become too low during summer to cover them. More upright banks of rugged or broken ground, such as are occasioned by the wash of rivers or large lakes, and from which patches of gravel may jut out here and there, are of another order, and may become really picturesque.

Numerous winding walks conduct the pedestrian sometimes between the new plantations and sometimes along the side of the water; but the public have also free access to the grass in all parts. In addition to a considerable number of fine old elms which yet remain, there is a large collection of ornamental trees and shrubs in the younger plantations, and most of the rarer kinds have their names, native country, year of introduction, and tribe to which they belong, neatly painted on iron labels. The borders are also filled with the common kinds of herbaceous plants and annuals, which, however, present but a starved appearance. Among the trees which thrive best here is the Western Plane (*Platanus occidentalis*), which is in a remarkably healthy and flourishing state, and retains its greenness during the driest summer weather, as well as late in the autumn. It seems, from what may be observed here and elsewhere, an invaluable town tree. The White Poplar is also very thriving; and there are many excellent young Thorns, of various kinds, which, with the Hollies, Pyruses, and *Ailanthus glandulosus*, seem quite at home. In point of effect, and keeping, and superiority in the plants, the south side of the lake is decidedly the best; though it is to be regretted that all the commoner plants, which are trespassing on the better sorts, and such as evidently do not thrive in a town atmosphere, and many of the weed-like flowers, are not cleared away. A great desideratum in all such places is to grow only or chiefly such sorts of plants as will maintain a healthy appearance, and successfully struggle against the atmospheric disadvantages of the locality.

The principal circumstance worthy of notice in this park is the glimpses or views which are obtained, in walking about it, of so many noble or striking architectural objects, to which the old elm trees form such varied and excellent foregrounds, supports, or frames. In no other place that we have seen, are so many striking combinations of this kind produced. From several of the London bridges, a far greater variety of objects may be taken in at a glance; but the wooding and the park are altogether wanting as a foreground. As seen from this park, however, we may particularly mention the towers of Westminster Abbey, which are well introduced and well accompanied from so many points; the New Houses of Parliament, which, when completed, will afford several excellent groups; Buckingham Palace, as viewed from the east end of the lake, near the Swiss Cottage, the entire length of the lake stretching out between the palace and the observer; the Duke of

York's and Nelson's Columns; with Carlton Terrace, Marlborough House, and a variety of other mansions. Even inferior houses, or such as have no great architectural pretensions, acquire a character, and make pleasing parts of a picture, when they appear half shrouded with venerable trees.

On the north side of the park, but not within the railing, is the Mall, which is composed of four broad avenues of trees, three of which are appropriated to pedestrians only. One of these avenues conducts to the centre of Buckingham Palace, which is thus advantageously seen at the end of a long vista. The trees forming these avenues appear to have been all elms at one period; but as some of these are dead, they have, unhappily, been replaced by elms, limes, and planes promiscuously. If the whole of the trees in these avenues could be allowed to stand on a broad strip of turf, the ground being well broken up and renewed before the grass was laid, they would certainly be shown to more advantage, have a more natural appearance, and probably stand a better chance of becoming and remaining healthy. Beneath the trees, a great number of seats are provided for the public use, as well as in the park.

The *Green Park*, separated only from St. James's along part of one of its sides by the Mall, is a more open area of fifty-six acres, which was at one period larger, but was reduced by George III. to enlarge the gardens attached to Buckingham Palace. A few years ago it was much improved, on the Piccadilly side, during the time when Lord Duncannon was Chief Commissioner of Woods and Forests, by the removal of the old ranger's house, and throwing the whole of the gardens, &c., into the park. From the higher ground near the reservoir at the north-east corner of the park, commanding and beautiful views into Surrey may be obtained, including the Norwood and Wimbledon hills, and more distant prospects. Along the east side are several first-rate mansions, especially Stafford House, at the lower corner. The close fence which surrounds the garden is curious, as being made of slate. Bridgewater House, which is next to Stafford House, has just been built for the Earl of Ellesmere by Mr. Barry, and is a particularly fine specimen of an Italian mansion, with the garden arranged architecturally, and intended to be surrounded, apparently, with a balustraded wall. Among the commonplace and paltry gardens attached to many of the best houses in this part of London, the visitor will be pleased to see this attempt to elevate one of them into something like character. But it is impossible to include in this commendation the mean bank of shrubs which screens the basement story of the building; which may, however, be only temporary, and be intended to be replaced by an appropriate ornamental wall. If this idea of an architectural town garden, where the area is so small, can be carried out effectively, and all the details be well filled in, it will be worthy of the mansion which it accompanies. Spencer House, the town residence of Earl Spencer, adjoins Bridgewater House. The purple lilacs and laburnums seem to succeed very well in the gardens here. There are some very flourishing young trees and handsome thorns in the park near this corner; and they here contribute greatly to relieve the boundary line, suggesting the advantage that would be derived from a few more, higher up, where they could be more boldly thrust into the park. At the entrance to this park from the west end of Piccadilly, there is a handsome triumphal arch, designed by Mr. Decimus Burton.

Hyde Park is entered from Piccadilly, opposite the triumphal arch, by a series of three arches, with a screen and lodge, also designed by Mr. Decimus Burton. Apsley House, with the gardens at the rear, is on the right-hand corner of the entrance to Hyde Park, which contains 349 acres. There are other entrances from Park Lane, from the end of Oxford Street, and from Bayswater, with one from Kensington, and two comparatively new ones at Knightsbridge, and another from Kensington Barracks.

A large portion of this park being high, dry, and very little cumbered by trees, it is, perhaps, the most airy and healthy spot in London. It is, therefore, an excellent place for walking in, and has many paths, which are well kept, and can be used at pleasure by the pedestrian, who may also walk anywhere on the grass if he prefers it. Excellent drives, which are diligently attended to, and from which all but private vehicles are excluded, likewise furnish the means of enjoying carriage exercise, and make this one of the most frequented resorts of the higher circles, at all seasons, but especially from April to July, and between the hours of five and seven, P.M. It was even thus fashionable for drives and promenades in Charles II.'s reign. There are here, too, peculiar facilities given to equestrians in a road known as Rotten Row, where the fine gravel is always allowed to remain loose, so that horses can gallop over it without the least danger from falling. And as the road is devoted solely to this purpose, while it extends, probably, almost two miles in length, it affords ample scope for horse exercise, and is much used. Adjoining this road, in a large open green space between the Cavalry Barracks and Kensington Gardens, is built the Exhibition Palace.

One of the park drives leads to a sheet of water called the Serpentine, part of which is in Kensington Gardens, the division being effected by an elaborate stone bridge, built by Rennie in 1826, which, having a fence along its centre, is useable by persons either in Hyde Park or Kensington Gardens. The Serpentine is a long canal-like piece of water, covering fifty acres, with no particular character, but expanding into a broad sheet at the south end. On the east margin, near the receiving house of the Royal Humane Society (which was designed by Mr. D. Burton), are several boat-houses, some of which belong to the Royal Humane Society, whose officers are always on the alert to prevent accidents from bathing or skating. At this point, also, sailing or rowing boats may be hired during the summer season, and, besides affording an agreeable recreation, they give a great deal of animation and finish to the water, which would otherwise have but a dull appearance. During a calm afternoon, when the water is thus studded with a variety of little vessels, and the banks are dotted over with gay company, and enlivened by passing equipages, this water assumes its most attractive aspect. Early in the morning, under certain restrictions, it is extensively used as a bathing place, as many as 12,000 persons sometimes bathing in it on a Sunday morning.

Behind the receiving house of the Royal Humane Society is a large government depôt for gunpowder and military stores, and on the south side of this are some of the best and oldest elm trees in the park. A little below the south end of the Serpentine is an ancient spring, from which a draught of pure water may be always obtained. Opposite the principal entrance from Piccadilly is a huge statue of Achilles. This and the equestrian statue on the triumphal arch at the Green Park entrance, are appropriate testimonials, in the immediate neighbourhood of Apsley House, of the national esteem for the Duke of Wellington's character and actions.

From the high ground between Hyde Park Corner and the Edgware Road, the best notion of the character and advantages of Hyde Park may be obtained. Here, looking westward, the old trees by the margin of the Serpentine form a broken fringe to some parts of the horizon, and occasional bursts of the gleaming water are caught through their stems, while the more ample woods of Kensington Gardens stretch farther into the distance. On the south, some of the Surrey hills are also visible, and several church towers and spires, on various sides, with a few other good buildings, rise as it were out of the midst of the park trees, near the margin, and furnish centres for some very effective groups. Over this high ground, too, are frequently, during the summer, spread some of the best metropolitan reviews, which, in themselves, often compose the finest pictures, and which set off the open space of the park to the highest advantage.

It will be observed that the three parks already described are in one continuous chain, occupying nearly 500 acres. Kensington Gardens, including 300 acres more, are virtually an extension of Hyde Park, thus bringing the whole of this fine park space into one area. Before George II.'s time, indeed, nearly the whole of these gardens were actually included in Hyde Park; Queen Caroline having enclosed them, and formed the Serpentine out of a number of small ponds. In the year 1550 the French ambassador hunted with the king in Hyde Park, which was then well stocked with game, and kept as a royal enclosure. The iron railing now extending along the south side was substituted for a close wall in George IV.'s reign; and the open railing along the Bayswater Road has since very properly been put up in place of a similar wall, so that passengers along the outside roads get the full benefit of the open space and trees. More recently still, a noted old half-way house, on the Knightsbridge Road, which had become a great nuisance, has been destroyed, and a new entrance made near the site of it. It is this entrance which will give access to the centre of the wonderful glass palace. Hyde Park, celebrated already for many interesting historical events, and as the place of daily concourse for all the aristocracy resident in London during "the season," will henceforth be noted chiefly as having supplied the site of, perhaps, one of the greatest and most important gatherings the world has ever witnessed.

Regent's Park, which probably comprises about 450 acres, is situated on the north-west side of London, and is of modern foundation, although it was once the site of an old Marylebone Park. In this park, the comparatively recent principle of letting off part of the land for villas and terraces has been adopted; and several fine villas, with ample pleasure grounds, besides a number of stately terraces, which are built so as to present two good fronts, the offices being kept in the basement, and concealed, adorn and improve the park rather than interfere with its effect. The handsome villa of the Marquis of Hertford, on the north-west side is, especially, a conspicuous ornament, but the plantations about it, chiefly composed of poplars, are of the commonest and most inferior character, and quite disfigure both the house and the park. Mr. Bishop's mansion and observatory is an object also of science and beauty.

Regent's Park was laid out in 1812 by Mr. James Morgan, from the designs of Mr. Nash, architect, by whom the principal terraces (with one or two exceptions, which were done by Mr. D. Burton) were planned. It was named after George IV., then Prince Regent, who is said to have contemplated building a palace on the north-east side. We are informed, however, that Mr. Nash reserved the inner circle, now the Botanic Gardens, as the site for this proposed palace. The park was not opened to the public till 1838. The full extent of this, which is decidedly one of the finest of the London parks, is nowhere seen, in consequence of the public road crossing it towards the south end, and the inner circle being taken out of it. And besides the inner circle, it includes the site of the Zoological Gardens, which are on the north-west side. The garden of Baron Goldsmid, near the inner circle, rather enhances the beauty of the park, being so well seen from the opposite side of the lake. The Coliseum, on the east side of the park, with its ample dome, contributes much to the effect from various points.

The leading characteristics of this park are the long straight walk, the ornamental water with its bridges, the broad open space on the north-western side, and the villas and terraces, already noticed. There is a great air of finish and neatness, too, in the keeping of the whole, the lines of the walks being well defined and maintained, and the edgings kept good. This may in part be owing to the limited number of visitors which find their way here, as compared with the other parks; but it must also be due to the greater amount of attention which is given to it.

The Long Walk is apparently about a mile in length, and extends from the south end nearly to Primrose Hill. It is forty feet wide, on a rise most of the way, and attaining the top of a low hill near the end. On either side of it, there are four lines of trees, which are all elms towards the upper end; but, unfortunately, the character is changed at the lower part, by the use of a row of horse-chestnuts in front, with three rows of limes at the back. The trees are now about twenty or twenty-five feet high, and rather stunted considering the diameter of their trunks. They are also becoming somewhat crowded. The public are permitted to walk amongst them, as well as on any part of the grass; and all the plantations have been thinned out, and the lower branches of the trees pruned off, so that persons and cattle may roam about amongst them at pleasure. There is, however, no kind of undergrowth to them, and low ornamental trees, shrubs, and bushes, have been quite excluded from the park, to the manifest injury of its character.

That part of the park near the ornamental water is in all respects the most interesting. The water itself is of a good form, with its terminations well covered, and several fine islands, which are well clothed with trees. It lies also in the midst of some villas and terraces, from which it receives additional beauty. It is on the south side of the park. Some noble weeping willows are placed along its southern margin. Three light suspension bridges, two of which carry the walk across an island at the western end of the lake, are neat and elegant, but the close wire fence at their sides sadly interferes with the beauty of their form. These bridges are made principally of strong wire rods. It is to be regretted that the material which came out of the lake at the time of its formation has been thrown into such an unmeaning and unartistic heap on the north side; although the trees which have been placed upon it in some measure relieve its heaviness. Here, perhaps, more than anywhere else, a good mass of shrubs, as undergrowth, would have been of the greatest assistance. Passing along the western road from Portland Place to the inner circle, there is a very picturesque and pleasing nook of water on the right, where the value of a tangled mass of shrubs for clothing the banks will be very conspicuously seen.

Between the water and the top of the long walk lies the broad open space we have before mentioned, which is on the slope of a hill facing the west. Perhaps, as this area is intersected with several walks, it may be a little too bare, and might possibly be improved by a few small groups of trees or thorns; but, in parks of this description, such a breadth of grass glade, especially on the face of a hill that does not front any cold quarter, is of immense value, both for airiness and for effect. It will only want some scattered groups of trees along the edge of the slope, near the summit, to form a foreground to any view that may be attainable from the top of the hill, and also to get a broken horizontal line when looking up the slope of the hill from the bottom. The space we are speaking of is by no means favourably circumstanced in the latter respect, as the hill is crowned by the fourfold avenue of the long walk, which presents an exceedingly flat and unbroken surface line. This consideration renders it very undesirable to carry avenues over any kind of eminence, when they are at all likely to be viewed from the side, and particularly when they are seen from lower ground.

The whole of this park is to be thoroughly drained; its clayey subsoil having long caused a damp unhealthy atmosphere to hang over the district during autumn and winter. The advantage of good drainage in such a locality cannot be over-estimated, whether as it respects the public health and comfort or the progress of the trees. But it can, at best, be only imperfectly done now, unless the whole of the surface be again broken up. In relation to this subject, a suggestion has been put forth, for connecting the Long Walk with Portland Place, through the present square, thereby bringing in a fine continuous vista from the top of one of our best London streets to Primrose Hill. The hint is one which well deserves to be carried out; as it would introduce a new and very noble feature in the arrangements by which our London parks are connected with the town.

Almost adjoining Regent's Park on the north-west side is Primrose Hill, to which the public have free access, and which is a very favourite spot for a summer ramble. It is in the form of a large roundish swell or knoll, and, being unplanted, affords views of a very ample and diversified character, besides yielding admirable exercise to those who are vigorous enough to run up and down its face.

Greenwich Park was laid out by Le Notre about the same time as St. James's, and contains 200 acres. Now, however, except in the remains of many of the avenues, there are happily not very strong traces of the formal style of that artist left, as it is not on a beautifully-varied surface like this that straight walks and regular lines of trees are at all tolerable. The natural advantages of this park are superior to those of any yet described. The ground itself is undulated with great variety, sometimes being thrown up into the softest swells, and in other places assuming a bolder and more sudden elevation. Around the site of the Observatory it is particularly steep, and attains a considerable height. Everywhere, too, it is studded with noble specimens of ancient trees; and in this respect there are none of the other London parks at all equal to it. Some of the best trees are Spanish chestnut, and the largest are on the south side. Many of these are truly fine and venerable, and would command admiration even if found in the heart of a purely rural district. The elms, which are abundant, are likewise large and noble; and there are some picturesque Scotch firs in the neighbourhood of the Observatory. These last are old enough to show the peculiar warm reddish colouring of the stems, and the characteristic horizontal or tufted heads. In this state, the Scotch fir is certainly one of the most picturesque trees we possess, and is the more valuable because each individual plant commonly takes a shape and character of its own.

The avenues still remaining in Greenwich Park are composed chiefly of elm and Spanish chestnut, the latter being mostly confined to the upper part of the park. They are of different widths, and take various directions, many of them not appearing to have any definite object, and some being formed of two single rows, others of two double rows of trees. But there is one avenue, perhaps the finest, which, widening out at the base to correspond with the width of the Hospital, is there composed of elms, but as it ascends the hill is made up wholly of Scotch firs, which are exceedingly good. In a general way, the trees in the avenues have been planted much too thickly, and have greatly injured or spoiled each other. In many instances, too, where plants have died out, they have been replaced by a most unhappy mixture of sorts, which, being also very poor specimens, detract much from the effect. At the upper part of the park are some aged and fine thorns, which have become very picturesque.

On "One-tree Hill," which is a bold and half-detached knoll, the tree which gave its name to the spot is dead; and here there are generally a number of old pensioners congregated, who while away their time here in summer by showing visitors views of the river, &c., through telescopes and through coloured glass of various shades, the effect of the latter being very peculiar. In the face of the Observatory Hill are several ice-houses, in which large deposits of ice are made, and disposed of, it is said, to the London fishmongers, and the Greenwich taverns. There is also a reservoir of water in the upper part of the park for supplying the hospital.

One of the most noticeable objects in this park is the Royal Observatory, situated on the most commanding site, and making a conspicuous feature in itself, while the platform around it is highly favourable for views. Standing here, or at many other points along this higher ridge, or on what is called "One-tree Hill," the observer has a very striking view of the river Thames, along which many large vessels are generally tacking their course either in or out of London, and the sight of these on a clear sunny day from Greenwich Park, with the old trees below partially to cover the town, is such as can nowhere else be matched. The Hospital, too, has an imposing appearance, between the park and the river, and several church spires come into view to break the outline. Behind the hill on which the Observatory stands, the park assumes a pleasing wildness of aspect, which, combined with the size and age of the trees, presents a marked contrast to the scene of habitation and bustle on the side towards the river, and at once seems to plunge the visitor into the very centre of the country. This thoroughly rural air is seldom realized at only the distance of a few yards from the great London population; for Greenwich is, in fact, almost a part of the metropolis. And those who have any taste for country scenes or picturesque beauties will wish to stay here some hours, in order to enjoy alternately the quiet and natural scenery of the park, and the varied and beautiful life of the river.

Victoria Park, on the north-east side of London, near Hackney, was commenced in 1842, and opened in two or three years from that time.

It contains nearly 300 acres, and is chiefly for the use of the large and crowded districts of Bethnal Green, Whitechapel, and Shoreditch. The site of it is in no way an inviting one, and it is severed into two parts by a public road. But it is marvellous what a few trees, well disposed, and a little skill in the shaping of ground, and in the arrangement of walks and roads, will effect for a place in five or six years. For even here, where everything has been done in the most imperfect manner, the trees in irregular plantations being placed in rows, the walks and roads made to follow every little irregularity of surface, and even to be more irregular than the ground itself, the ground, which was newly sown down with grass, not at all levelled, and the margin of a large sheet of water left with a steep gravelly bank from one to two or three yards in nearly perpendicular height, such is the softening and ameliorating influence of trees, that the mere plantations already begin to produce an air of comfort, and shelter, and variety.

Unfortunately for the character of this park for years to come, and, in some respects, for its permanent effect, everything about the execution of the work has been done in the worst possible manner. Even the roads will have to be formed afresh, the grass levelled, and the margins of the larger lake reduced to something like a slope, and rendered capable of resisting the wash of the water by some kind of pitching. The plantations, also, will require gradually remodelling, and single trees and groups must be dotted about the green-sward. This will all be a work of time ; but we are happy to observe that it has been begun in earnest by Mr. Gibson, who has now been appointed to the charge of the park two years.

Entering by a handsome lodge from the Hackney Road, and crossing the Regent's Canal by a bridge, the road diverges to the right and left, in a straight line for some distance, with an avenue of trees to each branch. Taking the road to the right, the larger lake presents itself, and is a fine sheet of water, formed out of some gravel pits, and having several islands, on one of which stands a pagoda. A collection of waterfowl is gradually being formed for this lake. Continuing by this route, and crossing the public road, a walk across the park leads to another lake, the margins of which have been better treated, and which is used as a place for bathing during certain hours in the morning. The park then extends a considerable distance eastward, and has the advantage of having a few old trees, with a prospect out into a wooded country, from this part.

In the plantations are a great variety of ornamental shrubs and low trees, which, when prevented from smothering each other, as they do at present, and distributed more equally through the masses, will supply the elements of a good collection, and will some day render this park a very interesting one. Common herbaceous plants and annuals are likewise grown in some of the borders, to make them a little gay in the summer. Mr. Gibson has further planted a number of the *Araucaria imbricata*, in different parts, for specimens ; and it is gratifying to learn that the chief authorities manifest a desire to render the collection of woody plants as perfect as possible. Everything but the Coniferous tribe seems to succeed very well in this situation ; and many of the trees, thorns, &c., have made an excellent growth, and are getting well established.

It is proposed, when the plantations are duly grown, to place a number of handsome terraces by the sides of this park, as at Regent's Park ;

and these will be of the greatest use in concealing the many mean-look-ing houses which now show themselves so repulsively. Nothing, in fact, could be more desirable, in the arrangement of public parks like this, than to provide in the plan for an irregular belt, on all but the more open sides, of villas and terraces ; as the formers of the park can thus shut out what is disagreeable, and obtain, by judiciously placing these structures, and adapting the plantations to them, and keeping a control over the elevations, a series of most delightful and ornamental accom-paniments.

Richmond Hill and Park.—Frequently as we have been attracted to Richmond Hill by the high estimate in which its scenery is popularly held, we have always returned from it with some degree of disappoint-ment. Much of the beauty of any scene will of course depend on the state of the atmosphere ; and there may occasionally be times when even the most common-place combinations will be so favourably lighted up, and so exquisitely tinted, while their defects are just sufficiently veiled in a kind of luminous mist, that they will appear perfectly charming. On the other hand, there will more frequently be seasons when, by a bad arrangement of the lights with respect to the position of the spectator, or by a deadening gloom, in which no individual features acquire their proper character, even beauty degenerates into dulness. But allowing for all these changes, the prospect from Richmond Hill, or that part of it where the terrace walk has been formed, opposite the Roebuck Inn, has never appeared satisfactory to us. Take away the river from the scene, and it at once becomes tame, and inferior to fifty others at a less distance from London. But as we are aware that the river is considered the chief object, we may remark that there does not appear to be enough of this visible to make a really fine landscape, and the nearer margin of the part that is seen is extremely bare and meagre. To render the view of such a river good, a considerable length of it should be seen, or several of its windings, or it should widen out and encompass two or three picturesque islands, while the banks should be clothed chiefly with herbage, with occasional tufts of bushes and shaggy weeds, or larger masses of trees. Nothing could be more defective than the margin of the Thames on the side next Richmond Hill. It is sim-ply a rough towing path, without any assistance from vegetation. And nearly the whole of the ground between the river and the top of the hill is similarly inharmonious. Indeed, the great and radical deficiency, which would ruin almost any such prospect, is the want of a proper fore-ground. If, near the top of the slope, which is admirably fitted for the purpose, a few irregular groups of trees and shrubs, with occasional tufts of such plants as thorns, or furze, or broom, a little lower down, were in-troduced, the whole would at once take a new character ; and though that would not alter the position of the river as viewed from this point, it would transform the entire scene into something infinitely better.

Higher up the hill, by the Star and Garter Hotel, a greatly superior view of the river may be had ; and in a warm calm evening, when the light from the setting sun, or the reflection from the clouds after he has gone down below the horizon, is thrown full on the still water, the aspect of the river from this spot is very lovely. There is still, however, the want of a suitable foreground.

But if the visitor wishes to catch all the beauty of the river view, and take in to the best advantage the principal features of the country be-yond, he must enter the park, and, strolling slowly along the top of the bank on the right, gradually find out for himself, through the fringe of trees, and between or over the other trees or bushes on the bank or in the hollow, the numberless delightful glimpses of river and country which will there be revealed. We may safely promise any one who will thus saunter as far as the top of the hill where the road turns off to the right to the Kingston entrance, and who will diligently use his eyes all the time, that, if he is at all alive to the charms of a landscape, he will have a very rich treat, and one infinitely greater than he could ever hope for on what is usually termed Richmond Hill.

The park at Richmond, which is 10 miles from London by the South-Western Railway, or 15 by the river, is of great size, including no less than 2253 acres. To those who are not so particular with regard to time, we recommend, in favourable weather, and when the tide is rising, the route from London by a Thames steamer, as one which would yield a much richer variety of scenery, reveal many pretty villas, and be altogether more pleasant. But on no account should this course be taken when the tide is flowing out, as the banks of the river are then most disagreeable, and very little can be seen, and there is always the chance of the boat running aground.

There are many entrances to Richmond Park. Besides the principal one, which is opposite the Star and Garter Hotel, there is one for Kingston, and another at Roehampton, and a third towards Putney, and a fourth at East Sheen, with some others. Entering at the Richmond gate the visitor will come at once to the bank before described, and if he is walking should strike off by the footpath to the right, and never touch upon the drive again till he crosses it where it descends to the Kingston entrance. Rambling along under the fine old trees, a group or two of handsome middle-sized horse-chestnuts will soon be observed on the left, exhibiting the desirableness of planting two or three trees of one sort together in parks. The house on the right, which is speedily reached, is the present residence of Lord John Russell, the site of which is a truly enviable one. Farther on, the bank begins to take a rougher and wilder character, and to be dotted about with tangled bushes, and clothed with fern. Along the sides of the footpath, too, among ancient oaks, of various character and sizes, specimens of fine old thorns, most picturesquely clothed or half-clothed with masses of ivy, begin to abound, and are thickly scattered over the brow of the hill at intervals, for nearly a mile. The lover of picturesque forms will find many a beautiful picture among these thorns, especially if seen just after the young leaves have expanded, or when they are in bloom, or after the foliage has begun to change colour and the haws to ripen. In all these stages, they present the most striking contrast to the ivy which invests them, and which is now seen jutting out in broad patches, then retiring, then just peeping forth and again retreating, and sometimes clothing the summit with a complete crown of dark green, the flowers and incipient fruit being very beautiful in autumn.

Advancing still further, the bank will be found quite covered with a younger plantation, which opens out here and there, and at length again gives place to bushes and trees. Below this part of the bank is Sudbrook Park, now used as an extensive hydropathic establishment, and very pleasantly situated. The excellent old trees in this park, and the gardens, which are distinctly observed from the top of the bank, form agreeable resting-places for the eye as it travels over the district. Proceeding in the same direction, Ham Common is next seen in the flat below, and then the country around Kingston becomes much tamer. But the internal features of the park are still as interesting ; and if the road to Kingston be crossed, and the opposite hill ascended, the park takes a more natural style, the ground being covered with fern, and studded with noble old oaks, while, looking to the right and still continuing straight onward, there are several interesting groups of thorns and bushes, over and among which the eye roams into the country towards the Surrey hills.

If the park be now skirted, in the direction of Wimbledon, an extensive young plantation of oaks on the right will be seen to have a quantity of Deodars and others of the Conifer tribe recently introduced in different spots, and protected from the game. These will no doubt some day become attractive objects in the park, when they have acquired sufficient age to be relieved from protection, and to stand out by themselves. Views of Wimbledon Common and Putney Heath begin next to unfold themselves, and the White Lodge, the house of the ranger, now occupied by H.R.H. the Duchess of Gloucester, is approached. In the neighbourhood of this villa there are some admirable park-like scenes, comprehending several beautiful specimen trees, broad and bold glades of turf, portions of an ample lake among the trees in the hollow, a finely-broken woody and hilly horizontal outline, and, on the north side, a splendid glade, which has all the effect of an avenue, without any of the trees being in lines. This is a most interesting and artist-like vista, which only wants terminating by some object large and good enough to justify its employment ; although the house, of course, supplies such an object from the other side of the park.

After leaving this point, about which there are some capital oaks, the drive continues through a richly-clothed and diversified tract till it nears the Roehampton entrance ; when some of the stately villas of that aristocratic neighbourhood begin to show themselves. A ride or walk round the other side of the park, till the Richmond gate is again reached, thus making the entire circuit of the park, will well repay those who can afford the time ; but the best portions are what we have thus briefly described. The park is appropriately stocked with deer, which seem the only (or the most) fitting tenants for a domain so ample and so ancient. Its surface is considerably undulated, and the plantations and scattered trees are, for the most part, happily placed. But, as in the parks nearer London, there is a great dearth of all kinds of bushes and lower trees, the absence of which is an immense drawback to the general effect, one of the chief beauties of grouping—that of blending the lines of a mass of plants with the sod from which they spring—being altogether lost. From the variations of surface in the ground, and the difference of character in the trees, there is necessarily an infinite diversity of view in so large an area ; and, in parts, the surrounding country is made to blend very agreeably with the arrangements within the park.

Windsor Park, which is now made less than an hour's ride from London by both the South Western and Great Western Railways, is divided into two portions, the Little and the Great Park. The former of these, occupying about 500 acres, lies more immediately around the castle, on the east and north sides, and is only so far accessible to the public as that there is a free path across it from Datchet to Frogmore, and the road which at present runs from Staines to Windsor is, for part of its course, within this park. The North Terrace at Windsor Castle further overlooks a large portion of the Little Park, and the South-Western Railway now crosses a corner of it. Since the Windsor-branch of the last-named railway was formed, a small new lodge has been erected near the terminus, and a drive made to conduct to the castle by going through the Little Park, and round the east end of the castle. The necessity for passing through Windsor town has thus been avoided ; and an avenue of Deodar Cedars has been planted along the straight portion of this drive, until it enters among the old trees of the park. The hideous wall which formerly bounded the Little Park on the northern side has also been removed ; and Her Majesty, with great liberality, has allowed space for cricket-playing in that part of the park.

But a most important alteration in the arrangement of the Little Park has further been commenced, and will probably soon be carried out. It is the diversion of the road which now enters Windsor, by way of Frogmore, along the south front of the castle, and throwing it into the Long Walk by carrying it at the back of the Frogmore Kitchen Gardens. The path from Datchet to Frogmore, which now crosses the Little Park, will then, it is said, have to be abandoned. This will get rid of the cramped appearance of the Little Park on the south side, and render that part of the park much more worthy of the castle.

HERNE'S OAK

The path from Datchet across the Little Park reveals nearly the whole of it to the public, except a portion immediately beneath the east front of the castle. Near the Frogmore end of this walk, at a short distance to the east, is the Queen's dairy ; and one of the shattered and decaying old oaks, which are seen about the highest point of the walk, and which is surrounded by a paling, against which ivy is planted, is said to be the famous Herne's oak spoken of by Shakespeare, and here portrayed. There are several other ancient oaks in the neighbourhood of this. Frogmore Lodge, the residence of the Duchess of Kent, is included in the Little Park.

Until the reign of Queen Anne, Windsor Castle was severed from the Great Park, which has been a part of Windsor Forest, by private property. At this period, however, sufficient land was purchased by the Crown to connect the castle with the Great Park by means of what is styled the "Long Walk," and its accompanying avenue. Magnificent as this avenue is, and nobly as it maintains the connection between the castle and the park, every visitor of taste will regret that so superb a palace should have anything but Crown property lying between it and the Great Park, and that the communication between the two should be so contracted. It may be allowed that nothing could better atone for or disguise during summer the meagreness of this strip of land than the double avenue which has been created, and which is one of the happiest possible ideas. But still the fences, and the houses and gardens, fields and farms behind, *will* force themselves into notice ; and, in spite of all effort, help to divorce this truly regal castle from the equally magnificent park.

The drive known as the Long Walk is described as three miles in length, in a straight line, and is supported on either side by two rows of elms, which have attained their full size, and, with a few very unimportant exceptions, are yet in the greatest vigour and luxuriance. This avenue will be sure to strike the visitor as exceedingly grand. It is somewhat marred, however, by being carried over a considerable swell in the ground about half way up it, which helps to shorten its apparent length, and to make the drive seem as if it were not straight, while a more decidedly objectionable feature is, that it ascends a hill *away* from the castle at the further end. If there are any two circumstances which, more than others, require to be kept in view in the formation of avenues, they are that the ground over which they run should be nearly level, or have one continuous ascent towards the mansion or principal object to which they lead ; and that, consequently, this object should be on the highest ground, at least as respects the avenue. Any avenue that commences on a hill, and passes *down* that hill towards its terminating object, even though it afterwards rise again near the end, must ever appear to some extent inverted ; and every undulation or swell of the ground in it will necessarily be a deformity. The idea which is conveyed to the mind by the elevation of the Long Walk at Windsor, as it reaches its termination in the Great Park, is, that the castle ought to be somewhere about the site of the statue of George III., by which this walk is so appropriately finished.

Those familiar with the Champs Elysées at Paris will remember that the Grand Avenue there, like this at Windsor, is partly on a steep ascent, *away* from the palace of the Tuileries to the Triumphal Arch at the summit. And although this circumstance enhances the effect as viewed from the front of the palace, yet, regarded as an approach *to* the Tuileries, it causes the latter to appear more or less buried in a low marshy tract.

Some notion of the length of the Long Walk will be formed when, in standing near the Castle, the visitor is informed that the equestrian statue of George III. at the top of the walk is, including the pedestal, above 50 feet high ; and that the statue itself (man and horse) stands 26 feet in height. It was designed by Westmacott, and erected by command of George IV. No termination to such a walk could be more felicitous ; and as the visitor approaches it, he will find that the pedestal or base has been very artistically constructed of large rude blocks of stone, to resemble a natural mass of rock ; and the peculiar roughness of the site, with the tasteful diffusion of a few large stones about the neighbourhood of the pedestal, fitly harmonize with and carry out the idea.

From this elevated spot, some conception—though a very inadequate one—may be formed of the character of the Great Park, which extends, however, a considerable distance to the south, where it cannot be seen, and embraces an area of 1800 acres. The views from this point towards the castle, and in an easterly and north-easterly direction, are truly magnificent ; and the steep ascent round the statue should by all means be climbed, in order to command the scenery more perfectly. Those who happen to be on foot should strike across the park in a south-easterly course from the statue, by a partially beaten foot-path, for Cumberland Lodge, where a greenhouse and small garden (once much frequented by George IV.) are shown to the public, and from whence Virginia Water will be reached in little more than a mile.

At Cumberland Lodge is a vinery containing a vine of the black Hamburgh kind, which is, in some respects, said to be even more extraordinary than the far-famed one at Hampton Court. It has a stem which measures two feet nine inches in circumference, and covers the roof of a house 138 feet long by 16 feet wide. In the autumn of 1850 it had 2000 bunches of grapes upon it, both bunches and berries being large and well ripened. No particular preparation seems to have been made for it, as it was only growing in a light, dry, shallow border.

Some of the most enchanting park scenery, with trees fully worthy of it, will be found in various directions around the statue, and between it and Virginia Water. The admirer of the picturesque will here be able to roam about amidst scenes that will supply new features for examination at almost every step. And yet the greatest unity and harmony of character will be observable.

Arrived at a line of fence and a porter's lodge, not far from Cumberland Lodge, those who wish to see the whole of Virginia Water should inquire of the porter for a path to the left, by way of a tall pillar which will then be visible ; and by this route, they will be able to make the entire circuit of the lake. The plantations will now be seen to have a far younger look, and there are some beautiful tufts of young birches (a tree much too seldom used in park decoration) on the left, among which, and mingling with the thousands of common rabbits which will be seen here, is a large quantity of purely white rabbits, which have a very lively and pretty appearance, and are quite worth introducing into extensive plantations, for their beauty.

Leaving the pillar, erected by George III. in memory of the military achievements of the Duke of Cumberland, on the right, and following one of the green walks or drives (with which the woods here are frequently intersected) in a nearly straight course, the visitor will come at length to a rocky waterfall at one of the heads of the lake, and taking a path to the left, if the gate is closed, he will speedily find himself on the grassy margin of the lake, where he will notice some extraordinary specimens of the Scotch Laburnum, and from which the views of both water and plantations immediately become very attractive. This lake is said to be the largest sheet of artificial water in the country, and covers several hundred acres. In its general outline, it has been particularly well treated, and presents a great deal of variety. With respect to the water itself, which is beautifully clear, it only wants the addition of a few islands of different sizes to enrich it, and these could be obtained without difficulty by extending the water round some parts of the present margins. It would then be perfect as a lake, though a quantity of water-fowl would also add to its liveliness and variety. But the accompaniments are in no way worthy of the water. Want of age in the plantations, and of the rich clustering character which older trees assume, can easily be allowed for. In no place, however, can be seen a more urgent necessity existing for the judicious use of the axe. A competent practitioner might, in one or two seasons, entirely transform this scene, by breaking up the plantations more into masses and groups, of ever-varying shapes and dimensions, with bold glades of grass, or fern, or other wild herbage, or heather, variously introduced among them ; especially making large occasional breaks into the plantations along the sides of the water, and introducing a great quantity of undergrowth and bushes, with such evergreens as Hollies, Yews, Rhododendrons, and *Berberis aquifolium*. The broad grass path or drive by the side of the lake, also, which is good in itself, and preferable to any kind of gravel road, requires to be thrown farther from the water at more frequent intervals, so as to get good masses of plantation down to the edge of the lake, and thus obtain more variety in the drive, and more of the beauty which trees dipping into and overshadowing water always produce. This is the more necessary along a portion of the south margin, to carry the drive out of the low swampy ground through which it at present travels.

Walking along from the point at which we have supposed the visitor to come first upon the lake, in about a quarter of a mile he will arrive at the overflow from the water, which is conducted over a number of bold masses of rock, so as to form a broken cascade. This waterfall has likewise rocky accompaniments at the side, and is best seen from the bridge below it. The whole has been much praised, as conveying a favourable impression.

From the site of the waterfall to a little beyond the classic ruins, the most satisfactory part of the whole of the scenery on the borders of this lake will be found. Here there is a good open glade of grass on the slope of a bank, upon which a cottage is situated, and the sides of the drive are more irregular, and groups of trees, with some tasteful masses of rocks, interpose at intervals between the drive and the lake. In a recess on the left, near a massive archway, which leads beneath the public road, there is a collection of the Elgin marbles, piled together in a variety of classic shapes, and very tastefully grouped. A number of middle-aged Scotch firs and other pines contribute additional interest to this pleasing nook.

Proceeding westward, still by the edge of the water, which is here most tamely accompanied by a young oak plantation on the left, the elaborate Chinese fishing temple, with its gilded ornaments, stands out by the side of an inlet on the opposite shore, and a small frigate is generally on the water in front of it. Looking back, however, a more harmonious object, in the shape of a neat church tower, of recent construction, at Egham, is seen mounting above the trees at the east end of the lake, and makes a fine break in the line of the horizon. Still keeping towards the west, the lake and the drive take a sudden turn to the left, and around this bend, the trees and margins of the water become more picturesque, and a long stone bridge, of an imposing appearance, opens to view. Here the visitor quits the lake, and passing over the stone bridge, still sees the water stretching away indefinitely on the left; leaving it with the desirable impression that there is yet a considerable portion of it which he has not explored. Taking the road towards Windsor, and winding through a pleasing hollow between plantations in which firs are the chief constituents, the open park is gained in a few minutes, and, a little further on, after scanning an ample landscape on the left, the horizon of which is almost lost in the blue distance, the eye falls again on part of a sheet of water in the valley beneath, thus prolonging and confirming the belief that the lake is continued indefinitely in that direction. A short distance further, through an open park in which there are a few gigantic beech trees, and we are again landed at the lodge from which we started, to resume the same or a more circuitous route by the road on our return to Windsor. Indeed, it will be worth while, even in walking, to go back by the road, which will present some fresh views of the park, and show the Castle in a better aspect than that which is caught from Snow Hill, where the statue is situated. As the hill crowned by the statue is descended, and the hollow is reached, the observant traveller will be sure to note how the castle rises in importance and grandeur when the road is so much below it, and appears to ascend towards it all the way.

From the eastern and southern fronts of the castle, as well as from the Little Park and Frogmore, that portion of the Great Park which lies eastward from Snow Hill exhibits a very varied and charming character. Extending along the ridge and slope of a hill, the trees about the summit are most pleasingly, yet softly, broken up, and the face of the hill is adorned with large masses of trees, here and there (but most irregularly) intersected with patches of greensward.

On the whole, the Great Park at Windsor is, like the Castle, quite unrivalled. Each is worthy of the other. And both together compose a fitting and most truly royal abode for the Sovereigns of Great Britain. The only cause for regret (which is of course unavailing) is, that this superb castle does not stand in the midst of its magnificent park. It should, perhaps, be mentioned that the Great Park is the Windsor Forest of former times, which has been celebrated by Pope and other poets.

Battersea Park, though not yet formed or even begun upon, is to supply a new recreation ground for the dense population of Vauxhall, Lambeth, &c., and to secure the present open space, which goes by the name of Battersea Fields, from that encroachment of dwelling-houses and streets to which it was rapidly yielding. This is an object for which an Act of Parliament has been obtained, and to carry which into effect the Government are only waiting for means. Battersea Fields,

c

the site of this contemplated park, include, we should suppose, more than 200 acres. The ground is situated by the side of the Thames, opposite Chelsea Hospital, and the South-Western Railway runs along within a short distance of its south margin. It is a low, flat, and in some parts swampy tract, having, at present, a most uninviting and desolate look, with scarcely a single tree upon it, except a few scrubby willows near the river.

To accomplish much with this park, it would perhaps be advisable to let in the tidal water from the river into an immense lake, to be formed somewhere in the marshy ground not far from the Thames, keeping this water to as low a level as possible, so as to make the surrounding land appear higher, and using all the material obtained from the excavation for it in raising and diversifying the rest of the surface. Doubtless, as the soil produces good crops of vegetables (it being now mostly culti-vated by market gardeners), it would, if properly drained and prepared, soon afford some thriving plantations ; and these, when they get large enough to blend with the trees on the higher ground about the Wands-worth Road and Clapham, and with the still older trees on the Chelsea side of the river, would give an entirely new character to the district. It is only to be hoped that its practical formation will fall into very different hands to those which produced the Victoria Park, and that those who have plantations not too remote from the spot will liberally present the thinnings of these, where they have attained the height of from 15 to 25 feet, that the flatness and barrenness of the locality may be immediately relieved, and that mere nursery trees alone may not be planted. It is not unworthy of note that Battersea Fields have been celebrated for the extraordinary quantity and variety of British species of plants which they yield, and which exceeds that of almost any other plot of similar size in the country.

A park for the *Finsbury* district of London has also been for some time contemplated, and the local authorities have repeatedly moved in the business ; but the Government do not appear, at present, to be in a position to allow them pecuniary aid, being in a manner pledged to proceed with Battersea Park, when funds can be spared. The proposed site of the Finsbury Park is in the neighbourhood of Highbury, and would include nearly 300 acres. From the astonishing quickness with which the suburbs of London are becoming filled up with streets and houses, notwithstanding the tendency which railways have to draw off the people to reside farther from town, every attempt to snatch a clear piece of country from the general fate, and to provide a belt of pure air, or the means of obtaining it, entirely around the crowded seats of business, should be delightedly hailed, and strenuously fostered.

To give an adequate conception of the full advantages possessed by the inhabitants of the London suburbs in regard to park space, we shall briefly point out some of the principal suburban *Commons*, which, with a very little aid in the way of planting, and the addition of a few walks in some instances, would become, for all ornamental and recreative pur-poses, most invaluable substitutes for other parks. Indeed, a few of them are already as good as parks ; and all possess the usefulness of parks in respect to affording breathing places, while they have the further merit of being always open to the public.

Clapham Common, which is in all respects the best, and the nearest to London, has an area of about 200 acres, and, being altogether on high land, is an exceedingly healthy and pleasant spot. It possesses a great many fine groups of trees, and, on the south side, we may specially notice a number of comparatively modern clusters, in which the principle of planting two or three trees of one sort by themselves has been adopted, and the heads are growing together so as to look like one handsome specimen. Several walks and roads traverse the common; and ponds—some of them deserving the name of small lakes, with islands—are of frequent occurrence. At one point, the material excavated in forming one of the ponds has been thrown up into a roundish knoll, which forms a favourite place of exercise and amusement. But the most characteristic and admirable feature of this common is, that the margins of it have been so irregularly planted, and the trees are thrown out from them so boldly in parts, that, though it is surrounded with villas and a road, the trees blend so well with those on the private estates, that from any part of the middle, the boundary is scarcely at all perceptible, and the private plantations seem merely to be denser woods belonging to the common itself. The appearance of a villa here and there does not at all interfere with this idea, but rather helps it, leading to the belief that they are only on inclosed portions of the common, and that there are other open and public spaces behind them. On the south side, where the ground falls away after it leaves the common, the illusion is, at one or two parts, still better sustained. At the northern end, nearer Clapham, where the village becomes more populous, there are fewer trees; but the church stands on the corner of the common, in a most appropriate and excellent position.

At a very little distance from this common, by either the upper or lower roads, Wandsworth Common is reached, and is also a large tract of ground. On the north side of this, fronting some villas which are locally known as the "Five Houses," the trees, again, are most judiciously arranged to cover the boundary; and along the south-east side, some open fields allow the eye to travel across to the villas, gardens, and plantations of Balham and Brixton Hills. Towards the western boundary, a number of old gravel pits have been converted into a very agreeable lake, with islands; and about this part, elegant young birch trees constitute the principal woody features, evincing how delightfully they harmonize with water, and how well they group together. The southern boundary of the common is almost all badly treated, and there have been some serious encroachments on it about the centre of this side, disfiguring it greatly with a number of ugly cottages and gardens. From the more open portion about the middle, however, admirable views across the hollow, in which Garratt Lane is placed, are obtained of Wimbledon Hill and Park. And some little attempts at planting a few groups of trees have been made on the barer common between this point and Tooting. The South-Western Railway crosses Wandsworth Common, but, being in a deep cutting, is not an eyesore. An enormous county prison has just been erected on the south side of the common, not far from Wandsworth.

A short walk, of less than half a mile, from the south-west corner of Wandsworth Common, will land the traveller on what is called Tooting Common, though it is actually in Streatham parish. A place on the right, shortly after this common is arrived at, with a park paling in front, was nearly all a part of the common a few years ago, and the ornamental water in front of it was made out of some old gravel pits. Taking the straight road onwards, a few yards further will conduct to the bottom of a fine avenue of elms, which ranges along the front of a house and park once occupied by Mr. Thrale, the brewer; and here the great Dr. Johnson was a frequent visitor, indeed, for some time, an almost constant resident. It is now occupied, we believe, by a Jewish family. Looking across the common to the left, a splendid mass of oaks will be seen spread over the grounds of a cluster of villas on Bedford Hill, and a small avenue to the left leads to another villa. Higher up the principal avenue, the common will be seen to be adorned with some handsome old pollard oaks, many similar ones having recently been cut down, and a few new clumps planted. It is a great misfortune that this stately avenue is not terminated by some good house, or by the church spire, and that in the changes of proprietorship which the adjoining property has undergone, a number of the largest elms have been barbarously cut down at the top of the avenue. The gigantic elm, previously described, is a short distance to the left from the end of this avenue; and the common extends, by a narrower strip, in a north-westerly direction, till it nearly adjoins Clapham Common.

Passing up the road to Streatham Church, and turning along the old Brighton road, with splendid elm trees overshadowing it on both sides, and a good deal of park-like scenery on either hand, a walk of ten minutes will reveal Streatham Common, a beautiful grassy slope, environed with trees, and having a number of villas on the south side. Unlike the other commons we have noticed, this is almost entirely free from furze, unless it be near the top, and has lately been well drained. Except, however, a tuft of old elm trees around a pond at the bottom, the sward is wholly unfurnished with trees, and a few small groups, scattered tastefully along the sides, and more sparingly towards the top of the first sudden slope, are only wanting to make this one of the most pleasing of the smaller commons. From the summit of the first slope, and various parts of the upper common, and from what are called "the Duke's Fields," a little to the northward, the prospects obtained are not surpassed in any other part of the suburbs, and the elm trees, in particular, are extremely grand. Towards the bottom of this common, on the north side, is a pleasant villa, now the property of John Gray, Esq., but built by the last Earl of Coventry, and lived in by the Dowager Countess until her death. Near the site of the present villa, a palace, which was once a favourite with Queen Elizabeth, formerly stood; and some hints for improving the grounds attached to this villa will be found in Repton's "Sketches" on landscape gardening.

Mitcham Common, two miles west of Streatham, is an immense but by no means pleasing tract, being so completely unplanted, and having very few villas on its margins. It is, however, an admirable open plot, with good views of the Norwood and Streatham Hills on one side, and prospects of other parts of the country on the south-west. We have also found it an interesting place for a botanizing ramble; *Genista anglica, Spiræa filipendula,* and many others by no means common plants, being plentifully found there. On the south side, too, it is bounded by the plantations which screen Beddington Park, once the magnificent seat of the Carew family, and still retained by a branch of the same, where some of the earliest specimens of exotics and of general gardening were formerly to be seen; and where, it is said, a cherry-tree was retained in fruit to a very late period of the year, by covering it up, in order to gratify and surprise Queen Elizabeth during a visit. Here, also, the first orange trees known in this country were grown in the open ground, and protected during winter. They were believed to have been raised from seeds of the earliest oranges imported into England by Sir Walter Raleigh. The severe frosts of 1739–40 entirely destroyed them. A trout stream (where there are some extraordinary fish), a glorious avenue of elms, and a few ancient trees in the park, are still interesting. Returning to Mitcham Common, let us hope that it will not be long before the very light expense and trouble of planting and inclosing some good clumps of trees in various parts of it will be incurred.

Scarcely more than two miles further westward lies the extensive and varied common of Wimbledon, including Putney Heath, which is not separated from it, and will yield a lengthened and most agreeable ramble. Indeed, this is much the largest common which the neighbourhood of London possesses, and furnishes a greater diversity of character. It must contain at least 1000 acres, and extends nearly to Kingston. On the north-east side it is bounded by Wimbledon Park, on the west by the villas and parks about Putney Heath and Roehampton, and, further on, by Richmond Park; while it is comparatively open on the south and south-west sides. For the most part, it is clothed with heath, which is short and small in the neighbourhood of Wimbledon Park, but strong and wild towards the vicinity of Richmond Park, where the ground becomes more rugged and broken, and the whole aspect is that of a wild moorland tract. Nearer Wimbledon village there is a smooth grass sward, and Putney Heath is a good deal covered with furze. There is an old telegraph station on Putney Heath.

Around the sides nearest Putney and Roehampton, the trees on the contiguous property keep the outline pretty well hidden and broken, and there are a few trees near Wimbledon. The rest of the common is, however, very bare, and the hard line of fencing round Wimbledon Park sadly wants covering in parts by masses of plantation. All the northern part of the common would, in fact, bear a great deal of planting; and the quantity of soil which is sold from it might well afford a small outlay for such an improvement. At the Kingston end, nothing would look so well, or thrive so freely, as masses of Scotch fir, which are admirably fitted for growing among wild and shaggy heather, and look most natural in such a position. From twenty to forty years ago Wimbledon Common was the scene of some of the most splendid military reviews, which are now rarely held there. Wimbledon peat is much celebrated among gardeners for heaths and orchids, and the great demand made for it causes it to be sold at a high price. It is a light-coloured and fibrous heath-mould, with no disposition to sourness or the retention of water, and having but little sand in it. Doubtless it is of first-rate quality for plant-culture.

Turning down either of the lanes between Putney Heath and Roehampton, Barnes Common will open out before the eye, after somewhat less than a mile of walking. This is a poor tame common, chiefly covered with furze, and almost wholly devoid of trees. There is a station of the Windsor Railway near the middle of it. The trees on the north and south help to relieve its dulness, and in the midst of some of those to the south, the tower of Barnes Church is seen. Eastward of Barnes Church, the woody park which bounds the common, and over which a beautiful church spire near Kensington now rises, belongs to Barn Elms, the former residence of Mr. Cobbett, and more recently tenanted by the late Vice Chancellor, Sir Lancelot Shadwell.

It will have been gathered, no doubt, from our description, that all these commons lie, as it were, in a kind of chain, none of them being more than a mile or two apart, and some being yet nearer to each other. Kennington Common, which is scarcely deserving of mention, but for its being almost *in* London, completes the chain. It is a thoroughly bare area, very much used for cricket and other games, and susceptible of infinite improvement by planting, which might be so arranged as very slightly to curtail the space actually now used by the public. A few years ago it had a large and disgusting open ditch along the south-east side, which has happily been covered in, and a row of neat houses have sprung up in its place. In so populous a district, it is matter of astonishment that no steps are taken to decorate and enliven this exceedingly dull-looking spot by planting, at least here and there round the margins. A better thing still to aim at, however, would be to convert the whole into a small park, retaining a good open plot, or large glades of grass, in the centre for public recreation.

On the west and north sides of London, beyond a few Greens (which make pleasing breaks by the roadside, and afford a nucleus for the smaller kinds of cottage villas to cluster round), and a small common at Ealing, Hampstead Heath is the only larger area which the public have the opportunity of ranging over. And this is certainly a very delightful spot. Situated on Hampstead Hill, and in part surrounded with the rich wooding of Kenwood and other estates, it is entirely open to the west, where the hill shelves away rather abruptly, yielding the most ample views into a fertile and well-timbered country. There are some large reservoirs of water on this heath, for the purpose of supplying Camden Town and the adjacent parts. Towards the south-east, ample prospects of London are obtained. The ground on the heath being somewhat broken, and full of rugged inequalities, great variety and much amusement may be had in walking about it. Some recent attempts to enclose this spot have fortunately been unsuccessful; the public and the press rightly considering that all such areas become additionally valuable in proportion as the outskirts of the town are gradually being absorbed in its insatiable vortex.

Many other commons—some of great magnitude—lie around London, at increased distances; and Epping and Hainault forests are brought within easy reach by the Eastern Counties Railway. But these are too remote to be classed with the London parks, and not of sufficient consequence to demand notice of themselves. A day's ramble in Epping Forest would, however, not be unremunerative to such as wish to study the natural grouping of trees and bushes; and many a garden or park group might, perchance, receive the characteristic breaks or finishings it requires, from those who have the management of such things sparing a day for earnest investigation of the manner in which nature deals with her combinations.

PUBLIC GARDENS.—Our account of these will include such as belong to the country, and are open without fee to the public at certain periods, together with those which have been created by subscription or by public bodies, and are accessible to the members of those bodies, and to the general public through the introduction of such members. In respect to accommodation of this kind, London, with its extensive pleasure-grounds at Kensington, its noble Botanic Garden at Kew, the more mixed garden of the Horticultural Society at Chiswick, embracing general gardening of all sorts, and including exhibitions which have acquired a world-wide fame, the beautiful promenade and scientific Botanic Garden in the Regent's Park, likewise distinguished for its exhibitions, and the ancient Physic Garden at Chelsea;—with such a combination of attractive and useful gardens—not to mention those devoted more exclusively to zoological purposes—the metropolis has advantages with which few other large towns in Europe can at all compete.

Kensington Gardens lie close to London, and are, as before remarked, in immediate connection with Hyde Park, to which they form an excellent adjunct, of quite a distinct character. Intended only for the pedestrian, they are conspicuous for presenting one immense and almost continuous mass of shade, beneath which the public may freely enjoy a most luxurious summer ramble, which, but slightly varying in its principal features, and only traversed here and there by a broad open walk, can be prolonged to a well-nigh indefinite extent.

The foundation of these gardens was laid by William III., but in his reign they did not occupy more than 26 acres. Queen Anne enlarged them to 56 acres, and had them laid out by her gardener, H. Wise, who afterwards became quite a celebrity in landscape gardening. Addison, in his *Spectator*, seems to have been delighted with those dawnings of the modern natural manner exhibited by this artist in his treatment of the old Kensington gravel pits, thus converted into a portion of Kensington Gardens. In the time of George II., however, Queen Caroline extended these gardens to their present size, by taking nearly 300 acres out of Hyde Park, and having the whole laid out by Bridgman. At this period, also, the Serpentine was formed out of a series of ponds; and a large and somewhat circular basin of water was made in the neighbourhood of the palace, at the point from whence the principal avenues diverge. Kent was afterwards employed to alter these gardens, and encountered much ridicule by endeavouring to imitate nature so closely as to plant a number of dead trees.

More recent times have witnessed comparatively few changes in Kensington Gardens, except that one or two of the broad walks up the centre of them appear modern, and a number of ornamental shrubs and low trees have been planted along the side of the wall near the Bayswater Road; while a new walk, bordered with a better class of ornamental plants, and adorned with summer flowers, has been made nearly parallel with Rotten Row on the south side, and the old kitchen gardens, behind the palace have been entirely removed, to give place to handsome villas.

Standing near the palace, and looking eastward, the leading features of the gardens present themselves, and consist in three principal openings or avenues, the best of which are terminated by Hyde Park, the intermediate and surrounding parts being filled in with dense masses of ancient trees. As the avenues are not sufficiently regular or contracted to acquire the dignity of art, and not expanded or broken enough to resemble nature, this scene is by no means impressive, like that at Hampton Court; and none of the vistas are at all happily terminated. But there is a massiveness about the trees, an appearance of age, and a total absence of anything that indicates the proximity of the town, which cannot fail to produce a striking effect on the observer, especially on a summer's day. The view down these avenues from the other side of the gardens, near the Serpentine, is much better, being terminated by Kensington Palace.

At various other parts of the gardens, these main avenues are crossed, at different angles, by a number of other avenues or vistas, which possess the great fault peculiar to that style of gardening, namely, that they are not properly connected with each other by any appropriate or necessary link, and that they have no sufficiently definite object. It cannot be too strongly urged that large straight walks will only be effective when they are obviously parts of some regular and symmetrical design, or conduct to some object important enough to justify their employment. One of the broad walks in these gardens is, however, very fine in itself; it has a row of excellent elms on each side, and is finished by a large rustic summer-house at the Bayswater end; an elegant church spire also form a conspicuous object behind the summer-house.

Of individual features, if we enter the gardens near the bridge over the Serpentine, and keep on the east side of the water, some noble old Spanish chestnut trees, which are well worthy of notice, will be found on the right, just within the gates. From this point to the head of the Serpentine, the walk beneath the fine old trees, with glimpses of the water and of the lawn and trees on the opposite bank, is one of the best parts of the gardens, the trees being more mature and more picturesquely disposed, and the ground less flat and tame, and the whole scene forming better and more varied combinations, than will be found anywhere else throughout the gardens. The new masses of shrubs on the western margin of the Serpentine, overrun with common laurel to an extent which almost conceals the Rhododendrons, of which they appear destined ultimately to be composed, are nearly the only deformities in this portion of the gardens.

After rounding the head of the water, the border of rarer plants, including a great number of good thorns, is seen on the right, and continues for some distance along the Uxbridge Road. The greater part of these plants are well labelled, as in St. James's Park. On the left, a kind of wilderness stretches far and wide, composed of tall trees alone, with no shrubs or undergrowth, but carpeted with grass, over any part of which the visitor may walk as he pleases. Nothing could be better adapted than all this part for a pleasant stroll in hot weather; although much variety, or any artistic arrangement, is by no means to be expected here. A little distance from the Serpentine, along by the northern boundary of the gardens, is a large mass of Scotch firs, some of which are interesting and picturesque, and their existence in this place forms a pleasant change from the comparatively monotonous foliage of deciduous trees. Considerably further on, and near the western boundary, there is a great number of evergreens, of large size, being chiefly hollies, cedars of Lebanon, and yews, often thrown together in groups of greater or lesser dimensions. From this quarter, too, the new villas, on the road formed after the destruction of the kitchen gardens, come into view. They are principally Italian, and assume some elegant and artistic shapes. Advancing towards the palace, the stately old orangery, which is not now used for plants, claims a passing glance, being one of the finest specimens of its class. Near the palace, a sudden change in the level of the ground is effected by a gradual slope in the broad gravel walk, and not by a flight of steps, as is more usual. This method has less of the dignity of art in it; but where the descent is sought to be disguised or rendered as little prominent as possible, the plan may be worth adopting. It certainly answers very well here in a position where steps would seem to be misplaced, and not sufficiently connected with the palace.

Immediately in front of the palace is a small flower garden, of quaint design, and inclosed with a low iron railing; while between this and Kensington there are some rows of capital old elm trees, which are here very rich and fine. At the bottom of one of the short avenues which they compose is a lofty architectural alcove, of the reign of Queen Anne. Keeping along the southern margin of the gardens, and crossing the end of the broad walk (which is 50 feet in breadth), the new walk already mentioned will soon be reached, and here the gardening visitor will find a large number of the newer and rarer kinds of shrubs, all legibly named; and, though not yet of any remarkable size, all appear healthy and flourishing. It is in the introduction of these rarer plants that the idea of a "garden" is perhaps better sustained than in most of the other features of the place, which are more those of a park. The demand, indeed, for evergreens and undergrowth in these gardens is most urgent; and if (which we greatly doubt) there exists a well-founded objection to the use of shrubs and bushes in tufts, or as single plants, there certainly can be no reason why solitary specimens or varied groups of the many kinds of thorn, pyrus, mespilus, laburnum, pine and fir, evergreen oaks, hollies, yews, &c., should not be most extensively planted, and a large proportion of the younger and smaller trees in the densest parts cut away to make room for them. We recommend those who wish fully to appreciate Kensington Gardens, to go there on a hot and sunny, or dusty, or windy day, when they will experience, particularly in the northern parts, the pleasure of having a shady and sheltered retreat, free from all the dust, and dirt, and bustle of the busy thoroughfares.

Kew Gardens.—The public gardens at Kew are at present divided into two portions, accessible by separate entrances and at different periods, and known severally as the "Botanic Gardens" and the "Pleasure Grounds." As some special reasons doubtless exist for keeping them apart, we can only express the hope that they will ere long be so far united as to be accessible from each other, that the public may thus have the additional privilege of taking a pleasant ramble and a scientific survey on the same day, and without the trouble of going round more than a quarter of a mile to reach the separate entrances. At present the Botanic Gardens are open every day, except Sundays, to respectable persons, from one o'clock till six; while the pleasure grounds can only be entered on Thursdays and Sundays, from Midsummer to Michaelmas.

An excellent guide to the Botanic Gardens at Kew has been prepared by the Director, Sir W. J. Hooker, and from this we shall glean only such particulars as a personal survey could hardly furnish; necessarily treating the subject somewhat lightly, because the gardens have already been so well described.

The history of these gardens may be soon told. They came into possession of the Royal Family through the Prince of Wales, father of George III., by whose princess both the pleasure grounds and exotic department were principally formed. In George III.'s reign, while Mr. W. Aiton was gardener, and under the auspices of Sir Joseph Banks, the gardens were greatly improved, and the extensive orangery, a large

c 3

stove, and other buildings, erected from the designs of Sir W. Chambers.
Until the death of George III., the collection of exotics and the number
of plant-houses were continually on the increase, and the gardens had
then acquired great celebrity. After this period, and until the year
1840, little or no progress was made, and the collection was chiefly
remarkable for the great size and richness of many of its specimens.
At that time, however, public attention having been drawn to the subject, and a commission of inquiry, headed by Dr. Lindley, having been
formed to report on the state of these gardens, the Commissioners of
Woods and Forests happily took them under their charge, and appointed
Sir W. J. Hooker—so distinguished as a botanist—to be director, and
Mr. John Smith—previously well known as a careful and intelligent
cultivator, and long connected with Kew—as curator.

Under the management of these gentlemen, and by the aid of liberal
parliamentary grants, the Botanic Gardens at Kew have undergone a
complete transformation. By the addition of a large tract from the
pleasure grounds, and by the destruction of all the old kitchen gardens,
the space has been extended from 11 acres to 75 acres. An immense
stove, with accompanying flower gardens, has been prepared; many new
and superior plant-houses have been erected; a museum is founded; a
pinetum planted; and, what is of great national importance, the whole
has been thrown freely open to the public for their unrestricted instruc-
tion and enjoyment.

A story is related, which it may be interesting to repeat, that the
well-known literary writer, William Cobbett, was once a common work-
man in these gardens, having been attracted thither by the wonders
they contained. It is said that George III., in one of his visits to the
gardens, noticed him, and desired that he might be retained in his
employ. Those who expect to see in Kew Gardens any superior examples of landscape arrangement, great beauty or symmetry of design,
or picturesque grouping, must lay their account with some little dis-
appointment. From the ugliness of the elevations and the defectiveness of the arrangement of the older buildings, from the difficulty of
blending new parts with old, and from the evident remains of a kitchen
garden on the site where the old one stood, with a hideous wall and
patch of unadorned ground (said to belong to the King of Hanover,
who refuses to surrender it) near the centre of the latter space, anything
really good in the way of landscape gardening was, perhaps, almost
impracticable. There are, however, some pleasant spots about the old
arboretum, where the visitor will find many magnificent specimens of
rare trees; and towards the great stove, the temples, and groups of trees
around them, both within the Botanic Gardens and the pleasure grounds,
present many very effective compositions. It is gratifying, also, to find
that Mr. Nesfield was commissioned to arrange the accompaniments to
the long broad walk, and the flower garden around the large stove.

It is with the greatest regret that we observe in the landscape features
of Kew, that the open glades in the pleasure grounds, as seen from the
Botanic Gardens, have been more than half planted up. Surely, with
such an immense mass of wood in the pleasure grounds, it would be more
desirable to employ the axe in the removal of at least half the existing
trees, and thus open up, instead of closing and covering, a great number
and variety of glades. The highest possible advantage, in a landscape
point of view, would result from such a breaking up of the old planta-

tions in the pleasure grounds ; and it is by no means clear to us that irregular glades might not extend from the verge of the Botanic Gardens quite into and across the little park near Richmond.

The entrance to Kew Gardens was formerly by a narrow alley from the side of Kew Green, along which the visitor proceeded, as it were by stealth. Now, however, a bold and highly appropriate entrance has been made at the end of Kew Green, where massive and enriched piers, gates, and open railing, extend across the end of the green. They are from the designs of Mr. Decimus Burton, and we have thought a sketch of part of them, here introduced, would be quite an ornament to our pages. Entering by these gates, *Taxodium sempervirens* and *Cryptomeria japonica* will be noticed on the lawn to the right. They are described as having stood three winters uninjured, and being plants which, from their novelty and the elegance of their forms, are much sought, it will be satisfactory to find them thus hardy. The *Taxodium*, we may mention, has even borne the much more northerly latitude of the neighbourhood of Liverpool, and is at present very flourishing.

ENTRANCE GATES TO KEW GARDENS.

As an accompaniment to the noble entrance gates, the large Architectural Conservatory on the right is very telling. It was brought here from Buckingham Palace. Though a good architectural feature, however, it was built at a period when the requirements of plants were little understood or little cared for; and hence it is far more heavy, and lofty, and dark than modern cultivators would approve. It is heated by an extraordinary number of small pipes, placed chiefly at the sides, by Mr. Perkins. This house, like all the others, is very conveniently numbered, and, from being nearest the gate, is known as No. 1. It contains a great many exceedingly fine Banksias, Dryandras, Grevilleas, Acacias, &c., and some huge and magnificent specimens of *Rhododendron arboreum*. The *Banksia solandra*, *Cunninghami*, *spinulosa*, and *latifolia*, with the *Dryandra formosa*, are particularly large and good. Nowhere in Britain—perhaps in Europe—is there anything at all equal to the plants of this tribe at Kew.

Passing out of the Conservatory westward, the long broad walk to the left will soon be entered upon. The large pillar which so happily finishes this walk is the chimney shaft to the furnaces which heat the great stove, and it also contains an extensive reservoir of water. The first house on the left is the old orangery (No. 2), built by Sir W. Chambers, in 1761. It is not at present used for orange-trees, but for storing a quantity of the less hardy trees and shrubs which will bear exposure in the summer, and do not require anything beyond shelter from frost during winter. These plants are generally placed about on the lawn, in the neighbourhood of the orangery, through the summer months. Many of them will be found at the back, and others are very appropriately used at the points of adjacent masses of shrubs, where they have a very good effect. Among them will be specially noticed some superb plants of *Altingia excelsa*, said to be the finest in Europe, and perfectly furnished with their flat graceful branches; *Araucaria Bidwilli*, which is rare and handsome; *A. brasiliana*, in an excellent state; the nearly hardy *Cunninghamia lanceolata*; several uncommon and rather tender pines; some large Camellias; with many kinds of Eucalyptus and other nearly hardy plants. The orangery is a very fine specimen of its class; but is now merely useful as a winter storehouse for such half-hardy plants as do not require much light at that season.

Advancing along the broad walk, by the sides of which an avenue of Deodar cedars has been planted, with subordinate rows of Juniper, Cypress, &c., and beds of Rhododendrons, other American plants, and summer flowers, a group of seven elm-trees stands out conspicuously on the right, and is called the "Seven Sisters," after the daughters of George III. At the end of this walk is a piece of water, of a kind of bell-shape, the broader end of which is straight, and finished with a balustraded wall, surmounted here and there with vases filled with summer flowers. The wall and vases are continued round each of the two ends for a short distance, and the rest of the banks of the water are of sloping grass, with occasional trees; and several masses of Rhododendrons have been newly introduced upon them. The object of the wall is evidently to form a sort of foreground to the great stove behind it, and to finish off the flower garden, which lies between it and the stove. The flower garden, of which there is a larger portion on the other side of the stove, is laid out geometrically, and acquires additional character by the aid of Irish yews and other dwarf evergreens, judiciously disposed, and by having many of the compartments sunk a foot or more below the general level. It looks best when viewed from the terrace on which the great stove fortunately stands, and which is continued all round the building. It has yet to be decorated with sculpture of various kinds. (See Frontispiece.)

One of the finest views of the great stove is that obtained from about the end of the long walk, where it is seen in perspective. Regarded as a whole, it cannot be considered a great architectural feature. The semicircular heads of the two lofty side entrances, and the attic in the middle portion of the building, appear to us particularly exceptionable. But in the superior height and breadth of the central part, in the adaptation of the whole to its intended object, and in the mechanical arrangements for ventilation, and for painting, repairing, &c., there is much to admire. Looked at pictorially, the building suffers—as everything of the same size would—by being so entirely unsupported. At present it stands alone, in a comparatively naked plain, with not a tree anywhere near it, to enter into a composition with it. This extreme nakedness and rawness—which the transparency of the material of which it is composed renders all the more glaring—are among its most defective characteristics, pictorially viewed.

As regards the building itself, we are happy in being able to furnish the following account, for which we are indebted to the architect.

This large building is constructed wholly of iron and glass, on a stone basement, and was erected from the designs and under the superintendence of Mr. Decimus Burton.

The masonry was executed by Messrs. Grissell and Peto, and the rest of the works by Mr. Richard Turner, of Dublin, who commenced in 1844, and completed the whole in 1848.

The whole of the ribs and sash bars are of wrought iron, rolled to the forms required while in a soft state by means of powerful rolling-machines; the ribs are composed of several pieces welded together, and bent to the curves required. They exhibit a method of construction which the contractor, Mr. Turner, was, it is believed, the first to introduce, and in this building. The glass used in the building is the result of many experiments made by Mr. Robert Hunt, of the Museum of Economic Geology, on the actinism of the solar rays, by which he found that the peculiar tint of green here adopted prevents the scorching effect upon foliage complained of in houses glazed with white glass. The glass is of great thickness, to resist the effect of hail storms.

The building contains upwards of 40,300 superficial feet of glass, or nearly an acre. The total length of the building is 362 feet 6 inches, the centre portion being 137 feet 6 inches long, and 100 feet wide, and 69 feet high to the top of the lanthorn light; the wings are each 112 feet 6 inches long, and 50 feet wide, and 33 feet high to the lanthorn.

A gallery runs round the centre portion of the house, at a height of 27 feet above the floor, from which fine views of the house and its beautiful inhabitants are obtained, and to which the ascent is by a light iron spiral staircase, inclosed by iron rods, which support climbing plants. The plants for which this house was erected, being natives of tropical countries, require that a heat of 80° should be maintained, while the external temperature is at 20° (Fahrenheit); this is effected by means of twelve boilers (Messrs. Burbidge and Healy's patent) placed in two vaults under the house, and upwards of 4¼ miles of iron pipes distributed under the floor and stone tables surrounding the house, giving a heating surface of about 28,000 superficial feet. As each of the boilers supplies a distinct set of pipes, the heat is readily and economically regulated by increasing or diminishing the number of boilers in use, and the house may be warmed in any particular portion, and climatised at pleasure. The heated air ascends through a perforated floor of cast-iron plates, supported on iron columns and girders, except where stone-paved paths interfere. The fuel to supply the furnaces is brought on a railway in a brick tunnel 550 feet in length, in which also are the smoke flues, which lead from the furnaces into one large vertical flue in a tower, which forms an ornamental object from various parts of the gardens.

The rain which falls on the Palm House roof is conveyed through the hollow pillars of support to a continuous tank under a stone shelf round the whole of the interior of the building, where its temperature is raised by its close contiguity to the heating pipes. This tank is capable of containing 42,000 gallons. Water also from the river Thames is supplied by means of a steam engine and pumps from an iron tank fixed at a height of 75 feet in the tower, from whence pipes distribute the water to the gallery and other parts of the house. The opportunity is thus afforded of throwing an artificial shower over the tops of the plants ; the steam engine also forces water into all parts of the garden. Ample ventilation is provided by means of rolling sashes on the roofs, by vertical pivot sashes, and by the panels in the stone basement of the building ; the whole of these ventilators, as well as the sashes, being readily opened and closed simultaneously by means of simple machinery. The cost of the structure, including the tunnel and tower, was about 33,000l.

Entering by the door at either end, the visitor will suddenly see before him one of the most extraordinary and perfect collections of tropical plants which is possessed by any garden in Europe. The wonderful variety of form in the foliage, and the extreme healthiness and richness of all the plants, are alike worthy of note. The mode of arranging the plants is to place a quantity of dwarf and showy ones on the narrow stages immediately under the glass, and all the rest along the centre, at the two ends, just leaving a sufficient path on either side of the house for visitors to walk comfortably on. All the plants are kept in tubs or pots, which stand on a kind of iron net-work or open grating with which the floor is covered, and through which the heated air ascends, as already explained. In the disposal of the plants, the highest are placed in the centre, and the lowest at the sides. This gives the whole a very formal appearance. In the central part, however, a more irregular and natural system of grouping has been followed, and with the happiest effect. This somewhat square middle space, with its broader and more varied masses of plants, just indicates the desirableness of making large houses of a squarer form than usual, and not so long and narrow. A house of the latter kind may be a very good repository for plants ; but a broader one would be equally suitable, and would, at the same time, furnish the means of arranging the plants far more artistically, and with much better effect.

The plants brought together in this large stove are all more or less interesting, and many of them very deeply so. Fortunately the visitor to whom such things are not familiar will easily be able to gather the required information from the labels which are attached to each plant, and which generally give the common as well as scientific name by which they are known. Here, besides the stately palms, some of which are superlatively fine, are most of the rich tropical fruits, together with plants which produce spices, gums, or other articles known in commerce. Here, also, in a small basin on the eastern side of the house, is the Egyptian *Papyrus*, from which paper was first made, many of the plants mentioned in Scripture, the *Valisneria spiralis*, also in water, where it uncoils its curious stems in proportion to the depth of the water in which it is placed, the sugar-cane, the cocoa-nut palm, the bread-fruit tree, the chocolate tree, the coffee tree, the celebrated banyan tree, the sensitive plants, and a great multitude of equally interesting objects. As more conspicuous features, the palms are extremely striking, and the bananas are also fine, and fruit well. Many of the palms flower and fruit abundantly ; and numerous other things, which are rarely seen elsewhere, except in a small state, regularly blossom and fruit here.

Among the more elegant and peculiar ornaments of this stove, the tree and other ferns will be sure to rank high in the visitor's esteem. The remarkable grace and beauty of their forms, and the tender green of their foliage, convey altogether a most pleasing and novel impression, such as scarcely anything else in the house produces. These ferns are especially to be admired when seen from the staircase or the gallery ; and, indeed, the view of the whole collection from the gallery affords quite a new idea of tropical vegetation, and should by all means be obtained. In going up the winding stairs, the observer will also notice how finely a species of *Bauhinia*, with its singular and large two-lobed leaves, is covering the railing, and how well both it and *Passiflora quadrangularis* are spreading along the sides of the gallery. The climbing plants, indeed, both in this and other parts of the house, will, when they have acquired two or three years more growth, immensely relieve and diversify the interior of the building. Towards the north end, we observed the singular club gourd, *Cucurbita maxima*, with its large pendulous club-shaped fruit. At present, the climbers at the sides of the house are grown in boxes beneath the stages, and trained up behind them ; a more regular provision for placing them in a better situation appearing to have been overlooked in the erection of the house.

About the centre of the house, particularly towards its eastern side, there is a great deal of *Lycopodium stoloniferum* scattered about, creating a very lively and agreeable verdure. If still more extensively used in such houses, it would greatly tend to relieve the appearance of dull-looking pots and tubs, or bare earth. In the great Winter Garden at Paris, it is actually employed as a lawn to carpet the ground between masses of plants, and has an exquisite effect during the winter months. There is no reason why it should not be used in much the same way in this country ; and it would make many a dingy back-ground look smiling and neat. The creation of small glades of verdure of this kind in a house like that at Kew, with larger or smaller groups of tropical vegetation scattered among them, and tufts of ferns filling in the lower parts of such groups, and blending them with the dwarfer herbage, might be rendered something quite enchanting. Of course it would require the pots or tubs in which the larger plants were kept to be sunk below the general level of the ground, so that they might appear to be growing out of a bed or border. And although the keeping of the plants in pots, as at Kew, unquestionably affords many advantages, and maintains their growth in proper check, yet every one will acknowledge that the pots and tubs themselves are very unsightly, and that the general effect would be better could they be sunk beneath the level of the paths, and covered over with something. It will be obvious, however, that nothing picturesque has been at all aimed at in this stove. There is no water for aquatics, except in small vessels, no rockery for ferns, no peculiar encouragement to tufts of rapid-growing plants (such as the bamboo and the plantains, which produce such a character in the great stove at Chatsworth), and no artistical grouping of any of the objects. Nevertheless, the magnificence of the general collection, and the grandeur of many of the individual specimens, together with the magnitude and lightness of the house, leave an impression on the visitor of deep admiration, and make him feel that in no other European country is gardening so munificently patronized and cultivated. For, however much we may be behind Continental States in our national galleries of art, it is quite certain that we stand unrivalled in our collections of plants.

Leaving the great stove, where so high a temperature is generally kept that caution will be necessary on returning to the open air, it will be noticed, looking in the direction of the pagoda, that some new lines of plants have been put down to form an avenue. Two of these lines are of Deodar cedars, which are to make the permanent avenue. The others are composed principally of scarlet thorns, with cypresses, junipers, &c., between them. Taking a north-westerly direction from the great stove, the plot of ground recently planted for a pinetum may be walked round. The plants are yet, of course, very young, and seem to have been dotted about in the usual common-place manner, without regard to their ultimately falling into groups. It may be admitted that it is no easy thing to arrange Conifers in a pinetum, where each plant is wanted to show itself distinctly, so that many of them shall in some degree blend into larger or smaller masses, and thus accomplish the double object of seeming specimens, while picturesque arrangement is also attained. But the very difficulty of the thing renders it all the more necessary that it should be attempted in a first-rate establishment; and that, instead of the ground being all pretty equally covered, there should be groups of two, three, four, five, or seven plants here and there, placed near enough to unite in a composition ultimately, but not so near as ever to interfere with each other, while single specimens are placed irregularly at the points of some of these, or between the masses, or in various other positions, but so that broad glades and decided open spaces are freely preserved.

Walking round the outside of the arboretum, the visitor will at length arrive at the Temple of Minden, in the southern corner of the garden, and pursuing the same walk, will pass the great chimney tower, and along the eastern margin of the water. Here some of the finest front views of the great stove may be had, and from this point the artist has taken the beautiful picture shown in our frontispiece. A little farther, on a mound of considerable elevation, is the temple of Æolus, very happily placed, and picturesquely embosomed in trees. This mound, with its temple and trees, make a very good picture from many points. A short walk to the right (though not to the extreme right, which leads to the museum) will conduct to the British Garden, where those who are interested in the study of native plants, will find most of the indigenous species arranged under the heads of the natural orders. A little to the left is also the grass garden, in which the student of exotic pasture or other grasses may correct his knowledge of them, and derive any fresh information.

Near this spot are the houses numbered 3, 4, 5, and 6. The first of these is chiefly filled with Mesembryanthemums and similar plants. No. 4 is a propagating house, which is commonly kept fastened up, but may sometimes be entered, when a number of curious or novel things will be found in it. In No. 5 will be seen some very interesting young stove plants, the extraordinary *Platycerium grande* growing on a board fixed to the wall, the lemon grass, a very curious strong-growing grass (*Andropogon Schœnanthus*), with a delicious scent, like *Aloysia citriodora*, and, on the other front stage, nestling among mosses and Lycopodiums, a number of charming little plants, with pitcher-like leaves, variegated Tillandsias, and other rare and pleasing objects, some of them with variegated leaves. The plants on this stage include the beautiful little *Cephalotus follicularis*, many Sarracenias, the *Dionœa muscipula*, &c. The manner in which they are arranged and grown is most happy and appropriate ; and the admirer of pretty exotic plants will be sure to be much pleased with this group.

Entering No. 6, one of the great modern wonders of this garden reveals itself. This is the house dedicated to the superb new water lily, *Victoria regia.* These gardens have the honour of first raising this extraordinary plant from seed, and distributing it throughout the country. And although it first flowered at Chatsworth, and next at Sion House, the plant in this stove has since bloomed abundantly, and is in excellent health. Indeed, it seems already to require a larger cistern to grow it in, which, as this is one of the very few places where it can be seen by the public, we hope it will speedily receive. The plant is now well known to have been discovered by Mr. (now Sir R. H.) Schomburgk in British Guiana, in 1837. Drawings were afterwards exhibited, and seeds repeatedly brought over ; but as these did not germinate, the idea of a plant with leaves from 5 to 6 feet across, and flowers 15 inches in diameter, began to be reckoned among those travellers' stories which men who go out of the beaten track are supposed to have a peculiar facility in concocting. At length, however, in 1849, Dr. Rodie, of Demerara, sent fresh seeds to the Kew Gardens, and as the plants from these have seeded profusely in this country, every one who will go to the expense of cultivating this vegetable phenomenon may easily obtain specimens. It

VICTORIA LILY.

appears to be a decided perennial; and is cultivated here in a high temperature, with a fresh supply of water slowly but constantly running through the tank. The leaves of the Kew plants have not yet reached the dimensions of those at Sion and Chatsworth, nor do they turn up quite so much at the edges: but there is every prospect of their speedily becoming in all respects equal. The flowers are large and very fragrant, of a creamy white, streaked and stained with deep pink towards the centre. A small sketch of both plant and flower is here furnished. Other aquatic plants are grown in the corners of the tank with the *Victoria*, and contribute much to improve its appearance. It has, in fact, rather a tame look unless aided by some taller-growing plants. When the leaves begin to turn up at the edges, however, it becomes more interesting; the extraordinary veins and spines on the under surface of the leaves, and their deep crimson colour on that side, imparting to it a much more striking character than when the upper surface alone is visible. In the *Nymphæa cœrulea*, and other allied plants which accompany the *Victoria* in this stove, the visitor will have an opportunity of comparing the giant proportions of this new water lily with the more common and familiar forms.

Leaving the Aquarium, and walking westward, the collection of grasses is nearly in front of us, and by keeping these on our left, we soon perceive the fine specimen of *Araucaria imbricata* on the lawn. This is the first plant of this favourite pine which was introduced into Britain, and was formerly protected with much care, but is now found perfectly hardy. Unlike all the other specimens in the country that we have seen, it has a bare stem to the height of 10 or 12 feet, and then expands into a broad, dense, hemispherical head. It is exceedingly curious and handsome, and has borne its large cones for the last four years. We noticed three of them on the plant last autumn. In Chili, where it is very abundant, the cones are said to reach the size of a child's head; and the individual seeds, which are about the size of acorns, though somewhat longer and less round, are eaten both for dessert and as articles of general food, being much like the Spanish chestnut in flavour.

In strong and admirable contrast with this singular Chili pine, the habit of which is so peculiarly rigid and bold, there is a lovely specimen of the weeping birch on the same lawn in the immediate neighbourhood. The extreme grace and elegance of this tree, whether with or without foliage, are particularly well set off by the strength and stiffness of its sturdy neighbour, and will not fail to command notice. Indeed, to the admirer of hardy trees, these are two of the most attractive plants in the garden.

The Greenhouse (No. 7) is a little to the westward of the spot just pointed out, and is very rich in the various kinds of New Zealand plants. The observer will, no doubt, be much struck with the great diversity of new and pleasing types which are here gathered together from one country. Nothing could be more beautiful than many of these are in point of form. The *Dacrydium cupressinum* is remarkably elegant, and there are fine plants of it here. Of the strange *Aralia crassifolia*, with its long, thick, and variegated leaves, there are also large plants; *Thuya Doniana*, a delightful new Arbor vitæ, some novel species of *Phyllocladus*, and many allied plants, are likewise to be met with in this house, and of very unusual size. The lover of rare plants and beautiful forms will, in fact, have a great treat from the examination of the treasures in this greenhouse, and will, if we do not mistake, be tempted to linger long in their inspection. He must by no means omit to notice the rare antarctic beech, which is so dwarf in its habit as almost to make one suspect it had been imported from China, and the yet more interesting evergreen beech (*Fagus betuloides*), which is almost equally dwarf, and is remarkable, as Sir W. J. Hooker tells us, "for its being the most southern-growing tree in the world; indeed, but little vegetation of any kind exists beyond it." Some large plants of *Magnolia fuscata*, well known for the peculiar scent of its flowers, will be found at the west end of the house, where *Sparmannia africana*—a plant that is more frequently found in a stove—flourishes and flowers most profusely; and there is also "one of the oldest and noblest specimens of the original *Rhododendron arboreum* in Europe."

Not far from the western end of this house there is a basin of water containing aquatic plants, many of which will be found worthy of notice; but the tussack grass of the Falkland Islands (*Dactylis cœspitosa*) is specially to be examined, because it is supposed likely, having stood out for three years, to become a valuable agricultural plant, on account of the great quantity and excellent quality of the herbage it produces.

A short distance from the back of No. 7, an old stove in two compartments (No. 8) may be entered, and will be found to contain, in the smaller or western part, a quantity of Tillandsias, Bromelias, &c., some of which grow naturally on trees like Orchids, and are very useful for suspending in stoves. Their flowers are often borne in long spikes, and are very showy. In the larger portion of this house, the members of the Aloe tribe are gathered together; and among their quaint forms will be distinguished the more beautiful and pensile species of *Littœa*, and the taller and conspicuous *Fourcroya gigantea*. Two plants of this latter kind "had been," says Sir W. J. Hooker, "in the royal gardens, first of Hampton Court and then of Kew, probably from the earliest introduction of the species into Europe, upwards of a century ago (in 1731). On one and the same day, in the summer of 1844, each was seen to produce a flowering stem, which resembled a gigantic head of asparagus, and grew at first at the astonishing rate of 2 feet in the twenty-four hours. So precisely did the twin plants keep pace with each other, that at the very time it was found necessary to make an aperture in the glass roof of the house for the emission of one panicle of flowers (26 feet from the ground), a similar release was needed by the other. The rate of growth then most sensibly diminished; still, in two months, the flower-stalks had attained a height of 36 feet! The flowers were innumerable on the great panicles: they produced no seed, but were succeeded by thousands of young plants, springing from the topmost branches, and these continued growing for a long while after the death of the parent plants, both of which perished, apparently from exhaustion." Only young plants are, therefore, now to be seen in this collection.

Near the centre of this stove is a strange-looking plant, with a stem not unlike the common Elephant's foot (*Testudo elephantipes*), but bearing grass-like leaves. It is from America, as we were told, and is unknown. Two extraordinary specimens of the Old-man Cactus (*Cereus senilis*) should likewise be pointed out, on account of their unusual size. They are actually from 12 to 15 feet high; but clothed with the white bristly hair, which gives its common name to the plant, only at the summit. Judging from the ordinary rate of growth in this species, Sir William

Hooker supposes these specimens may probably be as much as a thousand years old! If this be really the case,—and we know how careful Sir William is in putting forth such statements,—it gives a new and double significance to the name of the plant.

At the eastern end of this stove, on the outside, are a large *Photinia serrulata*, an immense old *Salisburia adiantifolia*, trained to a wall and kept pruned until very lately ; and, a little further on, three low trees, covered with ivy, growing into a very picturesque mass, and a magnificent plant of *Laurus sassafras.*

No. 9 is generally kept locked up, being a propagating house ; but No. 10, which is a large house devoted to Australian plants, is one of the best examples of modern construction and arrangement in the gardens. It is a long building, ranging nearly north and south, with what is called a span roof, which is only just high enough to enable persons to walk beneath it comfortably. There is a narrow flat stage on each side for plants, and the rest of the collection is placed on the ground in the centre, a walk running along on each side of this central mass. In the middle of the building it expands to a much greater breadth, which produces a good deal of variety and character. This house is light and well glazed, and peculiarly adapted for the tribe of plants generally placed in it. It is kept gay during the summer by retaining in it those plants which happen to be in flower, and by the use of the more showy but transient ordinary decorations of greenhouses. In the early part of spring, a very large proportion of the usual occupants of this house will be in flower. Perhaps April and May will be the best months. The collection of plants of this tribe is very perfect, and comprises most of the newest and best acquisitions, as well as those good old ornamental species which are now too seldom found elsewhere.

There is a large stove north of the Australian house, appropriated to orchids and ferns, of the former of which there is a very complete collection. This house (No. 11) is partly a new span-roofed building, and partly old, the division being only a glass one, and the doors being generally kept open between the two parts. The celebrated orchids of the late Duke of Bedford, and of the Rev. J. Clowes, of Manchester— both enthusiastic collectors—were added by gift to those previously existing here, and have greatly enriched the stock. On the whole, the orchids are well grown, and there are generally some of them in flower. The ferns on the north side of the house are in the best health, and furnish many highly interesting examples. Towards the middle of the house, near the partition, are some large pitcher-plants, with their singular goblet-shaped leaves.

Another stove (No. 12) contains a miscellaneous collection of plants, and is kept at a lower temperature than the Orchid House. The Begonias, of which there is a great variety, and some of which are very lovely, make a conspicuous appearance here.

Two greenhouses (Nos. 13 and 14) are assigned to an additional portion of Australian plants and cape heaths, the latter being grown in No. 13. In the house No. 14 are many excellent specimens. In the neighbourhood of these houses there is a bed of Cape heaths planted in the open ground, and apparently protected during winter ; and there are also several frames around this cluster of houses, in which will be found numerous plants that will afford interest to the more curious and inquiring cultivator.

The only other houses to which we shall refer are a stove (No. 16) at the back of the Museum, and the Cactus House, No. 19. Both of these are situated in what was the old kitchen garden, near the road from Kew to Richmond. In No. 16 are seemingly grown those rich and delicate tropical plants which will not thrive without a moist bottom heat. The nutmeg, clove, mangosteen, mahogany tree, Assam tea, the cow tree, the famed upas tree, and the Paraguay tea, are among the many plants which deserve to be examined here. The highly tropical forms of Cannas, Curcumas, Alpinias, &c., here abound. In this house, therefore, some time may very agreeably be spent; and the temperature, though high, is sufficiently humid to render it easily endurable.

No. 19, the Cactus House, is one of those best worth visiting, both because it contains a very first-rate collection, and because this is one of the very few houses in which any attempt at what we would call natural treatment or effect has been made. Let us add, that what is here done is with the happiest results. A walk passes through nearly the centre of the house on a raised level, between which and the front path there is a low pit, filled with the different kinds of *Echinocactus*, *Mammillaria*, &c. The specimens are planted out or plunged in the pots, among irregular masses of fused brick, so as to appear to be growing among small loose rocks. And though the material used is none of the most pleasing, and the forms into which it is thrown might with advantage be greatly varied on the surface, so as to take a less flat and more natural character, yet we cannot but point to the practice as a very decided step in the right direction, which we hope ere long to see extended to other departments and houses in these gardens, and executed with spirit. Plants of Lycopodium are growing here and there among the Cacti, and enliven the whole mass considerably; though they will undoubtedly require watching and restraint to prevent them from spreading too far, or producing too much moisture. It is difficult to conceive, without seeing them, what a change this system of treatment produces in the appearance of the tribe, and how well they seem to thrive under it. Of course the beds in which they are planted are most thoroughly drained, being filled with loose brick rubbish, or some similar material. Among the plants occupying this pit is the great Visnaga, of which the spines are used for tooth-picks in Mexico, from whence it derives its name. "The weight of this single specimen," observes Sir W. J. Hooker, "is 713 lbs., and it is in the most perfect health and vigour. It was drawn by oxen from the interior of Mexico (San Luis Potosi) to the coast for shipment, and arrived in excellent condition." Another specimen which weighed a ton was received at the same time, and appeared likely to grow, but it afterwards decayed.

Between the central path of this house and the back, the taller Opuntias, Euphorbias, species of Cereus, &c., are arranged, and the kinds of Stapelia, &c., occupy the front stage. As is well known, many of the larger forms bear the most splendid flowers. The cochineal insect, from which the brilliant dye called cochineal is obtained, may here be seen in abundance on the *Opuntia coccinilifera*. It is a small whitish mealy bug, and is so valuable in commerce, that Humboldt states there is exported from Mexico alone as much cochineal as yields annually the enormous sum of half a million sterling.

Many of the smaller members of this family here flower profusely, and produce very pretty blossoms, while some have showy fruit. From several of the Euphorbias a deadly poison is extracted, which is used on arrows and other weapons in South Africa. In this house, also, there is a small collection of plants from Africa, obtained near Ichaboe, where the great beds of guano exist. "More than one of them are remarkable (we quote again from the 'Guide' to Kew Gardens) for exuding gum resin, and that marked *Monsonia Burmannii* (the old *Geranium spinosum* of Linnæus) for becoming when dead a mass of gum resin, of which the quantity is so great in these burning sands, that it has been imported, in the hope of its proving valuable as an article of commerce. This particular plant on its arrival, and for four years, had been, to all appearance, perfectly dead, and more than half converted into a gum resinous substance, exhibiting only a few crooked lifeless-looking branches. Suddenly, in the spring of 1850, it has put forth leaves, and is full of life and vigour."

Before entering the museum, it will be worth while to take a walk through the herbaceous garden at the rear of that building, where several handsome plants, or tribes of plants, are usually in bloom. As this is a class which is now too much neglected, it is fortunate that particular attention is here given to them ; and those who will take the trouble to walk amongst them will be almost sure, at any period from March to November, to find some which they will desire to cultivate. Along the old walls, too, in this part of the garden, will be found a number of good climbers, from which a nice selection might easily be made by any one seeking to grow them.

We will now turn to the museum, which is quite a recent addition to these gardens, and by no means the least attractive or valuable one. At present it is confessedly but the beginning of what will, no doubt, some day include everything that such a depository could be wished to contain, not even omitting a herbarium. Even now, half an hour or an hour may be most amusingly and instructively spent in examining the specimens of the plants which produce hemp, flax, straws, vessels, caoutchouc, gutta-percha, and a variety of other things, with the numberless products manufactured from these, and articles illustrative of the different processes of manufacture. Here are also the plants which produce paper, and specimens of different papers, the opium plant, and the implements used in the preparation of the opium of commerce, sections of different woods, specimens of woods and barks, a great many sorts of seeds and seed vessels, specimens of plants used in medicine, or for chemical or other useful purposes, spices and dried fruits of many kinds, and an almost infinite variety of other vegetable products, mostly of a useful character. The museum is adorned, likewise, with models in wax of the *Victoria regia* and other flowers ; and with many drawings of the *Victoria*, the *Rafflesia Arnoldi*, and a multitude of other plants. Perhaps the article which is most perfectly illustrated—and to which public attention has been a good deal excited of late—is the gutta-percha, of which there are numerous specimens exhibiting its applicability to a number of ornamental objects.

After quitting the museum, the visitor will naturally return towards the entrance, and in doing so, he will cross the old arboretum. Here a temple, called the temple of the Sun, and erected by Sir W. Chambers, will be conspicuous ; and around that, the botanist, or admirer of hardy trees, will loiter a little to inspect the many fine specimens of old exotic trees. Among them will be particularly noticed a venerable old cedar, shattered by a gale in 1841, and rendered highly picturesque by the destruction of its head, although the greater part of its former beauty is of course gone. We need not single out any of the rest, because a stroll among them will show that, like all the other plants in the garden, they are each (except those which are too common to need such aids) conspicuously labelled,—a circumstance which, in gardens of this character and extent, is of the very utmost importance and value.

It may be well just to recapitulate that the houses which will most remunerate the enlightened visitor are—No. 1 for its splendid specimens of Banksias, &c.; the great stove for palms and tropical plants; No. 5 for the small pitcher-like and variegated stove plants on the front stage; No. 6 for the great water-lily; No. 7, as containing so many elegant New Zealand plants; No. 8, which comprises the aloes and their allies; No. 10, the Australian plants; No. 11, the orchids and ferns; No. 12, for the gesneras, gloxinias, and achimenes in summer; No. 16, for the tropical plants which require great heat; and, No. 19, for the cactaceous plants. And we are sure that, on leaving these gardens, the visitor must feel himself astonished and delighted with the magnitude and splendour of the collection of exotics in them, and with the excellence of the arrangements, and the liberality with which the public are so freely allowed to go everywhere unattended. We need hardly say that a whole day should be given to the inspection of this collection; or, at least, that persons wishing to see it well should be there directly the gates are opened.

If Thursday be chosen for visiting Kew, parties who have thoroughly looked through the Botanic Gardens may quietly stroll through the *pleasure grounds*, which are not closed till dusk, and which will not demand a lengthened survey. They can be entered at either of the two gates on the Richmond Road, or by one situated at the side of the Thames. As the latter is the one usually chosen by persons going from the Botanic Gardens, we will suppose the visitor to start from that point.

Allowing for the abstractions which have been made to enlarge the Botanic Gardens, these pleasure grounds now contain nearly 130 acres. Just before the gate is reached, two or three very large elms will be noticed, one of which is said to have been planted by Queen Elizabeth, but was blown down about eight years ago. The stump is still preserved. It may be well also to point out the long island in the river, opposite Kew Palace, where a plantation of trees was happily made to cover the town of Brentford, which it certainly does in the summer season, while at the same time it adds to the beauty of the river at this point, and would be a still finer object were there not so many common willows upon it. These last, growing up rapidly to one uniform height, and having all the same common-looking character, greatly detract from the appearance of the island, which might be much improved by a sprinkling of lower trees among them. Nothing would look better than alders of various kinds in such a position, and they are very fast growing. A few deciduous cypresses, also, which would flourish here, might greatly relieve the appearance.

On entering the gates of the pleasure grounds, it will be seen that there are a great number of newly-planted trees, evidently arranged with the intention of forming this ground into an aboretum. A collection of elms is commenced just within the gates, and other tribes will be noticed farther on. That it may be desirable to have a good national arboretum we readily admit; but that, in a place already so thickly covered with trees, and where very few glades of grass or openings of any kind exist, every little open space should be filled up with new trees, as is here done, so as, in time, to render the whole one dark and gloomy mass of shade, we, in our ignorance of the final intentions of the planters, can by no means understand or appreciate.

Proceeding by the walk which leads along near the river side, the ground soon loses some of its tameness, and a pleasant hollow on the left begins to show itself, and continues for some distance, the slopes and tops of the banks being rather profusely studded with evergreens, of which there is, in other parts, a great dearth. Continuing along this walk, beds of rare yews and other small and uncommon plants will be occasionally observed, newly dotted down in the strangest places. Views of Sion House and Park, with the noble cedars accompanying it, then begin to reveal themselves, and to take a shifting but generally pleasing character with the progress of the visitor. Portions of the Little Park at Richmond also come into sight, and here, at *the side* of a group of fine trees, we remarked a large Lombardy poplar, as an example of how much out of place this very effective plant appears when it is not actually *inclosed* by a group of other trees. At a much more advanced part of the walk, when the spectator comes more opposite this mass of trees, the poplar, from seeming to rise nearly out of the middle of them, becomes quite characteristic and beautiful.

Passing a large glade in the grounds, where the grass, from its rankness, appears to have been *burnt* off in order to be renewed, and where a number of old oak trees are scattered about, some signs of increasing cultivation prepare the visitor for coming upon what is called Queen Charlotte's Cottage, a picturesque building, with a thatched roof and deep eaves, now uninhabited. We noticed here how much character may be given to any building by the treatment of the roof ; for this cottage, which is certainly common-place enough in itself, is made to possess a degree of picturesque beauty, and a harmony with the masses of forest-like woods around, almost solely by the prominence given to the eaves of the roof. In the autumn, the effect of the building is further heightened by the Virginian creeper and clematis with which it is in great part mantled.

Formerly there was an inclosed garden around this cottage, and, as we were told, it was a favourite resort of Queen Charlotte, who used to keep kangaroos there. The remains of the garden are still visible in a smoother piece of lawn than is common in these pleasure grounds, and some good masses of Rhododendrons, which are nicely dotted about, and must be very showy in spring.

On the right-hand side of the walk, the little park of Richmond, comprising 400 acres, now opens out to view, and continues till the Richmond Road is gained. In this park the observatory is situated, and is now used by the British Association for the Advancement of Science, in order to carry on a series of experiments on terrestrial magnetism. This park is simply a large flat pasture, over which a few good old trees are sprinkled ; but we do not think it is accessible to the public.

Between Queen Charlotte's Cottage and the Pagoda, beds of hydrangeas, deeringias, ribes, berberries, &c., occur, but in places where thickets of native plants would seem much more appropriate. Indeed, we can in no way reconcile the introduction of dwarf and rare plants amongst old woods that are even destitute of suitable undergrowth with any principle of landscape arrangement. Uncommon exotic shrubs, especially such as are not often met with even in cultivated gardens, assuredly require to be planted in a dressed and polished scene, amid various rich and more ordinary exotics. In a wild woody spot like the greater part of Kew pleasure grounds, the principal enrichment wanted a tufts of common evergreens, and great masses of evergreen and other undergrowth;—yews, hollies, brooms, rhododendrons, berberries, &c., with such gayer deciduous plants as laburnums, thorns, crabs, viburnums, &c. And all these should not be disposed in quaint beds and regular figures, such as are here seen, but to suit the irregularity and partial wildness of the old woods. We can imagine this becoming a very delightful spot if so treated; but never being anything better than it now is by the system which seems to be adopted, unless the bulk of the old trees are cut down, and the place is converted into a huge garden.

Shortly before coming to the pagoda, a summer-house presents itself, from which, through a short and broken avenue of Scotch firs, a capital view of the pagoda is obtained. Here, supported and half shrouded as it is by trees, the proportions of this building assume a much more pleasing harmony than at a distance. When seen from any remote point, it appears so much above the trees as to look too slender for its height, and does not at all fall in with the vegetable forms around it. But from the summer-house just mentioned, and from another on the opposite side, it is a really fine object, and blends exceedingly well with the trees. Looking at it from the summer-house and the walk at its northern side, there are two or three Scotch firs near it which enter most admirably into a composition with it, and without which it would appear sadly blank and unsupported. We were astonished to find these trees marked for felling, and hope it must have been by mistake, and that they will yet be spared, as they are of the greatest consequence in a pictorial light. There are also four or five cedars of Lebanon, which group well together, near the pagoda.

From the vicinity of the pagoda, the avenues of Deodar, &c., before noticed as leading from the palm house in the Botanic Gardens to this point, again come into view, and the aspect of the palm house from this part of the pleasure grounds is much more satisfactory than any nearer view of it, because it is well supported by trees as seen from hence.

A considerable open space about the pagoda has been planted, on one side of the Deodar avenue, with numerous beds of rosaceous plants; while a similar space on the other side contains great numbers of the leguminous tribe, arranged in regular beds, with rows of acacias and other plants among them. A great many of the more tender acacias and other common inhabitants of the greenhouse are planted out here, —no doubt by way of experiment. As these new plantations occur in a sufficiently large and open area, and are disposed, apparently, with something like system and regularity, they will of course not lie open to the objections hitherto urged, especially as they will be connected with the Botanic Gardens, by the avenue of Deodars, and are in the immediate neighbourhood of the pagoda.

Along the back of the Deodar avenue, we believe, and in other less accessible parts of these pleasure grounds, have been put in clusters of new trees, with the members of one genus in a group, which will never, we think, unite well together, or form an agreeable whole, and which must greatly damage the effect of the handsome old trees before which

D

they are placed, and which last, in all probability, would have gone on improving for the next century, at least.

After leaving the pagoda, the walk runs nearly parallel with the Richmond road, and as the trees on the left are more spread about, and not so dense, an improved effect is obtained. Beds of fresh plants, here and there, still continue, with the same disregard to their fitness for the position in which they are placed. The temple of Victory, with some nice cedars of Lebanon as accompaniments, the Pantheon, another temple erected by William IV., well situated and backed by trees, and the ruined arch, all occur along the side near the Richmond road. The ruined arch is far from being an unpicturesque object; but an artificial ruin in a state of dilapidation, and revealing the superficial and delusive character of the structure, without any of the harmonizing and concealing drapery of ivy and other wild climbers, cannot be admired; and hence the present state of this ruin is not at all gratifying.

With respect to the temples, both here and in what are now the Botanic Gardens, it may be noted that they are generally well placed, and fitly accompanied, a sort of artificial mound having been raised to plant them upon, and a number of trees being judiciously disposed around portions of them. There were formerly other architectural objects in these gardens; but they became so decayed, or were considered so unsuitable, that they have been removed. The pagoda is unquestionably the finest now remaining. It is of an octagonal form, 163 feet in height, and 49 feet in diameter at the base. There are ten stories to the building, each of which has an outer gallery, inclosed by a rail, and covered with a projecting roof of sheet iron. The staircase is in the middle of the building; and the prospects from the several stories and from the summit are said to be very various and extensive.

A gate at the end of the pleasure grounds, near where they adjoin the Botanic Gardens, will dismiss the visitor into the Richmond road, within a few minutes' walk of Kew Bridge, where steamers, a railway, or omnibuses, will convey him to London or any intermediate place.

Horticultural Society's Gardens.—Situated at Turnham Green, which is better known from being in Chiswick parish, these gardens—taking in a far wider range of objects than the Botanic Gardens at Kew—have acquired great celebrity from their having been established at a period when gardening was in a very low condition in this country, and from having been the principal means of raising it to its present extraordinary and yet rapidly-improving state.

Founded in 1802, and incorporated by charter in 1808, the Horticultural Society issued its first volume of "Transactions" in 1812, and in 1822 arranged with the Duke of Devonshire for the lease of 33 acres of land at Chiswick, in order to form a garden. Previously to this, a small piece of ground had been temporarily occupied by them at Brompton. In 1824, the orchard and great part of the garden was planted and arranged, and in 1825 the arboretum was completed. During all this time, T. A. Knight, Esquire, so widely known by his valuable experiments and writings on horticultural matters, was the president of the Society, having largely contributed to its establishment, and, by his great exertions, laid the foundation of its subsequent usefulness. Mr. Joseph Sabine was then, also, the honorary secretary, and had much of the practical management of the Society's affairs.

About the year 1830, the financial difficulties of the Society drew the attention of its members to the faulty state of its management, and, as the result of much deliberation and inquiry, Professor Lindley, who had been previously the assistant secretary, was charged, in connection with the committee or council, with the whole of the executive business of the Society; and by his able and enlightened efforts it has been, in great measure, extricated from its difficulties, and settled on a satisfactory and sound basis. In fact, for the last twenty years, its course has been, for the most part, a highly prosperous one, and it has so far achieved its object in reference to some of the points contemplated by its establishment, as to be able partly to relinquish these, and embrace the wider field of ornamental cultivation.

Although we are chiefly concerned with such a notice of this Society as will illustrate the present condition of its garden, so important has been the influence which it has exerted upon horticulture that we think we shall not be travelling out of our way by still further explaining the intentions of its founders, and the manner in which they have been accomplished. At the period when it was first formed, the want of systematic and combined effort among the promoters of horticulture, and the absence of anything like a gardening literature by which discussion and intercommunication could be kept up, had incalculably retarded the progress of cultivation, except in reference to a few such things as the forcing of fruit and vegetables, which was looked upon as the highest attainment of horticultural skill, and in which the gardeners of that day had attained an excellence which has scarcely since been surpassed. In regard, however, to the kinds of vegetables and fruits more commonly grown, and to the means, and processes, and philosophy of cultivation, an immense deal then remained to be done which has since very largely been effected, and which the Horticultural Society has been one of the principal means of performing.

To act upon the then comparatively dormant horticultural mind, this Society, besides establishing frequent meetings in its rooms at Regent Street, at which superior gardening products were exhibited, and the cultivators stimulated by prizes, invited communications from all parties on subjects relating to horticulture, and published these in a combined form in their " Transactions." They also commenced a gardening library, which has been subsequently so much augmented as to become a most valuable repository of all that relates to the art, and which is readily accessible to respectable persons. When the garden was formed, moreover, they employed it for cultivating and testing all the known kinds of fruits and vegetables, trees and flowers, and trying various methods of treatment, and practically experimenting on every new sort of machinery or appliance used in the various branches of horticulture. The collection of fruits, vegetables, and ornamental plants thus became a living cyclopædia of reference as to every object of value to the cultivator; and, during successive seasons, every different mode of managing the numerous products of a garden has been tried.

At the same time, by opening communications, and establishing exchanges, with the various public, commercial, and private establishments throughout our own country and the world, the Society has been enabled to gather together, at various times, a prodigious mass of new and valuable plants as well as information, and the former of these it has distributed to its members through the medium of cuttings, &c., and the latter by means of its " Transactions."

Nor has it been at all inactive in adopting more direct methods of obtaining new and interesting objects from previously-unexplored resources. At different periods since its origin, it has sent out numerous collectors, specially commissioned to search for novel and useful plants in tracts before untrodden, save by the wild beast or the savage, and the aggregate of such acquisitions is now quite startling. There are, in fact, but few of our most prized modern ornamental plants which the Society has not, in some way, been the means of introducing, or of making more generally available. The list of its own exclusive collectors is now a considerable one; and among them the name of the unfortunate Douglas will long live as having introduced such excellent hardy plants as *Ribes sanguineum, Berberis aquifolium, Spiræa ariæfolia, Gaultheria shallon, Garrya elliptica, Acer macrophyllum,* several first-rate species of *Pinus* and *Abies, Nemophila insignis,* and many other annuals, *Mimulus moschatus* and *cardinalis,* some showy Lupines, and, in short, above 200 hardy plants, all of which are more or less ornamental. The more recent acquisitions, also, of Hartweg in Mexico and the neighbouring countries, and Fortune in China, are of great value, and will contribute much, in the present and future ages, to do honour to the Horticultural Society.

In addition to the shows periodically held at Regent Street, the Society began an exhibition—of fruits only—at the gardens in the month of June, 1831; and this was extended to flowering plants, and held in the months of May, June, and July, in the year 1833. These exhibitions have since been regularly continued; and, by the amount of the prizes offered, and the emulation which is excited among cultivators through having their objects examined by such multitudes of the higher class of visitors, have tended, almost more than any other means, to bring plant cultivation in England to its present truly wonderful state. Those who have the good fortune to witness one or more of these displays, when, besides the extraordinary richness of the plants and flowers, all the beauty and fashion of the metropolis are quietly promenading the gardens, and the best military bands are filling the air with delicious music, will certainly form a very exalted notion of what the Horticultural Society has done for gardening.

The exhibitions of the Society are still kept up in the gardens for one day in each of the three months above named, and for several years the Duke of Devonshire, who has been president of the Society ever since the death of Mr. Knight, has very handsomely allowed his beautiful grounds at Chiswick, which adjoin the Horticultural Gardens, to be thrown open to those who attend the July exhibition. For the year 1851, we are informed, the Society has made special provision for gratifying the visitors to the metropolis, by allowing Mr. Hosea Waterer, of Knap Hill, to exhibit his magnificent collection of rhododendrons and other American plants; and there is also, we believe, to be a special show of fruit, with other novel features, on some day in the month of August, hereafter to be announced.

Of the usual garden shows got up by the Society, that in May is peculiarly rich in azaleas, the splendour of which is surpassingly great. Orchids, too, which are now exhibited most abundantly, and have been brought to the very highest perfection, are perhaps finest at the May show. Indeed, almost every kind of flower here shown is commonly best in the month of May. Pelargoniums, heaths, roses in pots (in the culture of which an immense improvement has lately been made), and calceolarias, are mostly about as good in June as in May. The various kinds of cacti, with their gorgeous flowers, and collections of cut roses, constitute one of the great features of the June exhibition, which otherwise includes orchids almost as good as in May, and most of the other features of the May show, with such showy plants as ixoras, and some of the greenhouse specimens, often in better flower than in May. The July show is most conspicuous for fruit; but also contains many of the flowering things produced at the earlier periods, and comprises a more miscellaneous collection, in which no one class has any very decided or conspicuous prominence. Those persons who can only attend one of the shows, and who wish to see the greatest display of flowers, will ordinarily be safest in choosing the one given in May, unless the season be a very late one.

We must not omit to mention that the Society has done much for horticulture by endeavouring to raise the character and improve the education of gardeners in their establishment. Young men are only admitted to the gardens after undergoing an examination in various branches of the business, and they are subsequently examined as to their progress and proficiency. Within the last two or three years, likewise, a reading room and study have been formed for the young men in the gardens, where, without any expense to themselves, they can use the books in a good library, or instruments provided for drawing. And Dr. Lindley has kindly delivered to them a series of lectures on botany and gardening science, on which matters he directs their studies, and periodically examines them in class, awarding prizes in books to the value of 2*l.* and 3*l.* for those two among the young men who attain the greatest proficiency. All these things are admirably calculated to produce an intelligent, thinking, and skilful race of gardeners, fitted at once for raising the art in the scale of public estimation, and for carrying fully and successfully into practice those modern scientific principles, the development of which has rendered English gardening the occasion of envy and admiration to all the rest of Europe.

It is time, however, that we gave some account of the Society's garden; and we shall commence with the fruit department, which was that formed earliest, and constituted originally one of the leading features of the establishment. It is now, and has been for the last twenty-four years, under the superintendence of Mr. Thompson, whose knowledge of the fruits grown in this country, and skill in their cultivation, is justly considered unrivalled. If any proof were needed of the advantage of confining one man's attention to one department, in order to secure the highest knowledge and excellence, Mr. Thompson would supply that proof to demonstration. Earnestly devoted to his main pursuit, there is not a variety of fruit, or peculiarity in their habit, or delicate distinction of flavour, or aptitude for receiving any particular treatment, with which he is not thoroughly familiar. And this is the sort of acquirement which not only fits a person for such a position in such a garden, but renders him of the greatest use to science and art in general; for it is chiefly by exclusive application of this kind that science widens its foundations, and all the processes of art are advanced.

At an earlier period, when this garden was first formed, its fruit department embraced the culture of such things as pine apples, and the *forcing* of peaches, figs, cherries, &c., with the growth of mushrooms and such like objects. Now, however, nothing of this kind is attempted beyond trying a few grapes, and proving melons, cucumbers, or similar plants. After having given several years to ordinary forcing, and shown some of the best examples of it, the experiment was found too expensive, and the modes of cultivation, or the sorts of fruit used in that way, changed too little to warrant a large machinery being kept up solely to test them. The existing fruit department is therefore confined almost wholly to hardy things.

Guided by Mr. Thompson, who kindly explained the arrangements and objects of this department to us, we walked all over it in the autumn of 1850, and found that it had recently been re-arranged, and much of -it planted afresh. It occupies about nine acres, inclusive of the part devoted to vegetables. It is divided by walks into several quarters, of different sizes. There is a large quarter of old apple and pear trees occupying an acre and a half. A quarter newly planted with pears, to be trained as espaliers, contains about half an acre. Another quarter, of about a third of an acre, is appropriated to select plums ; and one of the same extent to cherries. There is also a plot, of similar dimensions, just planted with general fruits, in which every known method of training is to be exemplified. A trial ground, for new fruits of every kind, contains three quarters of an acre; and there is a large border for the newest and best strawberries, with a border for apple trees all round the orchard.

Much of the ground having been newly planted, the interest attaching to this department is not so great as it will ultimately be ; especially as that portion which has been freshly arranged, comprises all the more novel sorts of fruits. The great aim in this part of the garden, as in every other portion, is to ascertain and exhibit the best kinds of articles in any particular tribe, and to show how they may most fitly be treated. And to render the comparison between any given .varieties, or the exhibition of any one sort more perfect, there is an excellent fruit room, where fellows of the Society and their friends, or, we believe, any respectable gardener, may examine and taste the various fruits, while they can afterwards refer to the living tree, if they desire, in order to see its character and habit.

The fruit room is large, and situated at the back of a peach wall. It has a north-westerly aspect, and is entered through another small room, so as never to admit the external air when this is wished to be excluded. It is generally kept almost dark, and well ventilated, the windows being matted up in winter just to keep out frost, and no fire heat employed. The fruit is laid on wooden shelves, arranged in tiers, and formed of strips of wood about three inches wide, with small openings between each piece. The more valuable sorts of pear are wrapped individually in soft paper. Nothing could be more simple than the arrangement of this fruit room, the great point requiring attention being to see that it is just sufficiently ventilated to carry off the moisture which exhales from the fruit, without drying the air so much as to cause any of the articles to shrivel. Almost total darkness is also maintained.

As a very pleasing and useful adjunct to the fruit room, there is kept, in a small apartment through which it is entered, a collection of greatly varying fruits, admirably modelled in wax by Mr. Tuson, who was formerly connected with the gardens, and who has exhibited much self-taught skill in the execution of his task. Being coloured to resemble the several kinds of fruit which they represent, these models serve as a constant reference for visitors, even when the fruits themselves are not in season.

On the long wall behind the fruit room are some excellent peach and nectarine trees, with occasional grape vines intermixed. The border is divided into compartments by hedges of Arbor-Vitæ, at distant intervals, to prevent the winds from sweeping along it with such violence; but Mr. Thompson does not attach any importance to the plan. The pear trees on the other walls are models of excellence, and bear prodigiously. They are nearly all trained on the horizontal system, and the young shoots stopped twice or thrice during the summer, so that they require very little pruning in winter. We observed, also, that all the dwarf apple and pear trees, which are required to be kept within certain limits, are extensively pruned in the summer, by stopping back all their young shoots; and this plan, besides preventing the undue extension of the trees, seems to have a decided and valuable tendency to throw them into a good fruit-bearing state.

In preparing the new ground for orchard planting, no drainage is requisite here, on account of the porous nature of the substratum, and the manner in which this is kept open by worms. But deep trenching is of course practised.

With that part used as kitchen garden, it is customary to select certain tribes of vegetables for each year's experiments, and obtain seeds or plants from the most certain sources of each particular kind of vegetable belonging to such tribes. These are then planted in rows, side by side, and their relative merits, and true character, and comparative distinctness, may thus be noted by any visitor during the season; while a faithful record of the results of the trial is kept, and given to the world through various channels. It is impossible to over-rate the value of such experiments, directed impartially, in clearing away from our ridiculously long lists of vegetables such names as are merely synonymes, and such kinds as are quite unworthy of cultivation. Nothing could be more loudly demanded than an extensive weeding out of our vegetable catalogues; and no more satisfactory method than that pursued here could be adopted for accomplishing that object. For seeds of each sort are procured from the originator or principal grower, and the plants are placed in precisely equal circumstances, on one plot of land, where they can be inspected during their entire growth by every one at all interested in their culture, and where their relative excellence is afterwards most fairly made known.

In this part of the garden are likewise often tested those numerous chemical and compound manures which are so peculiarly the offspring of the present age, and of which we occasionally hear so much. Only two or three years back, indeed, the Society rendered great service to horticulture and agriculture, by commissioning Mr. E. Solly, jun., to carry out a series of experiments in the garden, on the efficacy of the different modern manures, and that gentleman also delivered a course of lectures on the subject at the Society's rooms in Regent Street.

At the western end of the kitchen garden, on the site of what was the miscellaneous fruit department, where all the useless fruits which will grow in Britain were formerly cultivated, just for the sake of having a full collection, some considerable improvements had, when we visited the garden in October last, been commenced, and will no doubt be completed by the spring. About an acre and a half of land is here to be converted into a sort of flower garden and American ground, to receive the exhibition of American plants in 1851. By excavating along the centre of part of this plot, and throwing up the earth into banks—chiefly at the eastern side, some variety of surface will be obtained, and the faces of the banks are, we believe, to be broken with masses of fused brick, irregularly disposed, to form a receptacle for rock-plants. Small walks are also to wind among these masses of rock-work, on various levels. As there are several old specimens of trees and plants remaining on the ground, the whole may no doubt be made to present, at once, a good deal of character.

It would of course be premature to give more than this general description of changes that were only in progress when we saw them. But we are delighted to find that in this and similar ways, the managers of the Society's affairs are alive to the importance of keeping pace with the general progress of gardening, and that they have determined to render their garden more attractive. Much yet remains to be done ; and though the flat surface of the ground, and the number of objects upon it, and the character of the original arrangement of the parts, render it to some extent intractable ; we believe that, if the Society had plans of the whole prepared on a moderately large scale, indicating everything that is now upon it, and submitted these to the landscape gardeners of Britain, with ample time for consideration, and the promise of certain privileges to those who supplied designs for improving it, there are very few who would not, without any pecuniary remuneration, and simply from a desire to see this garden made as perfect as possible, give them the benefit of their suggestions. In this way, perhaps, a plan might be struck out which, by being gradually executed, as funds could be obtained, would make the garden more worthy of ranking as the best British establishment of this class.

From the new American ground, an old walk, surrounding the orchard, and bordering this side of the garden, passes off eastward, and a great many trees and plants have recently been cut out of the border, partly to show the specimens of rarer things already existing in it, and partly to obtain room for a quantity of better shrubs. This border contains, near the boundary fence, numerous very fine specimens of different kinds of *Cratægus*, which are well worth examining. It is in future, we are told, to be fronted by the very lowest sorts of dwarf and trailing shrubs, so as to have no bare earth visible, and yet not to require a grass or other edging.

Leaving the American garden, however, in an opposite direction, and passing under a bridge which has been made to carry the kitchen-garden road across this newly-ornamented part, we soon rise into a straight walk, at the other extremity of which the large conservatory will be seen. And here we may mention that the whole of that portion of the garden which does not come within Mr. Thompson's department is now under the direction of Mr. Gordon, who is a kind of walking cyclopædia of plants, and of everything relating to his department, and under whose conduct we spent a very instructive half day in scrutinizing the various treasures which this part of the garden contains, and of which the mere casual visitor, who cares little about such things, or has not the advantage of such a guide, forms no adequate conception. Indeed, it would be of great assistance to those who visit the garden if the pits, houses, &c., were all numbered, and a more elaborate " guide book " than we can possibly pretend to furnish were provided at a cheap rate, as at Kew.

In the borders at the sides of the straight walk before alluded to, at the west end of the great conservatory, the visitor will find some highly interesting objects. Here are many of the magnificent Mexican pines, introduced by Hartweg; some of which, by the magnitude and boldness of their foliage, are quite startling, and will, in time, constitute splendid features in our southern English landscapes. Among the most remarkable, we noticed *Pinus macrophylla, Hartwegii, Devoniana, Russelliana,* and *Lindleyana,* which are truly noble in their character, and strikingly different from such as are commonly met with, both in the size and paler colour of their foliage. In these borders are likewise capital plants of *Cupressus macrocarpa,* one of the very best of modern introductions, with nearly horizontal branches, something in the style of the cedar of Lebanon; and *Cupressus Uhdeana,* which has glaucous leaves, and will constitute a novel and beautiful ornament to lawns or shrubberies. *Cryptomeria japonica* and *Taxodium sempervirens* are here, too, in excellent condition, and a multitude of other scarcely less rare and conspicuous plants, among which we may further note a large and healthy *Paulownia imperialis,* which seems to be quietly establishing itself in sheltered places throughout the country, and the common upright yew. This last plant, which is very rarely seen, has a good deal of the habit of the Irish yew, but is stronger and more dense-growing, and apparently superior. It never becomes so ragged, and is not broken down by winds or snows. There is here a particularly handsome specimen of it.

On the rockwork which supports the banks at either side of the entrance to the conservatory, large patches of the Russian pyracanth are appropriately placed. It is decidedly different from the common pyracanth, and has pale orange berries, which are borne, as on the ordinary kind, most profusely. Mr. Gordon says it is more hardy than the commoner sort; and it is admirably fitted for growing on rocks, to give projection to a jutting mass, on account of its close habit, and because it is evergreen, and is enlivened with berries in autumn and winter. It is even better than *Cotoneaster microphylla* for this purpose, being bolder, and presenting its berries more conspicuously.

Approaching the large conservatory at its western end, it exhibits a very light and elegant exterior; but, in conjunction we believe with most persons who have seen it, we cannot admire the mode in which the entrance is there effected. The walk is made to descend gradually for some distance, so as to get the door beneath the plinth of the house, and there are steps to the right and left after entering, to conduct to the level of the floor of the house. This is essentially awkward and inconvenient, and gives the impression, from the outside, of going down into the house, instead of rising to it as would be desirable. So far is this plan from improving the elevation, too, that we cannot but think a bold square-headed door, with proper mouldings, would be rather an advantage to the appearance of the building at this end.

Entering this conservatory, which is remarkably neat, and has, if anything, too much light for the plants—a fault which, if it exists anywhere, is peculiarly modern, and arises out of the excess of a virtue—the character of the house, and the arrangement of the plants in it, will be almost sure to please. It has a curvilinear roof, formed entirely of light iron, and glazed with patent sheet glass. The present portion, which is one wing of the proposed building, intended to be 500 ft. long, and to have an octagonal centre compartment, was erected by Messrs. D. and E. Bailey, of Holborn, in 1838, from the designs of Alfred Ainger, Esq. It stands in a direction nearly east and west, on a raised platform, and is 180 ft. long, by 27 ft. high, and about 27 ft. in breadth. The eastern end, which is upright, is only temporary, till the other parts are added. The glazing will be observed to be beautifully done, and all the work about the building is nicely finished. By the ventilators in the sides (beneath the stages), the air is caused first to pass over a gutter of water, collected from the rain which falls on the roof, and it thus becomes partially charged with moisture. It afterwards passes over the hot-water pipes; and in this way, whenever heat and air are required at the same time, becomes slightly warmed before it reaches the plants.

CONSERVATORY, HORTICULTURAL GARDENS, CHISWICK.

Within the house, there are narrow stages along the side walls, and a path on each side of a central bed. Small and showy flowering plants are generally kept on the stages, and on the north side, there is a limited collection of the cactus tribe, with Echeverias and other succulents. It is found that the strong light is rather prejudicial to plants on the southern stage, as it dries them up so quickly, and causes them to require frequent waterings. It may here be observed, too, that the leaves of the larger plants in the middle of the house frequently become burnt opposite a particular angle of the glass, and acquire numerous brown blotches; but those plants which have woolly leaves do not appear to suffer. It is only the leaves which have a smooth surface that are at all affected, and these simply, as we have said, where they happen to come within range of the rays which pass through a certain curve of the glass.

Down the centre of this conservatory is a bed of soil, in which the bulk of the plants are inserted, without pots. Here they grow most luxuriantly, and produce magnificent specimens, causing one greatly to regret that, in consequence of the rapidity of their progress, they have either, in a few years, to lose their leading shoots, or be removed. Even with this drawback, however, the effect they produce in giving an air of picturesque wildness and resemblance to nature, is so good and so very desirable, that it strongly inclines us to prefer sacrificing a few plants every year in order to attain this extreme healthiness, and variety, and vigour. By a very little contrivance, a succession of plants, in different parts of the house, may be kept advancing, so as never to render the practice of this system productive of bareness and feebleness. And there are so many plants, likewise, which will always keep within moderate limits, that are peculiarly fitted for planting out in this way.

Those plants which have most arrested our notice in this conservatory are the tea-scented roses placed here and there along the sides of the bed, and which thrive here in great splendour; the Hedychiums on the northern side, near the western end, which flourish and flower superbly; the Brugmansias, which are admirable conservatory plants, but want a little autumn pruning; the charming Hydrangea-like *Luculia gratissima*, which seems most congenially placed on the north side, and blooms profusely in November and December; *Polygala grandiflora*, quite a tree; *Acacia oxycedrus*, a variety of *A. pulchella*, and other species of the genus, singularly elegant when in flower; *Cestrum aurantiacum*, very large, and equally handsome, during autumn, whether in a large or small state, for its bright orange flowers; *Araucaria brasiliensis*, producing cones; the large Altingias at the eastern end, which one laments to see necessarily decapitated; and, without further multiplying examples, the many elegant climbers, especially *Kennedya* (*Hardenbergia*) *macrophylla*, which scrambles up some wires to a great height, and forms an immense mass of the richest foliage and flowers in summer, looking like the splendid drapery to some luxurious Eastern scene. In the wild and free manner in which this and other climbers are left to dangle about, there is much of nature, and at the same time indications of the highest art; for it is one of the last attainments of art to realize anything like a natural appearance. We shall be much mistaken if the visitor of taste is not as highly pleased with the *Kennedya* we have mentioned as with any other thing, however rare, in the whole garden.

Descending from the platform on which the conservatory stands, the visitor will find himself in the department called the Arboretum. The principal part of this section is comprised in a somewhat square plot of grass, over which are scattered, irregularly, specimens of various kinds of ornamental trees, with a few masses of the taller sorts of shrubs, and a small oval-shaped hollow filled with beds of Rhododendrons; the bulk of the space being devoted to lawn. Originally, the plants in this arboretum were arranged in masses, according to their affinities; but, with the exceptions already named, these groups have all now been broken up, and, during the autumn of 1850, an extensive thinning out of the specimens was further made. At present, then, it is a lawn, over which large single trees are freely dotted, without any grouping, and, except along the northern side, where there are a few clumps of shrubs, with the tribes of Mespilus, Thorn, &c., and the Rhododendron hollow just referred to, there is scarcely a single shrub, deciduous or evergreen, or even a low bushy tree. The whole breadth of lawn is therefore, for the most part, visible from any one point, and the only merit of this arrangement is that it allows visitors to promenade the grass on fête days without the interruption or the reduction of space which single shrubs and clusters of them would occasion.

Some years ago, a narrow and irregular strip of water crossed the lawn near the centre. Being thought, we suppose, to possess too much of a ditch-like character, this was filled up. It appears to us unfortunate that it was not deepened and enlarged; for nothing is more pleasant than the appearance and the coolness of water in summer, and it would certainly contribute materially to vary and enliven this lawn. If kept at a low level, too, and the material obtained in forming it judiciously used in varying the surface of the ground, it would tend much to redeem the garden from the lowness and flatness which now characterize it.

On the east side of the arboretum, there was, until the autumn of 1849, a long strip of irregular flower garden, enclosed by shrubberies, and a collection of roses on the side next the lawn. All this space has now been transformed; and a high broad walk extends along that side of the arboretum, from near the chief entrance in the Duke of Devonshire's new road, to a new entrance, in a line with the large conservatory, where it branches off into the walk leading to that conservatory. On each side of the new broad walk where the old flower garden stood, is ranged a series of flower-beds, varied by Irish yews and other plants, while a number of young specimens of rare plants have been put in between the beds on the eastern side of the walk and the boundary belt of the plantation. At either end of this walk, where it joins the branch walks, it expands into a circle, around which are raised beds, following the line of the grass edging, and having the soil in them supported by upright grass sods. They are about 6 or 8 inches above the level of the lawn. This slight elevation has rather a good effect; but they are filled with a mixed collection of plants, which has a decidely bad one. If occupied by such things as choice Rhododendrons, with a few standards placed among them at regular intervals, these beds would certainly look well. On the whole, this new walk, though unhappily destitute of terminating objects, is tolerably well treated in all but the working details; but we venture to suggest that broad straight walks, which only serve to render the narrow limits of the pleasure grounds more contracted, are not the features required in this garden.

With the long walk previously existing opposite the main entrance, and which has now been finished by an alcove brought from another part of the garden, and the pediment of which is unluckily much wider than the vista through which it is seen, the arboretum has three bold straight walks on its eastern, northern, and southern sides. There is also a walk, though of less consequence, along the western margin. The space by the sides of the northern walk, and between it and the boundary wall, however, is the most interesting part of the arboretum. Just within the entrance, at the left-hand corner of the lawn, is a large plant of the *Acer Lobelii*, said to be as thoroughly fastigiate in its habit as the Lombardy Poplar, and having its bark streaked with white. Should this prove to be the case, it will be very valuable in grouping, for at present there is a great dearth of trees of that class. In a border on the opposite side of the walk, is a pretty little variegated evergreen oak (*Quercus ilex variegata*), which has quite a shrubby habit, and is conspicuous for having so much whiteness in its leaves. Further on, and dispersed about the lawn on the same side, are many very excellent specimens of the coniferous tribe. There is a *Pinus insignis*, the branches of which spread over a circumference of nearly fifteen yards, and are very dense ; *Abies Douglasii*, a beautiful but not extraordinary specimen ; *Cedrus Deodara* and *Araucaria imbricata*, both exceedingly good and handsome ; *Abies pinsapo*, a small but very charming plant ; *Abies Webbiana*, singularly stunted, from having the shoots destroyed by frost ; *Pinus Lambertiana*, very fine ; and *Pinus Llaveana*, one of the new Mexican sorts, about 10 ft. high. Noble plants of different Cypresses, Thujas, &c., are further mixed up with the Pines and other things on this lawn ; and there are occasional tufts of such dwarf trailing plants as the various Savins, Cotoneasters, Mahonias, &c., which serve to vary and heighten the general effect. A few roses trained to poles, and *Wistaria sinensis* treated as a sort of tree, add to the variety and interest of the scene.

On the conservative wall along this side of the garden, there is a large collection of such plants as are naturally climbers, and either hardy or nearly so, together with those tender shrubs which, requiring the protection of a wall with a southerly aspect, will yet bear some little amount of training. Having been planted a great many years, the majority of these have become large, and outgrown the space originally allotted to them. *Arbutus procera* is here becoming a tree, having burst away from its former fetters. *Mahonia fascicularis* is particularly fine, and *Berberis trifoliata*, with its glaucous leaves, is in a vigorous state. The *Chimonanthus* and its variety have attained a great size. *Ceanothus azureus*, and some other species, are extremely beautiful. But the large Wistaria is the chief feature of attraction when, in the month of May, its numberless beautiful blossoms load the air with perfume. It extends along the upper part of the wall for fully sixty yards.

The plan adopted for sheltering the plants on this wall is to have a narrow border, not three feet wide, with a row of rude pillars along the front, and a light frame-work of wood at the top to support a thatch which is applied during winter. This thatch, which is only just sufficient to cover the border, at once turns off all the wet, and checks radiation, while it does not materially interfere with the action of light and air on the plants. Advantage is further taken of this warm border to cultivate several kinds of *Amaryllis*, and such like tender things; while we remarked a cluster of plants upon it of the curious Squirting Cucumber (*Momordica elaterium*), the fruit of which, when sufficiently formed, will, as soon as it is touched, discharge its seeds, accompanied by a quantity of juice, with considerable force, and often in the face of the rude invader of its liberty. It is a most amusing plant.

On the lawn at the other side of the broad walk, and not far from the council room, are good specimens of *Abies nobilis, grandis*, and *amabilis*, with a beautiful plant of *Sophora japonica pendula*, which, though grafted 5 or 6 ft. high, has branches that sweep the ground. Among the Rhododendrons, too, in the hollow, is a curious and elegant plant named *Cupressus sinensis*, the habit and foliage of which are not much unlike those of the Deciduous Cypress. From the lightness and gracefulness of its mode of growth, and the pale green colour of its leaves, it is of great use in mixing with such evergreens as Rhododendrons.

Leaving the arboretum near the council room, a walk on the left becomes pleasing by the row of climbers trained to pillars and hanging in festoons from chains attached to the poles, on each side of the walk, while there are likewise rows of the best sorts of Standard Roses.

Walking through a gateway in the wall opposite the council room, we enter a walled area, in which are a number of flower beds, generally containing some novel and showy kinds of summer flowers, with several excellent cold pits, for the protection of half-hardy shrubs. These pits have low walls, and span roofs. They are neatly constructed, and only covered with glass during the winter, when, in very frosty weather, the glass is further protected. No fire-heat is, however, employed. They are used for testing the quality and comparative hardiness of a variety of new shrubs, which are taken out and replaced by other more novel kinds when they have bloomed sufficiently and been duly examined; the great object being, both here and throughout this department, not so much to obtain and preserve large specimens, and keep up a great general collection, as to grow new and little known things, and thoroughly exhibit their character, capacities, and merits, making them at length give way to more recent introductions or less commonly known species. Hence, the plant-houses and pits in this part of the garden, though not exclusively used in the way we have described, are not to be looked upon as examples of the best method of selecting and combining ornamental plants, but more as repositories of whatever happen to be the current novelties of the day, with just a few showy old plants interspersed, and occasionally some common things placed about to produce a little effect. Display, however, is very far from being the leading object. The particular pits to which we now more immediately refer contain all Fortune's new Pœonies, which flowered well here last year; several new species of *Ceanothus*, *Weigela rosea*, which has a better appearance when protected, though quite hardy, and some other things.

At the back of the area on which we have been remarking, the plant-houses commence, and in front of them are some more small pits. In fact, throughout the whole of this portion of the garden, the visitor will require to be continually on the watch for attractive objects, as these are placed about in all sorts of odd corners. Just at the doors of these plant-houses, for example, we observed, on some small groups of stones, a few very pretty rock plants. On a wall a little distance behind these houses, too, among other good climbers, was the white variety of *Wistaria sinensis*; and in a small rough house close at hand, besides many similarly curious things, there were plants of the Japan Cocoanut, which, though a palm, is said to fruit when only 3 ft. high. Mr. Gordon had here succeeded in raising plants, also, of the common Brasil nut, *Bertholletia excelsa*. In another corner were a quantity of new oaks from California; and in some pits, nearer the kitchen garden, a wonderful variety of new or curious plants from Japan (obtained through Dr. Siebold); from Dr. Fischer, of Petersburgh; from Hartweg's Mexican collections; Fortune's Chinese gatherings; and a multitude of other quarters. Here and there, too, in some retired nook, one comes upon a set of plants which Mr. Strangways or some other enthusiastic lover of gardening has collected and sent here years ago; and for which no definite or conspicuous place can be provided. The treasures and curiosities thus scattered about are innumerable, and such as almost to amaze and bewilder the fortunate visitor who happens to be favoured with the secret of their history, and to learn their real nature and rarity. And to collect all these things properly together, and arrange them in something like order, so as to be easily inspected and understood, would be, we confess, a Herculean task. Yet it is one from which, for the benefit of the public, and for the credit of the garden, we hope the Society's officers will not shrink.

Without staying to describe the various houses and pits individually, which would occupy too much space, and answer no useful purpose, we may state that, in the area which we first supposed the visitor to enter, there is an orchid house, in which the pots containing the plants are placed on a thin bed of gravel, to keep them moist without making them too damp. This house is kept pretty hot, and rather above the average for moisture, and the plants look very healthy. A large specimen of the lovely *Phalænopsis amabilis* is nearly always in flower. A stove near this house, with a broad span roof, which is entered rather uncomfortably by two or three descending steps, contains a mixed collection of stove plants, with climbers trained to trellises in pots, and many pretty little plants of rare kinds of *Begonia, Achimenes, Gloxinia, Centradenia, Columnea,* &c.

Another house used as a stove (formerly a vinery) has many newer things in it, and is better deserving of a visit to those who are in search of novelties. The gigantic specimen of *Lælia superbiens,* which blooms freely every year, is usually kept in this house; as is likewise a very large plant of the old *Dendrobium speciosum,* which few persons can flower, but which here produces an immense number of blossoms, though not every season. A low span-roofed greenhouse, with a path in the centre, and broad flat stages, the glass coming down nearly to the level of the stages at the side walls, is described as a very useful house, with a particularly simple heating apparatus, which is capable of doing a good deal of work at a light expense, and with little trouble. The boiler used is called the Exeter drum boiler, and supplied by Mr. Jervis, of Exeter. The upper part of the boiler is a sort of hemisphere, connected with the lower part by upright pipes, and the fire is in the centre of the lower part, as it is in most of the conical boilers. Shewen's boilers are also used in these gardens, with the happiest results.

Another span-roofed greenhouse, of more pretensions, and ranging north and south, stands near the one last mentioned, and was presented by Messrs. Hartley & Co., of Sunderland, to exhibit the application of their patent rough glass. It is a neat and elegant house, and the large panes of glass give it a very superior appearance.

A little way off, in the other direction, a plain span-roofed pit, with a path down the centre, has just been completed at a trifling expense. It is entered by two descending steps, and, without being much (if any) dearer than those pits which are only accessible from without, it enables the gardener to get into it in all weathers, for the purpose of watering and for other tendance, without exposing the plants to rains or cold, and at a much less sacrifice of convenience. Through the multitude of other pits and frames which lie in this quarter we cannot pretend to conduct the visitor, although we can assure him that, if he at all understands plants, and takes an interest in them, he will derive much pleasure from the inspection of these, with the aid of a competent guide; for, unlike such things in general and more ornamental establishments, these pits contain some of the most novel and singular plants in the garden.

The experimental ground, in which these pits occur, is used for raising new annuals, for testing different kinds of produce, for examining the properties and value of agricultural plants, for trying experiments with manures, for gourds, vegetable marrows, general flowers, or any object or thing which happens to require examining, and for which there is not a regular place provided elsewhere. And while thus referring to experiments, we may state that Mr. Gordon raised a very good hybrid variety of *Anemone japonica* here, which found its way into many of the gardens about London last year, and, like the original species, is much esteemed as a summer bedding plant.

Returning through the arboretum to the principal entrance, we will just remark that access to the gardens can be easily obtained through the order of a Fellow of the Society; and gardeners, we believe, are always admitted on application at the Turnham Green Gate. Candidates for membership must obtain the introduction of three Fellows of the Society, and the yearly subscription is four guineas. Tickets for admission to the gardens on fête days can be had through the medium of Fellows of the Society; or respectable parties may apply to the Vice-Secretary, 21, Regent Street. The exhibitions in Regent Street are open to any one introduced by a member, and are held once or twice in every month, on Tuesdays. The days on which the garden exhibitions are held are always duly advertised in the newspapers. We must not omit to add that the Society distributes the plants which are introduced through its means with the greatest liberality, as well to nurserymen as to its unprofessional members, and that grafts of the best kinds of fruits are likewise freely distributed.

Royal Botanic Gardens, Regent's Park.—When these gardens were first projected, those at Kew were in a wretched condition, and difficult of access, while the Horticultural Gardens were formed and conducted on a much wider basis than was here contemplated, and did not embrace at all many of the objects which the founders of these sought to compass. It is well known that the Horticultural Society never attempted to establish a botanical collection, or, indeed, any collection at all, except of hardy shrubs and trees, and fruits. There was, therefore, a legitimate field open to this Botanic Society for the formation of a botanical collection, and the site which they chose for their gardens would necessarily, by its proximity to the better parts of London, give them another claim to support. The success with which their exertions have been crowned, notwithstanding the great improvements which have been effected at Kew, shows at once the reasonableness of their plan, and the deep hold which gardening has taken of the English mind; for it now appears that there is ample room for this new claimant to patronage, without detriment to the older institutions.

The Royal Botanic Society was incorporated by Charter in 1839, and the garden commenced in 1840. This garden stands on the site of the Inner Circle, Regent's Park; a spot said to have been reserved for a palace by George IV. It was long occupied as a nursery-garden by Mr. Jenkins, and derived the advantage from this circumstance of having a number of ornamental trees, some of which are of a respectable size, already existing upon it. The many specimens of Weeping Ash, the large Weeping Elms, and the numerous more common trees on the south-western side of the gardens, are among the older tenants of the place.

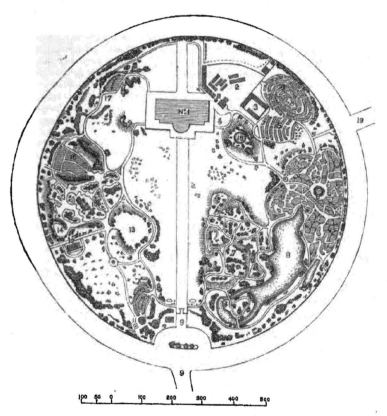

PLAN OF BOTANIC GARDENS, REGENT'S PARK.

Some first-rate specimens of *Andromeda floribunda*, too, for which Jenkins's nursery was celebrated, still exist, and are in the American garden.

Although situated, as it were, in London, this garden does not suffer much from the smoke incident to the metropolis, being on the north-western side of it, and in a not very populous, though highly aristocratic district. Comprising only about 18 acres, too, this place, by being in the midst of Regent's Park, and having the ground falling away from it on most sides, while conspicuous hills and swells rise in the distance, is made, by a wise treatment of the boundary, to appear at least twice as large as it really is; for, from the middle of the garden, the fences are scarcely at all seen, and the plantations are now beginning to blend with those outside, and with the surrounding country, so that a great indefiniteness of view is procured.

In the year 1840, before the garden was begun, the Society appointed Mr. Robert Marnock, the designer and former curator of the Sheffield Botanic Gardens, to the curatorship of this establishment; and from the plans, and under the direction of this gentleman, assisted by Mr. Decimus Burton as architect, the garden has since been laid out.

In a landscape point of view, we may safely affirm that Mr. Marnock has been particularly happy in the arrangement and planting of this garden. As a whole, the avowedly ornamental parts are probably superior to anything of the kind in the neighbourhood of the metropolis. Much has been attempted, especially in the variation of the surface of the ground; and almost all that has been proposed is fully and well achieved. We would particularly point out the clever manner in which the boundary fence is got rid of on the northern and north-western sides, as seen from the middle of the garden; the beautiful changes in the surface of the ground, and the grouping of the masses of plants, in the same quarter; the artistic manner in which the rockery is formed, out of such bad materials, and the picturesque disposal of the plants upon it; and the treatment of the large mound, from which so many and such excellent views of the garden and country are obtained. We might also refer to the singularly delightful arrangement of the American and Coniferous plants, brought last year for exhibition, in which a great deal of the highest taste was displayed, and which we understand has now been re-arranged in a still more interesting manner.

Entering by the principal gate (9 on the ground plan), not far from York Gate, the first thing deserving notice is the very agreeable and effective manner in which the entrance is screened from the gardens, and the gardens from the public gaze. This is not done by large close gates and heavy masonry, but by a living screen of ivy, planted in boxes, and supported by an invisible fence. There are, in fact, two screens; one close to the outside fence, opposite the centre of the principal walk, and having an entrance gate on either side of it; and the other several feet further in, extending across the sides of the walk, and only leaving an opening in the centre. By keeping the ivy in boxes, it does not interfere with the continuity of the gravel walk, and has a neater appearance, and can, we suppose, be taken away altogether, if required. At any rate, it has a temporary look, which is of some consequence to the effect. These screens are from 6 to 8 ft. high. In a small lodge at the side, visitors enter their names, and produce the orders of Fellows of the Society, which are necessary for seeing the gardens. Gardeners are admitted by a gate on the east side of the Circle, nearly opposite the road which crosses the Park from the neighbourhood of the Colosseum.

After passing through the screen we have thus described, a broad, bold walk is entered upon, at the end of which, on a slightly-raised platform, is that portion of the great conservatory which the Society has already been able to complete. But before advancing to an examination of that building, we would recommend the visitor to turn to the right, and, taking the various features of the garden in regular course, accomplish the entire circuit of it without having to travel over the same ground twice.

Adopting this route, the ascent of the large mound (7) will be one of the first things that commands attention. And directly the visitor gets upon these walks, he will perceive that an entire change of character has been contemplated. From the highly-artificial features of the broad walk opposite the entrance, we are here introduced to an obvious imitation of nature. The surface of the ground is kept rough, and covered only with undressed grass,—such, we mean, as is only occasionally and not regularly mown; the direction of the walks is irregular, or brokenly zigzag, and their sides ragged; the plants and trees are mostly of a wild character, such as furze, broom, ivy, privet, clematis, thorns, mountain ash, &c., and these are clustered together in tangled masses. Such a style is too seldom thought of or well carried out to render a fair specimen of it otherwise than agreeable, or indicative of real taste. But we must be permitted altogether to doubt its fitness for this locality. In the very midst of a highly-cultivated scene, which is overlooked at almost every step, and adjoining a compartment in which the most formal systematic arrangement is adopted, in beds, and almost within the limits of the great metropolis itself, such an introduction of the rougher and less cultivated features of nature is assuredly to be deprecated. It cannot be too strongly insisted on that art is not a thing to be ashamed of in gardening, although, in general, it should in no way be obtruded. And whenever the rougher characteristics of nature are brought into a polished garden, there is just as much necessity for keeping them secluded and by themselves, as there is for isolating the conspicuous evidences of art in one of Nature's wildest scenes.

Several platforms on the face of the mound, and especially one at the summit, afford the most beautiful views of Regent's Park and its villas, Primrose and other neighbouring hills, and the more distant country. On a clear day, with the wind south-west, west, or north-west, these landscapes are truly delightful. There is a mixture of wood, grass, mansion, and general undulation, which are singularly refreshing so near London, and which abundantly exhibit the foresight that has been displayed in the formation of this mound. Unquestionably, when the atmosphere is at all favourable, the ascent of the mound is one of the greatest attractions of the garden to a lover of landscape beauties. The classic villa of the Marquis of Hertford in the Park, is a very conspicuous object in the view.

Descending the mound on its eastern side, a small lake (8), out of which the material for raising the mound was procured, is seen to stretch along its base, and to form several sinuous arms. Like the mound itself, an air of wildness is thrown around this lake, which is increased by the quantity of sedgy plants on its margins, and the common-looking dwarf willows which abound near its western end. In this lake, and in some of the small strips of water by which it is prolonged towards the east, an unusually complete collection of hardy water plants will be found, and these are planted without any appearance of art, so as to harmonize with the entire scene. Being all labelled, as is almost everything else in the garden, there will be no difficulty in ascertaining their names. There is a rustic bridge over one arm of the lake, which, being simple, and without pretension, is quite in character with the neighbouring objects.

Between the lake and the boundary fence, in a little nook formed on purpose for them, the various hardy ferns and Equiseta are cultivated. The plants of the former are put among masses of fused brick, placed more with reference to their use in affording a position for growing ferns, than for their picturesque effect. This corner is, in fact, altogether an episode to the general scene, and does not form a part of it.

On a border near these ferns, and extending along the south side of the lake, are several interesting collections, illustrative of one of the Society's objects, which is to show, in a special compartment, the hardy plants remarkable for their uses in various branches of manufacture.

Commencing at the western end of this border, we find first the plants which afford tanning materials. The *Rhus cotinus* and *coriaria*, the Scotch Fir, the Larch, and the Oak, are among these. It is unfortunate that the whole of the plants in this border have not more room ; because, being of such very different habits, they will soon outgrow their position, and will then require to be thinned out or removed. Next in order are the plants whose fibre is used for chip plat, comprising *Salix alba*, the Lombardy Poplar, &c. Then follow the plants whose fibre is adapted for weaving cordage, &c. The *Spartium junceum*, Flax, and Hemp, rank in this class. The plants used in making baskets or matting, &c., next occur, and embrace the Lime and Osier among others. Grasses of different kinds then illustrate the plants whose straw is used for platting. The Cork tree and *Populus nigra* furnish examples of plants whose bark yields cork. A collection of plants whose parts furnish materials for dyeing finishes the series, and includes some species of *Rhus, Hippophäe, Salix*, &c. Altogether, this is a very instructive border, and all the objects are labelled under the respective heads here given, so that they may be readily referred to. If they had proper room to grow in, the compartment would be one of increasing interest.

A large herbaceous garden (6) adjoins the lake at its eastern end, and the plants are here arranged in beds, according to the natural system, the species of each order being assigned to one bed. Of course the beds will thus vary greatly in size. They are edged with box, and have gravel walks between. Three or four crescent-shaped hedges are placed here and there across this garden, partly for shelter, but principally to act as divisions to the larger groups of natural orders. These hedges separate the garden into the great natural divisions, and each of the compartments they form is again subdivided into orders by walks 4 ft. in width, the sub-orders being indicated by division walks of 2 ft. in width. The inquiries of the student are thus greatly aided, and he is enabled to carry away a much clearer impression of the natural system than can be had from books. This is an excellent place for ascertaining what are the best and most showy herbaceous border flowers.

Further on, in the same direction, is a garden (5) assigned entirely to British plants, disposed in conformity with the Linnæan system in long beds, with alleys between. In this division will be seen how very ornamental are some of the plants to which our soil gives birth ; and the less informed will be surprised to find that many of their garden favourites are the natural products of some part or other of our own country.

A well-stocked Medical Garden (4) terminates this chain of scientific collections, and is more pleasing than the other two, on account of the plants being much more varied. The arrangement of this tribe is founded on the natural system, and the plants are in narrow beds, which take a spiral form. If the visitor will commence with the Ranunculaceæ, and carefully observe the way in which the names on the labels read, so as to keep these names constantly before him, he will easily be able to follow through the whole collection in the order adopted. All the hardy plants used in medicine are thus brought together, without reference to their habits, a great deal of useful knowledge being thereby conveyed in a compact form.

This last feature of the garden may possibly be deemed a superfluous one in a metropolis which possesses what is termed by way of distinction a Physic Garden. And we are not by any means certain that a botanical collection of plants with various habits, arranged solely with relation to heir natural alliances, can ever be satisfactorily kept up. It is clear, ndeed, that in a few years many of the plants in this medical department must be abandoned, or renewed with smaller specimens; for such as grow to the size of trees would soon fill all the space, while there will not be room for any of them, except the very smallest, to grow to their full and natural dimensions. This evil is, it seems, proposed to be remedied by replacing the plants with younger ones as soon as they get too large.

Near the Medical Garden are the plant-houses, pits, and reserve ground (2), in which all the plants are grown for stocking the conservatory, flower-beds, borders, &c. Here we were happy to notice, during a visit last autumn, that three useful new span-roofed houses had been erected, in a kind of series, which is to be yet further extended. A detached greenhouse contained a considerable number of Pelargoniums, pruned and trained into tall upright plants, which are very useful among masses of smaller things in the conservatory during summer. The plan is worthy of imitation in any place where the plants have to stand on the ground, as, by being rendered thus tall, their flowers are brought more on a level with the eye. There were likewise some standard Azaleas here, of the Indian varieties, which are serviceable in a similar way to the Pelargoniums.

The new houses are constructed in a very simple manner, with a path down the centre, flat shelves or stages at the sides, the hot-water pipes under the stages, near the walls, the lights resting on the side walls, and all fixed, with ventilators in the shape of small sashes here and there along near the top of the larger lights, on both sides of the centre. One of these houses, which is used for orchids, has no means of ventilation at all, except at the end, over the door, where there is a small sash capable of being opened. And with proper shading, it is found both here and elsewhere that orchids very seldom require fresh air. The collection of orchids here, as of stove and greenhouse plants in general, is not at present extensive, but is continually increasing. The beautiful *Phalænopsis amabilis* was producing seed-vessels, which appeared likely to contain sound seeds.

One of the span-roofed houses is almost wholly occupied with a cistern containing the great *Victoria regia*, *Nymphæa cœrulea*, and other aquatics. Although kept at a high temperature, and planted in a tank of great dimensions (27 ft. by 17 ft.), through which hot-water pipes pass, and where the water is maintained in motion by the action of a small revolving wheel, the *Victoria* did not seem, last October, in a happy or healthy state. Since that period, however, the water having been changed, it is, we learn, progressing as satisfactorily as could be wished, and is now one of the finest plants in the country. At the farther end of the aquarium, is a cluster of handsome plants, including a very large and striking specimen of *Asplenium nidus*, a new species of *Ficus*, with singularly fine leaves, and, trained to the roof, a very luxuriant plant of the snake gourd (*Trichosanthes colubrina*). This last curious object bears long thin fruit, sometimes from 3 to 4 ft. in length, like a very slender cucumber, but strangely twisted, especially towards the end, and having white streaks on a green ground. When ripe, it changes colour to a bright red, which renders it exceedingly showy.

From the reserve ground, a few steps will lead to the large conservatory, which is more appropriately termed the Winter Garden. At the eastern end of this conservatory, and in a corresponding place at the other end, there is a very large vase placed on the gravel, no doubt for containing plants in summer, but without either plinth or pedestal. Along the front of the conservatory, at the edge of the terrace, are several more vases, of a handsomer kind.

This large conservatory is doubtless the most remarkable thing in the garden, and is, perhaps, of its kind, the best in Europe. It is rather more than a third part of an extensive design, which is intended to be carried out as soon as the means of doing so can be realized. The original intention was, we believe, to connect this great glass house with the outside road, by a long glass corridor, so that visitors during winter might step from their carriages into the building at once, and proceed, between rows of plants, to the main portion of it, without having to walk through the open garden. This part of the plan has, however, been abandoned.

Examined architecturally, and with an eye to beauty of design, nothing worthy of note will be observed in this structure. It is of the very lightest description—almost too light for effect—being built wholly of iron and glass. The front is simply adorned with a kind of pilaster, composed of ground glass, neatly figured, which gives a little relief, without obstructing the light. And the central flattish dome has an ornamented kind of crown, which helps to break the outline. Otherwise, on the exterior, there are no pillars—not even to the doors—and nothing but the very lightest cornice, and no decorations of any kind on the ridges of the roof. The roof is for the most part composed of a series of large ridges, the sides of these being of an inverted sort of keel shape, and a transverse ridge extending along the principal front from either side of the projected domical portion. There are smaller lean-to additions at each end, but these are only temporary, and the back is finished with an upright face till the building can be enlarged to its proper width. At present, the extreme length is 176 ft., and the width at the widest part 100 ft. Ultimately the greatest length will be 375 ft., and the utmost width 200 ft. The house is ventilated at the top by small sliding lights, worked by little winches attached to the pillars. These pillars themselves are so exceedingly slender as scarcely to be noticed when the house is well stocked with plants. It is fairly open to debate whether, in the effort to secure the greatest amount of lightness, too much character has not been sacrificed; and whether, in such a large building, the introduction of more massive exterior pillars or pilasters, a bolder cornice, some broad and decided frame-work for the doorways, and a slightly enriched roof, would not have signally improved the elevation without in the least degree unduly interfering with the supply of light.

Be this as it may, there can be no question, on getting within the house, that the right sort of general shape for a house of this kind has been hit upon, and the true idea of treating it as to the internal arrangements adopted. What is evidently wanted in a conservatory, and what will unquestionably, ere long, be more generally realized, is a sort of in-door garden. It may be some years, perhaps, before we attain to anything like conservatory lawns, with masses of plants and single specimens scattered about them, and walks made only a concealed and subordinate feature; or to in-door fountains, vases, statuary, and the classic arrangements of an Italian garden, disposed as they would be in front of a villa or mansion, and aided by beds of flowers; or the wilder and more purely natural features of a rocky waterfall and irregular basin for aquatics, and an accompanying tangled mass of luxuriant vegetation, combining only rugged and picturesque forms. Still, we do not despair of seeing any of these, something approaching them having already been in part effected in one or two places, on a small scale. But there is every probability of a great change passing over the interior arrangements of conservatories, whether large or small, and tending to the multiplication of walks, the grouping of the plants, whether on stages, on the floor, or in beds, and the placing of single specimens at certain points to give variety, with the more frequent introduction and more natural treatment of climbing plants, and the use of trailing or pendent species suspended from the roof.

Surveying the Winter Garden now under notice from near the door by which entrance is gained, the grouping of the plants in masses, the planting out of good single specimens, the great variety in the walks, the climbers hanging down so loosely from the roof, the noble large vase filled with flowers, and the numerous other neat stands of flowers, with the small statues here and there placed about, convey the impression of really being in a garden, and one of a novel and delightful character. There is the advantage, too, that visitors do not so much come in contact with each other, and that a party may be exploring any portion of the house without being exposed to the gaze of every one else who happens to be in it.

The great subject for regret, and that which makes the whole defective, is that such specimens as are planted out, and those which are grouped together in pots, are all surrounded by gravel alone. The gravel is even spread up to the very stems of the planted-out specimens; and there is not an inch of soil, or any kind of edging, or substitute for grass, anywhere visible. Gravel and plants, with very few of the latter having branches and leaves that extend downwards to within nine inches or a foot of the ground, are the only things to be seen by looking on the ground. And we should suppose it would be altogether impossible, even by the most fortunate selection of dwarf plants for surrounding the groups, to make these two things harmonize satisfactorily. If the specimen plants had the soil left bare for a small space around them, and neatly edged with stone or slate, or with *Lycopodium*, and the plants in the principal masses were plunged in the ground, and the outline of the groups similarly edged, or alike bordered with *Lycopodium*, the character of the arrangement would be redeemed, and made artistic, without at all limiting the space left open for visitors;—and we are aware that the conservatory is regarded as a great shelter house for visitors in showery weather, and that it is calculated to contain nearly 2000. Perhaps, also, a better general appearance might be secured by throwing the plants into somewhat larger masses, and not having so many groups. The principal outlines would thus be improved ; though the variety, in walking about the house, would certainly be slightly lessened. As viewed from the raised bank at the eastern end, such a change would throw the collection into better and more broken shapes, and create less sameness of surface.

There is a glass partition towards the eastern side of the house, separating off a portion that is dedicated to stove plants; and here the ground is raised into a bank two or three feet high, over which the walk passes. Here, too, is a collection of the hardier sorts of cacti, aloes, mesembryanthemums, &c., planted among lumps of rock, and very appropriately treated. A little more variety of this kind in the house —such as will no doubt be added when it attains its full dimensions— would be a decided relief, and produce a more lively interest.

One of the most effective plants in this house is the *Chamærops humilis*, a dwarf palm, of which there is a first-rate specimen. It is found to be so hardy that it stood several degrees of frost without damage. A huge specimen of *Cereus speciosissimus*, planted out, must be a splendid object when in flower. There is also a magnificent aloe. Camellias and orange-trees, of large size, are numerous; and there are many beautiful acacias, especially some standards of *A. sophora*, and other Australian plants, with large specimens of the showy *Habrotham-nus elegans*, and a great number of charming climbers. Being trained up the pillars, and allowed to hang about loosely, or fastened to the roof, and covered with long pendent lateral shoots, which bloom most freely, these climbers are quite an important feature in the house. Some Passion-flowers have side shoots at least two to three yards long, depending from the roof, and waving about gracefully with the slightest agitation of the air.

In the part appropriated to stove plants, a far more decided and pic-turesque character is obtained than in the cooler compartment. Besides the leaves and forms of the plants being bolder, and fitter for grouping, they are disposed more irregularly, and in broader masses. A small basin of water, too, with a broken margin, and containing several good aquatics, and overshadowed with much beautiful foliage, contributes largely to heighten the picture. Among the masses of rock which surround this basin, many strong-growing ferns are dispersed. The Egyptian Papyrus is here growing in the water, and the noble leaves of *Strelitzia augusta* behind are sure to command attention. All the plants in this division appear extremely healthy: and we have no doubt that the pictures here produced will be contemplated and studied with the highest satisfaction.

The conservatory is marked No. 1 on the ground plan which we have given. We have been favoured with the following account of it.

This building stands on the north side of the Society's grounds. Its construction is simple in character, and without architectural pretence, the principle on which it was designed being, with limited funds, to obtain the largest possible extent of garden covered and enclosed with glass, and temperately warmed, as a promenade for the Fellows of the Society and their friends, in winter as well as summer.

Its length, as already stated, is 176 ft., and breadth 75 ft., exclusive of a centre circular projection, where the internal width is 100 ft. The upright sides are 14 ft. high, and the roof at the centre 32 ft. high.

The roof is supported in the front by a cast-iron moulded gutter, and by iron columns in the interior of the building, placed at 12 ft. distance from each other, in bays or divisions of 25 ft. span. These columns afford support to a variety of climbing plants.

The warming is effected by means of hot water circulating in cast-iron pipes, 2500 ft. in length, placed in brick chambers under the surface of the floor; and by a continuous iron tank 18 in. wide and 6 in. deep, placed in a brick chamber around the building, having a heating surface equal to 2000 ft. of 4 in. pipe. The top of the tank has openings, with circular covers, to emit vapour when required. The heated air escapes by perforated castings level with the floor. Air ducts communicate with the chambers containing the pipes and tank, bringing air to be heated from parts of the house most remote from the heating surface.

Two boilers for heating the water are placed in a boiler-house about

30 ft. to the north-west of the building, one for heating the water in the pipes, the other that in the tanks. An auxiliary boiler is also provided, for giving increased temperature to the water circulating in the pipes, when required. An outer chamber of brickwork is constructed around the furnace-room, from whence also heated air is transmitted to the interior of the house. Additional boiler power is now being added, to compensate for the extra heat required for the stove.

Ventilation is provided by means of sashes made to slide on the roof, and worked simultaneously by means of simple machinery; and at the ends of the house, and in the front, by casements hung on pivots. The roof water is conveyed by the iron columns and under-ground pipes into three large tanks. The total cost was about £7000.

The Architect was Mr. Decimus Burton, and the Contractor Mr. Richard Turner, of Dublin.

On the west side of the conservatory the ground takes some beautiful sweeps, descending rapidly towards the site of the rockery (17). Here a walk winds through masses of fused brick, very well disposed, and now just becoming sufficiently clothed with the ivy and rock plants scattered throughout. Exit is given from this rockery through a rude arch of the same material, formed and clothed in the best manner. And at a little distance there are several old half-decayed stumps of trees, which have been stuck in the lawn, and are rapidly getting well covered with ivy and Virginia creeper, so as to yield a particularly desirable feature in the vicinity of so decidedly rustic a scene. Much as the celebrated Kent was laughed at for having planted dead trunks of trees in Kensington Gardens, it is here proved that, if intended as the ground work for a mass of ivy or other climbers, they may be rendered in the highest degree picturesque and desirable.

Standing opposite the stumps thus noticed, a very superior view of the rockery and rustic arch is afforded. The spruce firs and other living accompaniments are now of just the right size to finish off and furnish the rockery, and they here fall into a really good outline, and compose an excellent picture. As the subject for an agreeable sketch, few garden scenes, in a small way, could be met with that excel this; and its merit is that it owes its attractiveness almost entirely to art.

Continuing along the walk from the rockery, the spot devoted to the American exhibition will now be passed through, and another fine feature will be witnessed. The plants are supplied by Mr. John Waterer, Messrs. Standish and Noble, and Mr. Baker, all of Bagshot. At the right-hand side of the walk from the rockery, an opportunity will be afforded for examining the actual treatment of the boundary plantations, and it will be seen that there is no elaborateness or great effort about it, and that the effects are occasioned by a few of the commonest elements. A more studied and finished treatment of this part would, indeed, be advantageous, when looked at from the walk on which we are supposed to be standing. And this is likewise the case with all the boundary plantations, which want more attention given to the dwarfer plants of which the front of them is composed.

Adjoining the American garden, a compartment nearly as large has just been arranged and planted with roses, by Messrs. Rivers, Lane, and Paul, on the same principle as that adopted with the American garden, each having his own separate division. An iron framework has been

E

constructed to support a canvas covering, during rough weather and bright sunshine, while the plants are in bloom. There will now be nearly an acre of this kind of garden under awnings, and it will be arranged to form one great exhibition.

A rude arch to the left formerly conducted to a little secluded spot where the smaller American plants were grown; but this part of the garden has, we are told, been entirely changed, and a broad terrace walk is formed leading to the American and Rose gardens, the exhibition tent, and onwards to the great conservatory.

A short distance further south lies a flower garden (13), in a kind of hollow, and likewise shut in by itself. On one side of it is a tall pillar, surmounted with a vase. The beds in this plot, which has no regular figure, are filled, in spring, with gay early flowering bulbs, such as early tulips, hyacinths, narcissi, &c. After these are off, they are stocked with the usual summer flowers. It is intended to remodel this flower-garden shortly.

Along the walk on the west side of the garden there are many noble weeping ash trees, sometimes in pairs. Advancing towards the entrance gates we come upon a small rosary (10), the beds in which, though chiefly occupied with roses, are filled in with gay herbaceous flowers. At the back of it is a rustic summer-house, thatched with reeds and lined with *Polytrichium commune*, from the moors near Chatsworth, the rude pillars being clothed with ivy. On a table in the centre is a wax model of *Victoria regia*. At the side of the rosary, next the lawn, 61 sorts of thorns have been grouped together on the grass, and will at some future period, with a little thinning, make handsome masses. Near these, too, are 14 kinds of *Robinia;* and we observed a dwarf plant of *R. macrophylla*, making a capital specimen for a lawn. These are only part of the general collection of ornamental hardy plants, which is arranged round the borders, and which, except the Pine and Fir tribe that will not flourish here, is rather noble.

Throughout the borders of the garden a good display of such things as stocks and mignonette is kept up in early spring by rearing them in frames, and planting them out after the frost is over; and the same attention to maintaining a stock of showy and fragrant border flowers is continued all the season; so that the garden always has a festive air, and furnishes evidence of superior care and cultivation.

As in the Horticultural Society's Gardens, three great exhibitions are held here, for flowers and fruit, in the months of May, June, and July. The same kind, and about an equal quantity, of objects is brought to each of these gardens. But the visitor to London, who happens to include a show at both the gardens during the period of his stay, should by all means go to both. The grounds of the two are so very different that it is quite worth while to see the effect of a large number of elegantly-dressed persons promenading in them, apart from the interest of the exhibitions themselves. The annual subscription to the Society for membership is two guineas, and the entrance fee five guineas.

Chelsea Botanic Garden.—The primary object of this garden was to cultivate all the medical plants which were known in this country, so as to form a constant source of reference to medical students. Another, but more secondary purpose, was the gathering together a collection of rare exotic plants; and many of the most ornamental inhabitants of our gardens were first distributed from this establishment.

It is decidedly one of the oldest of existing gardens. Some of the earliest greenhouses known in Britain were erected and heated here. The ancient cedars of Lebanon, supposed to be the first known in this country, are said to have been planted in 1683, being then about 3 ft. high and 5 years old. In the year 1720 Sir Hans Sloane, Bart., a celebrated physician and naturalist, having purchased an estate at Chelsea, gave the site of this garden to the Apothecaries' Company, on condition of their making an annual present of plants to the Royal Society. Philip Miller, the well-known author of the "Gardeners' Dictionary," and one of the earliest writers on gardening subjects, was, we believe, the first curator of this garden, and had the management of it for fifty years, having resigned in 1770, at the age of eighty.

At the time the garden was formed it must have stood entirely in the country, and had every chance of the plants in it maintaining a healthy state. Now, however, it is completely in the town, and but for its being on the side of the river, and lying open on that quarter, it would be altogether surrounded with common streets and houses. As it is, the appearance of the walks, grass, plants, and houses, is very much that of most London gardens—dingy, smoky, and, as regards the plants, impoverished and starved. It is, however, interesting for its age, for the few old specimens it contains, for the medical plants, and, especially, because the houses are being gradually renovated, and collections of ornamental plants, as well as those which are useful in medicine, formed and cultivated on the best principles, under the curatorship of Mr. Thomas Moore, one of the editors of the "Gardeners' Magazine of Botany."

This garden is situated by the side of the Thames, near Chelsea Hospital, and is entered by a gate in a side lane. It covers only a small area, and is not laid out for much ornamental effect. On entering by the gate we have mentioned, the principal plant houses are nearly straight before the visitor, being only a trifling distance to the right. The herbaceous garden and more decorated part lies to the left, and the medical department, with the lecture room and offices at the back of it, are on the extreme right. The first thing to be noticed is an ancient cork tree, which is a good deal enfeebled by the bad atmosphere, but is large and tolerably sound. This must have been one of the first specimens introduced into Britain. In the middle of the garden is a fine marble statue of Sir Hans Sloane, by Rysbach, with all the smoothness taken from its surface by the action of the weather, and thus made to resemble stone. It is an example of what may be expected from marble when a great many years exposed in our climate.

Between the statue and the river, on either side of a walk which leads to the margin of the water, are the two venerable cedars already spoken of. They are not remarkably large nor particularly handsome, some of the branches having been shattered by a storm in 1809. The circumference of the trunk of one of them is 15 ft., and that of the other 12 ft. Their conspicuously flat heads give them, however, a most striking character; and standing so near the river, in a low district, they are seen for some distance, and always tell powerfully on the landscape. Every passenger by the steam-boats must have noticed and admired them.

In the neighbourhood of the statue, a large *Cratægus mexicana*, which has acquired a drooping habit, is very beautiful. Other fine specimens are seen at various points; and at the back of the houses, in the medical department, is a handsome *Pavia rubra*, having mistletoe growing upon it; a noble tree of *Quercus cerris*; *Salisburia adiantifolia*, by the side of

E 2

the wall, grown to an immense size, and partly overhanging the outside street; with *Pistacia terebinthus*, also very large, and against the wall.

The medical garden is opposite the lecture room, and contains about 150 species of plants, arranged scientifically. While of course possessing a peculiar interest for the medical student, these plants, many of the products of which are familiar to most persons, are not without attractions to the ordinary observer. They furnish, also, the subjects of lectures, delivered to medical students each year by Dr. Lindley. In this part we noticed the double Feverfew, which is very pretty, and *Artemisia annua*, a very elegant border plant, with a tall and partially drooping habit, quite worthy of general use. Near the lecture room, too, is the oldest plant in the country of the beautiful *Thuja pendula*, in a pot and greatly stunted. Here, also, the original single-flowered species of Dahlia from Mexico, the parent of all those splendid things which now adorn our gardens in autumn, is grown; and reminds us that botanic gardens might secure a very pleasing addition to their more common stock by giving a collection of the types or originals of those numberless showy hybrid plants which skill in cross-breeding and cultivation has developed from such seemingly unpromising materials.

Clustered around a kind of winter depository for plants that merely require a little shelter in frosty weather, is a quantity of old-fashioned greenhouse plants, in pots, mingled with some more novel and rarer things. In the corner of this room, moreover, which adjoins the lecture room, is preserved the flower stem of an aloe (*Agave mexicana*), which bloomed in 1849. It is of a great height, with nearly upright small branches, and bore about 4000 flowers.

Among the plant-houses, that used as a stove is of wooden construction, well arranged and finished, glazed with long panes of sheet glass, and containing a first-rate collection of dwarf stove plants, kept in pots, and each plant treated as a specimen. In the neatness and order of everything in this house, the perfection of each individual plant, and the remarkable verdure and healthiness of the whole, there is a great deal to admire. The species are likewise well chosen, in regard to their ornamental properties, those which are conspicuously attractive for either foliage or flowers being almost exclusively cultivated here; though some kind of systematic arrangement is, we believe, maintained. Many rare objects may further be seen in this house, and among them we remarked *Jatropha podagrica*, a fine species, of which we were told that there are only three specimens in the country. The true sensitive plant (*Mimosa sensitiva*) will be found here, along with the species (*M. pudica*) more commonly known as the sensitive plant. Both are alike susceptible on being touched, but the former has flatter and larger leaves. *Dioscorea discolor*, a singular and elegant climber, with parti-coloured leaves; a good species of *Cordia*, with white convolvulus-like flowers; the *Illicium religiosum*, so much venerated in Japan; and excellent specimens of the different pretty species of *Æschynanthus* (a tribe possessing the greatest merits, and capable of being suspended in baskets, or on logs of moss-covered wood), with numerous climbers trained to dwarf trellises, and grown in pots, were a few of the other things we noted.

The Fern-house is very rich in the species that require heat, and these are nicely cultivated. As we have elsewhere remarked, the tribe is most prolific in elegant and novel forms; and the variety of tender green, and silvery white, and golden yellow tints in the foliage, with the peculiarities in the arrangement and colour of the inflorescence, renders them a highly delightful group, either to study or grow. With Mr. Moore they are, we understand, a favourite class ; and the proofs of this are seen in the extent of the collection, the health of the plants, and the fact that he has, we believe, published an interesting little book in relation to them.

Temple Gardens, London.—Those who have only seen these gardens at a dull season of the year will at once assume that, except for their historical associations, and as presenting a rather dusky green plot of open ground in the desert of London houses and streets, we can have nothing worth communicating with respect to them ;—nothing, at least, that would render a visit remunerative. Such, however, is not the case. We have ourselves been both astonished and delighted by an inspection of them in the later autumn months ; and from the information of two of our kind friends, as well as from our own cursory glance at them, we now furnish a brief account of what is here to be seen.

These gardens are divided into two parts, one belonging to the Inner Temple and the other to the Middle Temple. The former of these is a considerable area, of about three acres. Except a slight extension to the west, along the water side, it is of a nearly square figure. A border for flowers extends round three of its sides, that towards the river being kept open. The rest is neatly-mown grass, with broad gravel walks in good condition, the one by the side of the river being largest, and affording a good river view at high water. A few small trees are scattered about, three elms on the grass appearing to be very healthy and thriving. There is an ancient sycamore on the lawn, now unfortunately dead, which once stood close by the side of the river, that here formed a bay. The trunk and branches of this tree are now very judiciously being covered with ivy, and with the aid of props will last a long time. Nothing could be plainer than the whole of this garden, which wants a few masses of shrubs and some good fountains. In the borders, however, many old summer flowers, such as sweet-williams, wallflowers, irises, mignonette (which is a first-rate town plant), and other well-known but frequently discarded herbaceous plants, with numerous crocuses and snowdrops in spring, are successfully cultivated by Mr. Brome, the gardener. But the chief feature of the garden is the chrysanthemums, which we shall presently describe.

Of much more contracted dimensions, the garden of the Middle Temple is arranged with superior taste, having more trees and shrubs, and a number of beds happily placed about the lawn, so as in some measure to disguise its shape and limits. Here, too, besides the flowers before mentioned, and stocks, and annuals, chrysanthemums are the leading element.

Nearly adjoining this is a smaller plot, half enshrouded with trees, in the middle of which is one of the few fountains of which London can boast. Although of the plainest description, with a simple half-inch jet, which throws the water 10 ft. in height, it is difficult to convey an adequate notion of the cheering effect which its sound, and sparkle, and coolness, communicate to the passers-by in the heart of the metropolis on a hot and dusty summer's day. Were the jet of a different character, and made to scatter the water more, the pleasure it occasions would be still increased. When looking at it, even as it is, however, one cannot help regretting that such objects are not of frequent occurrence in a town of such magnitude and with such resources.

At the back of the Temple Church, in a small piece of ground fronting the master's house, is a remarkable Jargonelle pear-tree, fully 35 ft. high, well branched, and with a proportionately stout trunk. In this dingy corner, where everything is darkened with soot, it is pleasant to see such a vigorous specimen, and to learn that it last year bore nearly a bushel of tolerably good pears.

Returning to the two gardens in which the chrysanthemums are grown, we may observe that, during the months of October and November, these afford little or no evidence of being kept in the midst of a great city. They look as green and fresh, and their flowers appear as clean and large, as if they were placed in some essentially country garden. In fact, we have seldom seen any out-door collection so good in the most favourable places. From the superior warmth of the atmosphere they bloom a little earlier than they do in the country, and many sorts that would perish during winter in a country garden, are here preserved in perfect safety. The whole of the plants were, when we saw them, covered with bloom, and being arranged so that the colours mix and blend as well as possible, they have the gayest and most enlivening effect. The individual flowers of some of the sorts were as much as 4½, 5, and even 6 in. across, the latter being protected by small glasses, suspended over the flowers on the top of stakes.

In the treatment of the plants there is no kind of difficulty. They are divided every two years (or the choicer sorts every year), and re-planted among the other flowers, without any renewal of the soil, and only with the addition of simple manure, and the subsequent use of manure water for them occasionally. None but the more delicate kinds are propagated in frames by cuttings ; and, as there is no convenience for that here, the gardeners trust to their friends in the country for a fresh supply of these few sorts each spring.

If a tribe like this, which is so exceedingly showy, and which blooms so far into the dullest month of the whole year (November), and which is likewise so very readily managed, were but sufficiently known as town plants, what an aspect of liveliness our numerous little town gardens might present in the autumn ! And how does the circumstance of these chrysanthemums flourishing so well in the Temple Gardens awaken and justify the belief which we confidently entertain, and which other cases have strongly confirmed, that one reason why plants do not thrive in London and other large towns is that the soil is so poor and often so thoroughly worn out. We incline, indeed, to the notion that there are a great many ornamental plants which would make a most respectable figure in town gardens, if the soil were occasionally renewed, or manure yearly supplied, and large trees were not suffered to fill the ground with their roots. The elm is particularly injurious in small plots on the latter account.

At the back of a border of shrubs in the Middle Temple Gardens, Mr. Dale has begun a rather novel system of growing chrysanthemums, in order to procure large flowers. The plants are inserted, pretty closely together, at the foot of a wall, and only one shoot to each plant trained up the wall, and arranged in various heights, so as to fill the wall well. On each of these shoots or stems just one flower is allowed to develop itself, and thus some most extraordinary blossoms are procured. As soon as the flowers begin to open they are protected from rain by a narrow-glazed calico awning, extending about 2 ft. from the wall, and they thus remain much longer in perfection. The flowers we saw were truly superb, and we noted the following names of a few of the sorts :—

Queen of England (a new and very handsome variety); Fleur de Marie, very fine ; Orlando, with the flower 5 in. across ; Lucidum ; Temple of Solomon, having a flower of the almost incredible size of 6 in. in diameter ; Princess Marie ; Beauty ; and Anna Salter. Some of these flowers were more like small quilled dahlias than chrysanthemums ; and those who are only accustomed to see the commonest border or greenhouse varieties could scarcely conceive it possible that a chrysanthemum should be so handsome and so perfect.

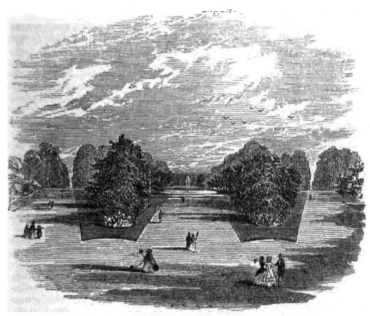

HAMPTON COURT GARDENS.

Hampton Court.—The great merit of this very striking place is that it has a *character of its own*, and that this character is alike adapted to the situation and country in which it happens to be placed, and to the palace of which it is the accompaniment. Perhaps there is not another garden round London of which this can be so truly said, or one of which the visitor will carry away such a clear and lasting impression. And though it has lately been the fashion to decry the style of gardening of which Hampton Court presents one of the very few remaining specimens, we doubt whether, in its leading features, anything more suited to the dignity of such a palace, or more in harmony with the flatness and tameness of the surrounding country, can be found. In this praise, however, we do not include what is called "the wilderness," which is only a subordinate and inferior part of the whole, and which might be removed without any loss, beyond the shadiness of walks which it affords.

It is most unfortunate, as far as the effect of the garden is concerned, that the public are only admitted through the wilderness. If access could be obtained by what are termed the "flower-pot gates," the noble terrace walk, which passes the east front of the palace, and which is probably one of the finest in England, would then be entered at once. Starting from these gates, after just glancing at the beauty of the flower baskets and groups of fruit by which their piers are surmounted, let the visitor imagine the wall on the right to be architecturally treated, in a manner worthy of the palace, and carried through in the same style to the margin of the river, the walk being terminated by appropriate iron gates and piers, or by a handsome small temple or summer house, and a more majestic picture can hardly be conceived. Passing along this walk towards the palace, the wall on the right will be seen to be covered with a variety of climbers, and, just by the side of the Tennis Court, which is the first part of the building that is reached, there is a very fine specimen of *Catalpa syringæfolia*.

When the centre of the palace is gained, the outline of the garden and the avenues in the park will be distinctly perceived. The principal part of the garden is comprised within a semicircular figure, from the sides of which, running north and south, a broad and lengthened oblong strip is extended. Besides the main walk along the palace front, there are three leading walks radiating from the centre of that front, flanked with lines of yew trees, and prolonged to the very entrance margin of the park by avenues of lofty limes. At the end of one of these avenues, the tower of Kingston Church gives an excellent finish to the vista. But this happy circumstance reminds one too strongly of the defectiveness of the terminations of the other avenues, which would acquire much greater dignity by having a tower, pillar, or some object of the kind to stop them. A very artistic group of trees, carried up to a point by a large Lombardy poplar, would even be a sufficient finish to the broader avenue.

About the middle of the central walk in the garden, is a large architectural basin of water, with a fountain, and a number of remarkably fine gold fishes. From the boundary of the garden, along the middle of the central park avenue (which, it should be observed, is much broader than the side ones), is a piece of water about three-quarters of a mile in length, and with straight sides, which is quite in harmony with the rest of the place; and a narrower canal, with a walk by its side, behind a noble grove of lime trees, is continued from this, near the margin of the garden, throughout its entire length. It is filled with aquatic plants and fish; but, from the proximity of the lime trees, is seldom perfectly clean.

With the exception of the long walk past the front of the palace, by the side of which a row of various kinds of hollies has been placed, (though some of these are now dead), the walks in the garden, and a grass glade extending the whole length of it, have had common yew trees planted on each side of them, at regular distances. The original intention and practice with regard to these was to clip them all to some regular shape, or into a variety of symmetrical figures. And though modern artists affect to rejoice in the emancipation of these trees from the rule of the shears, it is easy to conceive how such objects, if dressed in some pleasing or classic form, would, as the adjuncts of such a palace and such a garden, give the last and most characteristic touches to the picture. At present, many of the plants (both yews and hollies) have become exceedingly beautiful and venerable by being completely mantled with ivy; but, highly picturesque as they are, it is very doubtful whether, in this state, they at all accord, except in the antiquity of their appearance, with the character of the place. In some instances, where the yews seem to have died out, their place has been supplied with climbing roses, trained to pillars; and we noticed, around the central basin of water, that standards of *Robinia inermis* had been inserted between every two of the yews. These certainly produce contrast, but give an air of crowding, and evince a total want of harmony.

Chiefly beneath the yews and hollies, in a continuous broad band, which is, however, occasionally divided into beds, a great variety of summer flowers and herbaceous plants is grown. But as the plants do not flourish under the trees, and no proper system of massing them can be adopted, for want of regular divisions, their effect is extremely meagre. Some better arrangement of these flowers, so as to throw them into beds, and allow all the trees to stand on the grass, is the principal thing wanting in the garden, the walks of which are exceedingly well laid and well kept. In the lime trees which surround the garden, and form the park avenues, there is an unusual quantity of the common mistletoe, which is very conspicuous during winter. From the south end of the long terrace walk, near the river, one of the best views of the palace can be obtained. Here the old hollies and other trees in the private garden form an excellent foreground to the south front of the palace, and the east front is seen in perspective.

By ringing a bell, near the gates at the south-east corner of the palace, access can be obtained to the private garden, orangeries, and vinery. In the private garden are some remarkably old and picturesque variegated hollies, which are here the principal objects. On a raised terrace bank, at the west side of the garden, is an avenue of very ancient elms, trimmed into the form of a gothic colonade, and celebrated as a favourite walk of Mary, Queen of William the Third, of whom there are here many reminiscences. The effect of constant pruning is most remarkable in these elms, which, although so old, and most of them supposed to be hollow, are quite small in the stems, and appear, from their size, to be only young trees of forty or fifty years' growth. A handsome old dial-stand, in front of the orangery, bears the initials of William. The end of this garden abuts upon the river Thames, which has no particularly attractive features in this part of its course.

In the orangery, which is now never heated, but simply protected with shutters during winter, are some of the oldest and most perfectly formed orange trees in Britain. Several of them are said to be 400 years old; and many of the best were presented by Charles the Tenth of France. They are usually in flower throughout the months of June and July, when their fragrance is delicious. Among the orange trees are a small-leaved myrtle, and plants of *Pistacia lentiscus* and *Rowenia lucida*, which have been preserved since William the Third's time, and are even supposed to have been brought by him from Holland.

Between the orangery and the house in which the vine is growing, there is a very large plant of *Wistaria sinensis*, trained to a wall. The base of the stem is fully 14 in. in diameter, and the plant must have been one of the first specimens that were introduced.

At the south-west corner of the garden, fronting the orangery, is a large lean-to house containing the famous vine. The inside dimensions of this house are about 72 ft. in length, and 30 ft. in breadth. The vine is planted inside the house, and the whole of the floor is paved with flag-stones. The roof is almost entirely covered with branches, which are not trained in any particular method. One of the branches is described as 110 ft. long. The tree bears a pretty equal annual crop, neither the bunches nor berries being large, but the latter generally ripening and colouring well without any fire heat. About 1200 pounds was stated to us as the average yearly produce of the vine; and the grapes are sent to supply her Majesty's table. In the autumn of 1850, when we last saw it, the crop was healthy, and quite free from mildew. It has been conjectured that the roots of this vine have found their way into an old sewer near the house, and that this helps it to retain its vigour. The tree is believed to have been planted in 1768, by Lancelot Brown, who was once gardener at Hampton Court, and who afterwards became so much noted as one of the first practitioners of the English style of landscape gardening.

Returning from the private garden past the front of the palace, the wilderness will be entered through a gate on the left, and here, besides a few rather ancient cedars and yews, there is nothing but shady walks, until the labyrinth is reached. This is composed principally of hornbeam hedges, with walks between them nearly half a mile in length, and was formerly overlooked by a stand, which has been removed. The hedges are yearly becoming thinner and more broken.

Near the labyrinth is an entrance known as the "Lion gates," which are particularly handsome; and on the opposite side of the road is Bushy Park, with its magnificent avenue of horse chestnuts. These splendid trees are remarkable both for their size and for the great variety in their character, as regards the period of their coming into foliage and shedding their leaves, the shape and surface of the fruit-shell, and the appearance of the leaves. From the time when they first begin to unfold their leaf-buds till the autumn has quite stripped them, they are always interesting, but particularly so in June, while they are in full flower, and towards the end of September, when the leaves are changing their tints. The avenue is broken, not far from the Hampton Court entrance, by a large circular basin, with a figure on a pedestal in the centre. The trees are made to follow the outline of this basin, and although an interruption to the line is thus occasioned, they acquire more variety of character at this point. The avenue is backed up on each side by several rows of lime trees, and there are many picturesque thorns scattered about the park on the east side.

Hampton Court Gardens were originally commenced by Cardinal Wolsey, who formed the wilderness and the labyrinth. In the reign of Charles II. the large semicircle on the east side of the palace was planted. But it was reserved for William III., who resided a good deal at the palace, to bring the garden to its best state. At this period, the art of clipping yew and other trees into regular figures reached its highest point, being greatly favoured by the King. Four urns, said to be the first that were used in gardens, were also placed by William III. in front of the palace. Walpole says that the walls were once covered with rosemary, and that the trees were remarkable specimens of the topiary art.

The gardens at Hampton Court are the only ones of their class that we shall have to refer to, and are, in fact, almost unique as illustrations of the ancient or French style of gardening; very few places—certainly none near London, if we except the terrace gardens at Beddington Park, which have, perhaps, undergone little modern alteration, but are neither extensive nor remarkable—remaining at all like what they originally were. Hampton Court is therefore a valuable relic of the kind of taste formerly prevalent in this country, and is especially interesting to those who can discover beauty in a geometrical arrangement of lines and objects, dignity in a broad straight walk, and grandeur in a fine bold avenue, and who, with us, can lament that the sudden and violent changes of style which have successively occurred, have swept away so many noble examples of a period singularly rich in works of art of various kinds. With the more enlarged views of the present age, when no one style is proscribed, merely because another happens to be more generally suitable to the natural features of the country, such places as Hampton Court will be venerated and admired by the lover of art, and its more prominent characteristics would not be deemed unworthy of adoption in the like circumstances.

The greatest defect about Hampton Court is that the palace does not stand on a raised platform. The whole arrangement thus loses materially in dignity; and an elevated terrace—one of the richest features of the style, if fitly carried out—is consequently unprovided. If the building stood 3 or 4 ft. higher out of the ground, and the present broad walk in the front of it were raised to the same height throughout its entire length, or merely opposite the actual front of the palace, and supported by an ornamental wall or grass bank, with flights of steps in the centre walk and at other suitable points, a much grander appearance might have been created, and a very characteristic illustration of the style would not then have been wanting. In the private garden, where raised banks are introduced, the one on the right-hand side, as seen from the palace, is not properly balanced by the other side, and, from being higher than the base of the house itself, has an injurious rather than a desirable effect.

Although deficient in terrace banks, however, Hampton Court has the other peculiarities of the style well carried out. The straight walks are broad, flat, and long, affording a good survey of the best parts of the garden, without breaking up its breadth and repose. The design is not frittered away by narrow walks, nor by others starting off from the principal ones at an oblique angle. The grand central walk has its appropriate architectural basin and fountain about the middle of the garden; and the character of this walk is well prolonged into the park, to the very end of the avenue, by a bold and straight-sided canal. The other avenues, again, being of grass in the park, are properly carried through the garden to the palace as grass glades, so that there is no want of harmony between the park and the garden in this respect.

For so tame a country, too, the avenues of Hampton Court, confining the views to vistas, of which the central one is much the broadest, is a convenient and happy circumstance, well sustaining the dignity of the place, and imparting, by the contraction and consequent length of these views, a greater apparent extent to the park. In a better position such avenues and vistas might of course have been multiplied to advantage. But they are not disfigured by any inequalities in the surface of the ground; and the lime trees, of which they are composed, are among the most beautiful, the most regular-growing, and the least liable to accident or decay of any trees that could be selected. They are also easily kept within the proper limits, by pruning, whenever their branches are disposed to straggle across or interrupt the vista. Of the lime-tree avenue, which half encircles the garden, it may, perhaps, be said that it is too lofty for the purpose, and becomes a nuisance there by its shade, and by the scattering of its foliage in autumn. Yet without it, the other avenues would appear unsupported, the irregular groups of trees in the park would become visible and seem out of harmony; and it is in itself so beautiful in spring, when the leaves take their first tender green, and so grateful in summer for its shade, and so delicious when the flowers are in perfection, that, being far enough from the palace not to diminish the height and grandeur of the edifice, it must be considered an advantageous accompaniment, and it serves also to cover the boundary of the gardens.

In respect to the other, or garden avenues, the hollies, by the side of the longest walk, being of various kinds, and, as is here proved, being liable to fail when they become old, have not been happily selected for the object. The yews, however, from their having been so much pruned formerly, and having thus acquired a stunted character, are, for this reason, and because of their dark hue, contrasting so well with the palace, the gay flowers around them, and the lime trees, particularly suited for the purpose, and make, in the main, capital parts of the entire picture. When it is remembered how few kinds of plants there are which could by any possibility be substituted for these yews, the Irish yew being too small, arbor-vitæ and cypresses and junipers either too slender or of a less decided and desirable colour, standard Portugal laurels or rhododendrons or acacias being more fitted for Italian gardens, cedars of both kinds acquiring too great a size, other evergreens being too rambling or too deficient in character, and deciduous plants being quite out of the question, it will be seen and acknowledged that great judgment has been displayed in the choice of the common yew, even though it be admitted that its capacity for being reduced to a regular form by clipping was at least one of its original recommendations. Perhaps, if these avenues had to be replanted, and the use of the shears or the knife were forbidden, the Irish yew would be altogether the best substitute, and would look well when it acquired age and a somewhat spreading shape. At first its stiffness would require softening off by alternate standard acacias, or something of that description.

The whole of the ground in the garden being brought to a perfect level, and the grass kept smooth and even, the best possible finish is given to the place. Irregularities of surface, even of the smallest kind, are never tolerable in this style; no change of level being allowable, except by means of a regular bank, of uniform height, or a terrace wall.

What the flower-beds at Hampton Court may have once been we have no means of knowing. At present, as we have already hinted, they are the worst parts of the garden. It may safely be assumed that flowers are never proper beneath specimen trees or plants, particularly when these have so important an office to fill in composing avenues. If they do not stand on grass alone, such plants should never have anything but a small circle or square of dressed earth around them. And when they become old, nothing appears so proper as grass. Between specimen plants arranged in lines, as at Hampton Court, beds of 4 to 6 ft. in width, with straight sides, in accordance with the line of the walk and that of the plants, and the ends made semicircular either with an outward curve, or, more fitly, with an inward sweep, as if to allow for the spreading of the specimens, would, if not too crowded, and nicely filled with flowers, make a beautiful border at once to the lawn and the walks. Of course the ends might be finished in many other ways, as by making them square, and adding a small semicircle in their centre; and the effect might be varied by placing them in lines of two, three, or more together, and then leaving blank spaces between some of the plants, provided the whole were done regularly, and with due regard to symmetry.

It is very doubtful whether the introduction of any other beds than such as follow thus the line of trees would be at all admissible in such a garden; and, we believe, it has not been attempted. But some such simple alteration of them as we have thus sketched, and the arrangement of the flowers in them judiciously and symmetrically in regard to colour and character, would be an easy, yet most effective, mode of upholding the dignity of this garden.

Of architectural enrichment these gardens are almost wholly destitute, which is accounted for by the fact, that in William III.'s reign, when they were raised to their highest condition, such things as vases and similar ornaments had not become the fashion, and Hampton Court has been little used since by our sovereigns; while, we believe, several things of this kind were taken from hence to Windsor. Evelyn, however, in his Diary of 1654, long prior to the time of King William, speaks of the "rich and noble fountain in the garden, with *syrens*, *statues*, &c., cast in copper, by Famelli." The fountain, as we have shown, remains; but there are now no statues, nor any other architectural embellishments; a fact to be deplored, as they would agree so well with the style, and exhibit themselves in excellent relief amongst the sombre-tinted yews.

Although not properly coming within our province, we cannot forbear reminding the reader that these scenes have been rendered classic by the sad fate of Cardinal Wolsey, who founded them; by the birth here of Edward VI.; by a sort of imprisonment to which the unhappy Charles I. was here subjected; by the occurrence here of that conference of episcopalians and presbyterians, in James I.'s reign, which led to our present translation of the Bible; and by the existence in the palace of the renowned Cartoons of Raffaelle.

Beulah Spa.—Situated at the southern end of the range of low hills on which Norwood stands, and being not more than seven or eight miles from London, this place was formed sixteen or eighteen years since, and became one of very fashionable resort. It is made, for the most part, out of a young oak plantation or coppice, on the south slope of the hill, and, with the exception of a small open lawn about the centre, and a diminutive piece of water near one side, consists of an almost infinite series of walks cut through the wood, these walks being hidden from each other by low bushes, brambles, and wild brushwood, the whole forming a very agreeable summer retreat, on account of its wildness, and rusticity, and indefiniteness, and shade. On the upper side, however, there is a more open terrace walk, from which, as well as from a point where a camera obscura once stood, extensive views are obtained. Around the lawn already mentioned, and in other parts, several good rustic buildings, some of which have possessed considerable merit, exist; but these and the entire place are all now more or less decayed and neglected; and the remains of Penge Wood, which lie between it and the Annerly Station of the Croydon Railway, and which formerly had a fine forest-like character, will afford more pleasing wood walks, while better views of the country, on all sides, may be had from various other points in this most agreeable and picturesque neighbourhood.

In dismissing the *public gardens* of the metropolis, on which we have dwelt longer, because they are more decidedly national, and because, also, we can point to them with a good deal of general satisfaction, we must remark, by way of excuse for having offered what may seem to be so many objections and hints for improvement, that we have considered these gardens, from being the property of the nation, or from belonging

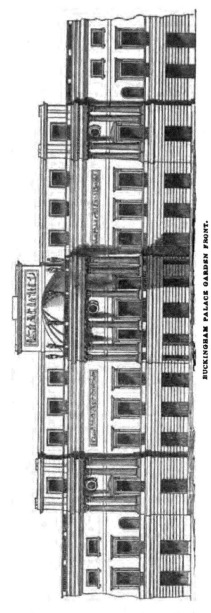

BUCKINGHAM PALACE GARDEN FRONT.

to public bodies, as legitimately open to criticism. In these cases, therefore, we have departed a little from the plan laid down, partly because a free discussion of such matters, when it does not trespass on private feelings and rights, is always beneficial, but chiefly to carry the visitor away from the contemplation of the defects by showing him how, with a few trifling alterations, particular points may be restored to their proper influence. In accomplishing the remainder of our task our hope is to be able to adhere better to our first rule.

PRIVATE GARDENS.—The environs of London are, as might be expected, rich in almost every variety of these; though they are more generally such as belong to the villa class than those which are proper to the country mansion. Among them, however, will occur some fine examples of different kinds of gardening. But as these gardens are not so readily accessible, and do not comprise such a variety of objects, as the public ones before described, we shall sketch their principal features more lightly, endeavouring merely to show the more distinctive characteristics of each.

Buckingham Palace Gardens are attached to the London residence of her Majesty the Queen; and those who have not actually been through them will be surprised to learn that they comprise about 40 acres, of which nearly 5 acres are devoted to a lake. Considering how thoroughly they are imbedded, as it were, in the town, this is an area, for exclusively private use, quite worthy of even a Royal Palace; especially as it is bordered on the north side by the open space of the Green Park, while the east front of the palace overlooks the whole of St. James's Park, with its large sheet of water.

On the south and west sides, these gardens are inclosed by streets and their accompanying houses. The buildings on the southern side being most inconveniently near the palace and gardens, and being mostly of an inferior character, have been happily shut out by a large bank of earth, raised in George IV.'s reign, and planted with both trees and shrubs. The existence of a number of fine old elms, too, in the western part of the gardens, excludes all but here and there a portion of the lofty houses in Grosvenor Place, so that in fact the gardens are rendered almost entirely private during summer; while, by the arrangement of the planting in many parts, the most perfectly secluded spots are secured, where no effort is required to imagine oneself in the midst of a purely country district.

In the front of the palace, no attempt has been made to obtain anything like an enriched garden. A plain lawn, with nothing but some groups of old elm trees upon it, stretches away between the palace and the water, taking more the character of a small park scene than a garden one. The water has, however, a good effect.

Along the south side of the gardens, at a very short distance from the palace, a profusion of shrubs and exotic plants begins to appear. And here, also, there is a small flower-garden, the flowers in which looked healthy and flourishing when we saw them. Walks winding among masses of shrubs bring us occasionally to the margin of the principal lawn, affording a variety of pleasing views across it to the lake; and they sometimes carry us along the side of the wall next Constitution Hill, where the boundary has rather happily been disguised by dense plantations of shrubs and trees, the branches of the former now extending out on the lawn, with a nice fringy line, so as to show no dug ground or border. There is a good deal of the same kind of treatment throughout the gardens, and it has a very pleasing effect in such a place as this, where flower-borders are not desired. The masses of rhododendrons and other evergreens are in excellent condition.

The walk adjoining Constitution Hill gives exit from the gardens near the Triumphal Arch opposite Hyde Park Corner. But another walk is continued round in the direction of Grosvenor Place, and a branch walk also crosses the lake by a bridge. Both these walks conduct to the foot of the large mound on the western side of the gardens, where another path is carried over the mound, so as to afford many different glimpses of the gardens, through the openings in the screen of shrubs. The face of this mound is planted chiefly with lilacs and other deciduous flowering plants, which must be exceedingly gay in the spring of the year, but which are rather dull in autumn and winter. They are for the most part growing on a grassy slope.

About midway along the top of the bank, we come upon a charming little Italian temple, called the Queen's summer-house, which is most admirably placed for commanding views of the lake and gardens, and has a broad terrace in front of it to afford space for enjoying these. In regard to both its position and character, it is quite the leading feature of the place. But its interior is still more worthy of attention, as containing eight frescoes, illustrative of Milton's Comus, executed in 1844 and 1845 by Eastlake, Maclise, E. Landseer, Dyce, Stanfield, Uwins, Leslie, and Ross. The ornaments and borders are by Gruner. This is a perfect gem of art, and is a most fitting ornament to the gardens of our Queen.

A set of winding steps descends from the terrace of the summer-house to the lower part of the garden, and the higher walk also continues along the top of the bank till it nears the palace, when it gradually descends, passing the Royal Mews, till it falls into the level of the broad walk along the front of the palace. Before leaving the summer-house, however, we must point out the large statue of the Duke of Wellington on the Triumphal Arch at the top of Constitution Hill, which from this point appears to be standing on a broad pedestal, none of the arch being seen. This is decidedly the best view we have anywhere had of that statue ; and, looked at against the clear strong light of a north-western sky, towards evening, it becomes an exceedingly bold and impressive object.

The face of the large mound we have described being clothed with grass, and the shrubs and trees being scattered about upon this without any bare soil being visible, the artificial character of the bank is in great measure subdued. In this and some other respects, the gardens evince tasteful management, and are under the charge of Mr. Mann, who has likewise, we believe, the superintendence of the neighbouring parks. One or two singular sheep, and some tame deer, have generally the run of the gardens ; and, though by no means conducing to their good order, or to the well-being of the plants, furnish some amusement to the junior members of her Majesty's family.

Windsor Castle Gardens.—With the exception of the flower-garden on the eastern terrace of the Castle, these gardens are more commonly known as "the Slopes." They extend from the town of Windsor, at the north-western corner of the Castle Hill, to the public walk which crosses the Home Park from Datchet to Frogmore. Occupying, as their name implies, the face of a long hill which is picturesquely varied in parts, and commanding the most splendid occasional prospects into an extensive country, and always having the magnificent accompaniment of the Castle, of which the most delightful peeps or open views are sometimes obtained, a walk through these gardens will do little more than satisfy the curiosity of the visitor. In all matters of taste, they certainly cannot be taken as models. And it is greatly to be deplored that so glorious a palace, on a site so peculiarly favourable for picturesque treatment, and overlooking such a number of interesting and classic scenes, should have no ground attached to it which really deserves the name of a pleasure-garden.

Before entering upon the Slopes, however, we shall carry the visitor to the Castle terraces. That on the northern side is always accessible to the public, and, in walking along it, just within the wall, some highly beautiful scenes will be unfolded, to which the trees on the slope of the hill often form appropriate foregrounds. To the west, especially of an evening, the windings of the river Thames, somewhat disfigured of late by the long wooden bridge and viaduct of the branch from the Great Western Railway, stretch away in great beauty and variety into the distance, and are often exquisitely illuminated. On the north, a little below the terrace, Eton College, of which there is an excellent view, frequently becomes visible through the trees. In the north-east, Harrow-on-the-Hill, with its gleaming church spire, is a very conspicuous object. And the bank itself, beneath the Castle, has, in parts, a beautiful clothing of shrubs and trees, as viewed from the terrace, particularly towards the western end.

The eastern terrace is only open to the public on Saturdays and Sundays, after two o'clock. This terrace, which is a continuation of the northern one, and on the same level, surrounds a sunken area of between three and four acres, which, being on that side of the Castle where the private apartments are situated, is formed into a geometrical flower-garden. Nothing could be finer than the views from this terrace into the open country, across the Little Park. A few old elm trees in the Little Park serve to break up the scene into several portions, the out-lines and character of which change as the visitor shifts his position; and after the eye has ranged over an immense tract of country, richly clothed with trees, and diversified with smaller swells and undulations, the view is terminated by some of the Surrey hills that lie nearest to London, and by here and there a glimpse of one or two of the Kentish eminences. To the south-west and south, the nearer high ground of the Great Park, with its noble woods, forms the line of the horizon; and much of the country seen from the north terrace is observable also, in a different aspect, from the eastern one. Bastions are thrown out at the angles of the terrace, which contribute to heighten its effect: and the visitor can pass from it along the south front of the Castle, from which the best idea of the long walk and the statue which terminates it will be obtained.

Steps from the raised terrace conduct, at several points, down into the flower-garden, which is further connected with the terrace all round by a sloping bank of grass. The general shape of this flower-garden is oblong, with a semicircular end. But it is not entirely regular, the northern side being the widest, and having some extra flower-beds in front of the orangery. The terrace itself forms an irregular pentagon.

A broad walk leads from some steps in the centre of the Castle down the middle of the flower-garden to another flight of steps which carries it on to the terrace. In the centre of the garden there is a circular basin, containing a fountain composed of numerous small jets; and round this basin the middle walk passes, diverging right and left into other walks, at right angles from it. These side walks join another walk that passes entirely round the garden. Between the cross walk and the Castle are two oblong areas, around the edges of which flower-beds are ranged, on the grass, the centre being kept as open lawn. These beds are slightly raised, with sloping grass edges, and are filled with roses, and a variety of the usual summer flowers. In the space between the cross walk and the terrace other beds occur, and are fur-nished chiefly with shrubs. There are also a few beds between the surrounding garden walk and the terrace banks, and these, too, are supplied with shrubs. In both these latter cases, the shrubs are commonly arranged in masses of one sort, occupying either the whole or a portion of a bed. We observed groups of *Phillyrea, Arbutus, Laurus-tinus*, and many others; but nothing either very rare or very effective, and nothing at all, in the way of shrubs, having any reference to the style of the garden or the character of the Castle.

Beneath the terrace on the northern side of the flower-garden is a conservatory or orangery, furnished with the hardier sorts of old green-house plants, and having a grass slope from it up to the level of the flower-garden, with a number of flower-beds on this slope. This orangery appears most unhappily placed, being so much below the level of the flower-garden, and having the ground sloping directly down to its front.

Scattered throughout the flower-garden, but arranged symmetrically, are some exceedingly handsome urns, of considerable size, and the high-est character and keeping. But, placed among these, there are likewise many bronze and other figures, brought from other Royal gardens, and only fit to be the accompaniments of an Italian palace. A noble bronze cast of the celebrated Warwick vase is placed near the Castle, opposite the centre. The wall of the terrace immediately beneath this east front of the Castle is covered with good climbing plants of various kinds.

In the choice of flowers to fill the beds in the flower-garden, and the levels of the verges to the walks, and the line of edgings to the walks, and the general keeping of the garden, nothing like a high tone of gardening, or first-rate order, was at all observable when we saw the whole last autumn. Everything seemed to be arranged and kept in a decidedly inferior manner.

A door through the back wall of the orangery leads us at once to the Slopes ; and here we immediately begin to see the country on this side in fresh aspects. The trees, through the openings among which we look, acquire additional height and importance now that we are on a lower level, and it is more easy, by choosing a position, to use them as changing frameworks to the various pictures, or for excluding things that are not wished to be seen.

Taking the walk towards the west, in order to get to the bottom of the Slopes, we see, in descending, more of the boldness of the hill on which the Castle stands, and learn how beautiful this bank might easily be made by the free introduction of an appropriate undergrowth of different sorts of bushes, grouped a good deal into irregular masses, thrown carelessly about as if they had been dropped there by Nature, and tangled over occasionally with the wild honeysuckle, briar rose, clematis, and ivy. No place could be better adapted than this bank for such semi-natural treatment.

Having reached the bottom of the slope, and turned along the margin of a small formal piece of water, of recent formation, we begin to get views of the Castle through the tops of the trees which clothe the bank. These views are of the most varied description, sometimes only presenting a tower, next a broader mass of the building, and then, perhaps, a larger portion, embracing several towers. Nearly all these views are good, and some of them very effective. But the visitor must be on the alert to look out for them, as they often occur suddenly, and are as speedily lost. There being, however, nothing else to attract attention in this part, the varying aspects of the Castle may be duly watched. We should here note, however, that the finest view of the Castle which we have anywhere had is from the South-Western Branch Railway to Windsor, within a few hundred yards of the terminus. From this point, which is just sufficiently near to enable one to appreciate the elevated position on which the Castle stands, and yet far enough off to give the great Round Tower and other towers their full height and consequence as parts of the composition, the whole northern front, and a perspective view of the eastern front, are seen at once, and the trees on the northern slope form an excellent support and accompaniment to the pile. Anything finer than this, as a whole, can scarcely be conceived.

On leaving the side of the new straight canal at the bottom of the slope, the bed of a stream, with an infinite number of little sinuosities, may be traced, till it arrives at an open space, in the midst of fine lime and other trees, which has now, we suppose, been converted into a lake, to be used principally for skating purposes. The stream is to supply it with water from the Thames. Before reaching the lake, however, a small rosary, with an attendant summer-house, will be passed. Further on, the face of the hill has, in one part, been covered with masses of chalk, obtained from the interior of the hill itself, but crumbling away fast beneath the action of the weather; and some excavations into the hill for chalk have been converted into small galleries, that at present appear without an object, and are simply lined with brick.

Advancing, but again ascending the hill, we meet with a bronze figure of Prince Albert's favourite greyhound, on a pedestal of Aberdeen granite, and then the Little Park, with all the country to the east and south of it, opens out before us. In a short time we gain the rockery, which is approached through a tunnel of flints of a very formal kind, and has a plain grotto, lined only with pebbles, at its side, with a wall of pebbly stone extending along its summit. A small stream meanders through the lower part of it. Near this rockery we noticed a rather nice vase, in artificial stone, the pedestal of which is composed of five small circular pillars, which have a light and pleasing appearance. And a little further on is a rustic temple, well placed, and superior to anything else in this portion of the estate. It is of an octagonal shape, the whole of the wood of which it is composed having the bark left on it, and a small gallery surrounding it. The pillars are furnished with rude bases and caps, and between them and the roof is a band of open trellis work. It has a thatched high-pitched roof, with broad eaves. Occurring in this distant and rude part of the grounds, and being well finished, it is a very picturesque object.

Following the path at the top of the bank, where many kinds of pine and fir have been planted, we come at length to a venerable old oak, and discover that within its trunk, on the northern side, a rustic seat has been contrived. This oak had become partially hollow, and had decayed into a hole on one side, to about 4 ft. or 4 ft. 6 in. from the ground. This hole, which is just large enough to accommodate one person, has been formed into a seat, and lined with strips of oak, having the bark outwards, so as to look not much unlike a part of the tree itself. When seated within this oak the aperture is only high enough to admit of a person seeing out, while the upper part of the head and the hat are in a higher portion of the hollow.

Not far from this oak we enter the garden around what is known as Adelaide Lodge, a small summer cottage, prettily situated, and completed under the superintendence of the late Queen Dowager. The ground about this lodge takes some very pleasing undulations, and falls away very gracefully, many firs and other large evergreens, with mixed masses of several kinds of shrubs, being judiciously placed on the lawn and round the margins of the garden, so as to give the whole an agreeable and picturesque air. Numerous flower-beds, used for verbenas, pelargoniums, and similar summer ornaments, are arranged on the lawn in the neighbourhood of the lodge; and not many yards from it a gate will discharge us into the path across the Home Park, proceeding by which, to the right, we may visit her Majesty's kitchen gardens.

The *Royal Kitchen Gardens* at *Frogmore* exhibit as fine a specimen of kitchen and fruit gardening, in all the departments of the latter, as is to be found in Europe. We doubt, indeed, whether there is any other garden of the kind which will, in its principal features, bear the least comparison with it. And this is precisely as it should be; for, in a country where gardening is carried to so high a point, we naturally expect to see some of the most perfect examples in the royal gardens.

These kitchen gardens are of comparatively recent formation, having been begun at the end of 1841. They are the result of the abandonment of the old royal kitchen gardens at Kensington, Hampton Court, Cumberland Lodge, Maestricht, and Kew, and the determination to concentrate the whole into one first-rate establishment. It having been found so very unsatisfactory to have the royal gardens scattered about as they were before, this method of combining them, and thus increasing their efficiency, was adopted at the recommendation of a commission of inquiry, of which Dr. Lindley was the head.

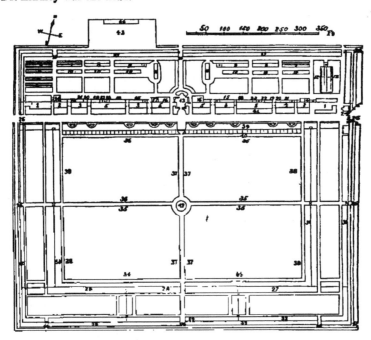

GROUND PLAN OF GARDEN AT FROGMORE.

In order to enable the reader better to understand the general arrangement of these gardens, we present a ground plan of them, on a small scale, as they existed in 1849, which we are obligingly permitted to use from cuts which have appeared in the *Gardener's Chronicle*. A slip of 8 acres has been added to the lower part of them, making the entire area of the gardens about 32 acres.

Being only about a mile from Windsor Castle, the pleasure grounds at which are destitute of any kind of plant structure except the orangery, one of the aims in forming these gardens has been to combine ornament with use, and render them sufficiently neat and attractive to be worth visiting by her Majesty and the guests at the Castle. Hence, in the great range of houses, a compartment at each end has been reserved for greenhouse and stove plants; a broad terrace walk, with flower-beds and borders, and vases on a low terrace wall, extends along the front of the range; a handsome fountain, with a large basin composed of Aberdeen granite, occupies the centre of the garden; the walls are adorned with sculptured ornaments at the end of the terrace; and rooms are fitted up, in the front part of the gardener's residence, for the use of her Majesty.

An air of extraordinary cleanliness and order pervades every part of these gardens. The walks are all gravelled, with neat box-edgings, and kept scrupulously free from weeds or soil; the sides of the walks are furnished with well-trained and regularly-trimmed fruit trees; the crops are all even, and free from weeds, and arranged with great regularity; the range of houses is, both in its structure and keeping, a perfect model of neatness and elegance; and even the back sheds, and the department filled with pits and the smaller forcing houses, are equally tidy, and seem to invite inspection. The walls of the back sheds are, indeed, covered with pretty climbing plants in summer, and look more like a row of beautiful little cottages than the places in which the materials of a kitchen and forcing garden are stored, and its processes carried on.

We proceed, however, to describe the gardens, with reference to the plan. Entering by a bold gateway, adapted for carriages, at 25, the porter's lodge (24) is on the right, and the broad terrace walk immediately opposite the entrance. The range of glass, extending to the length of nearly 1000 ft., inclusive of the gardener's house, stretches to the right of this terrace walk, and has an aspect a little east of south. On the left-hand side of the terrace walk is a broad grass verge, with a few semicircular flower-beds and an herbaceous border (39), backed by the terrace wall, which has vases on it in the centre and at either end, and 40 is a series of oblong flower-beds. The vine border (41) is also kept filled with flowers, and, when we saw it last autumn, looked very gay with alternate rows of the Tom Thumb and a pale pink Pelargonium, which were particularly luxuriant. Gates and piers finish the terrace walk at 26, which number indicates a gate or door wherever it occurs.

Just within the entrance gates, between the lodge and the range of glass, there is a very handsome plant of *Clematis montana* on the wall. It is treated somewhat like a vine, being trained to several upright stems, and spurred back every year. The result is that it throws out great tufts of its charming white flowers from each of the joints, and has a curious as well as beautiful appearance.

In examining the range of glass houses, it will be seen that the tameness of their front line is broken by the additional projection of the stove and greenhouse at the ends (No. 1), and also by the greater width of the large vineries (5). The houses on either side of the great vineries are likewise broader than the two smaller vineries which adjoin the gardener's house, and the pine stoves (2). And the heights of all these correspond to their width. The end plant houses are highest and broadest, and the pine stoves next them are lowest and narrowest. Between every two of the houses there is likewise a small glazed porch, 7 ft. square, which makes a further break both in the front line and the elevation. And the handsome gardener's house (13) in the old English style, which occupies the centre of the range, contributes yet more to vary and enliven it*.

* Other Numbers on the plan indicate the following:—3. Peach houses; 4. Apricot and Plum house; 6 and 7. Pine pits; 8 and 9. Cucumber houses; 10. Pits for melons, strawberries, &c.; 11. Cherry houses, exhibiting improvements in ventilation; 12. Asparagus beds, heated by hot water; 14. Dwelling and sleeping rooms of the workmen; 15. Mushroom houses; 16. Fruit rooms; 17. Seed rooms; 18. Store rooms; 19. Open sheds for barrows, &c.; 20. Potting sheds; 21. Work rooms for indoor operations; 22. Sheds for washing vegetables; 23. Tool sheds; 27. Apricot wall; 28. Peach and nectarine walls; 29. Cherry wall; 30. Walls for plums; 31. Walls for pears; 32. Walls for currants and gooseberries; 33. Walls for figs, mulberries, &c.; 34. Dwarf plum trees; 35. Dwarf apple trees; 36 and 37. Pear-trees on trellises; 38. Dwarf cherries; 43. Manure and compost yard; 44. Stables, cart-sheds, &c.

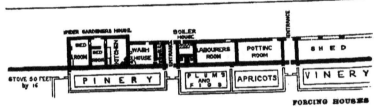

FORCING HOUSES

There is much in the construction of these fruit houses which is calculated to excite our admiration. They are of the usual lean-to character, with low upright sashes in front. But the roof is entirely of iron, except that the rafters are capped with light strips of wood, to prevent them from becoming too hot, and the sash bars, which are made hollow in order to allow for their expansion and contraction, are of copper. The doors, too, are of iron, with brass hinges to avoid rust. The houses are ventilated by means of the front lights; the whole of the lights in each house being raised simultaneously, to any required extent, by one or more turns of a winch placed at each end, and connected with a horizontal bar passing through them. Every alternate upper light is also made to slide down with the utmost facility on pulleys, by a "quadrant wheel jack," which acts most perfectly, the ropes being formed of patent copper wire. Other ventilators, for winter use, are placed above the houses, in the wall, where a grating is inserted, and communicate with the houses through openings in the upper part of the back walls; these being furnished with flap doors, all which can be opened or shut at once by simply turning a winch attached to the proper machinery. The most complete ventilation can thus be secured in safety at all seasons, and with the smallest possible expenditure of labour. The whole arrangement is of the simplest description, and appears to answer well, very rarely getting out of order. The only improvements that have been made upon it are in some smaller new houses which have subsequently been erected, and in which the front lights are made to open outwards, turning on a centre pivot, and not upwards, while the winch for working

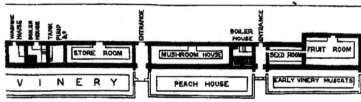

AT FROGMORE.

the apparatus is kept within the house, and thus is not exposed to the action of the weather, and can be more conveniently worked.

A more thorough control over the atmosphere of the houses is further kept up by means of the small porches which are placed between them, and which prevent any direct accession of cold or damp air, or sensible loss of heat, in passing in and out of any part of the range. These porches are likewise of use in giving access to each house, separately, from the back sheds or other parts of the back forcing ground ; and by placing a few ornamental plants in their corners, they enliven the appearance of the range as it is passed through, while they further give shelter to a few small vines or other fruit trees, which supply a limited quantity of late or intermediate crops. The houses were all erected by Mr. Clark, of Birmingham.

Hot water, conveyed in 4-inch pipes, is the sole mode of heating adopted for these houses. The dots (.) in the range of back sheds on the plan indicate where the boilers are situated. Over the upper pipes, along the front of the houses, small troughs for containing water occur at intervals, and are cast along with the pipes. These are supplied by a perforated pipe which passes over them.

Nothing can be more perfect than the state of the fruit trees in these houses, and the crops of fruit obtained from them. The two large vineries especially, which are each 102 ft. long, were, when we saw them last summer, in a magnificent condition, the bunches of grapes hanging, at nearly equal distances, over almost every square foot of the roof. These grapes were in moderate-sized bunches, well swelled, and, as far as they were ripe, excellently coloured. The peach trees in the house numbered 3 were equally good, as were the Muscat grapes in the house 5, on the west of the centre lodge. All the other fruit trees were in the best order. The houses numbered 2 are pine stoves, and 4 is an apricot and plum house. In the greenhouse at the east end of the range, some Passion flowers and other climbers are trained along the sides of the central pit, so as to cover the wall with verdure, and look particularly well. The stove at the other end of the range likewise contains a remarkable plant of *Ipomæa Learii*, which fills the whole house (50 ft. by 16) with festoons of its splendid flowers, a succession of these being produced every day throughout the greater part of the summer and autumn.

Following the order of the numbers on the plan, the pits marked 6 are filled with succession pines, which are all grown in pots here, and heated chiefly with hot water. The fruiting pine pits are at 7. The two houses marked 8 are for cucumbers. In those numbered 9, as well as in some of the others, which are occasionally changed from their original purpose for a time, plants of various kinds are grown. There are here small collections of stove and greenhouse plants, and orchids, cultivated principally for keeping up a succession of bloom in the larger houses in the range, for supplying cut flowers and flowering plants *to* the Castle, and for filling the beds and borders both here and at the Castle. There are, however, a few of the rarer kinds among them, such as the *Amherstia nobilis*, and some other stove plants, with several uncommon Orchids and ferns. We observed here also a pretty little trailing plant, *Sibthorpia europœa*, which seems as useful as Lycopodiums for covering the soil in pots, &c., whether in the stove or greenhouse, and, being of a very different character, ought to become more generally used. Many of the houses in this part have wooden roofs, with no iron in them. The *Amherstia* has lately flowered here, while in a small state.

The cucumbers are all here planted out in the houses devoted to them, and either trained to trellises, or treated as large bushes, the branches being supported with stakes as soon as they begin to bear fruit. We saw a house filled with plants grown as bushes, just as these were beginning to flower. The plants were between 4 and 5 ft. high, and about the same diameter, being full of branches. They were placed down the middle of a pit in the house, one plant being under each light. As they were very healthy, they had a novel and beautiful appearance.

That series of pits numbered 10 is for melons, French beans, strawberries, &c. Two span-roofed cherry houses, of an exceedingly neat and pleasing character, and exhibiting the improvements in ventilation before referred to, are shown at 11. These are of iron, like the houses in the large range. They have upright lights at the sides and ends, and a path down the centre; the cherry trees standing in pots on either side of this path. There was a particularly good crop in the later of these houses last summer.

Two new houses, for vines and cherries, have lately been erected between the span-roofed cherry houses and the centre walk. They are of iron, with a slightly-curved roof, and are finished, like the rest, with every attention to modern principles. Some extra ventilation is obtained by pipes which pass through the lower part of the back wall, and communicate with the outer atmosphere. They are intended to circulate the air a little more freely in summer.

At 12 there is a quantity of asparagus beds, heated by hot water, and used for forcing. They show clearly how such things can be forced without the mess and litter commonly occasioned. The asparagus is planted in long brick pits, 4 ft. deep and 7 ft. in width; and these are covered, when in work, by light span-roofed wooden frames, supporting close-fitting wooden shutters. Between the pits are small spaces 20 inches wide, each containing two hot-water pipes communicating with a boiler at the end, and diffusing the heat into the pits through pigeon-holes of the usual kind. The heat is prevented escaping from these middle spaces by their being flagged over in a very secure manner. By using one of these pits at a time, a succession of forced asparagus may be procured, and the plan is found to answer most satisfactorily.

We have already said that 13 is the residence of the gardener, Mr. Ingram, under whose direction the garden has been formed, and the houses erected, while the present state of everything in it is most honourable to his skill and judgment. At 14 are commodious dwelling and sleeping rooms for the foremen and men, while 21 are workmen's rooms for any indoor labour, or for meals, &c. The figures 15 point to two mushroom houses; 16, are fruit rooms; 17, seed rooms; 18, store rooms; 19, open sheds for barrows, &c.; 20, potting sheds; 22, sheds for washing vegetables; and 23, tool sheds. It will be at once seen that these arrangements, comprising every sort of convenience, are of the most compact description, and that the relative position of the several offices has been duly studied. Thus, the fruit rooms are close to the gardener's house, as they should be, and the seed rooms are properly put next. The foremen's rooms are also at either end of the range; thus distributing the surveillance of those who have to manage the garden over the greatest possible surface. There is a further advantage in having the open shed, the potting shed, and the tool shed grouped together, as the materials used or kept in these are often wanted at the same time. The manure and compost yard is at 43, with the stables, cart-sheds, &c., at the back of it (44), thus keeping everything of a littery or displeasing kind entirely by itself, where it cannot be seen, and affording the means of maintaining the whole place in the highest order. Even the back entrance to the gardener's house is covered with a clump of shrubs.

At 27, behind the pits, there is an apricot wall, the trees on which cover nearly every inch of its surface, and are in a remarkably good state. In order to preserve the blossoms from spring frosts, this wall is covered with canvas in spring, when necessary; the covering being rolled up and down by pulleys or bars of wood fixed into iron sockets at the base, and fastened against the wall near the summit. The whole of these are removed after they are quite done with; and the effect of this covering, in preserving the crops, is most striking. Another apricot wall is at 27, in the lower part of the garden.

The figures 28 refer to peach and nectarine walls, the trees on which, like the apricots, are trained on the fan system, and have nearly covered the wall. They were suffering very much from insects last year. 29 is a cherry wall; 30, walls for plums; 31, for pears; 32, for currants and gooseberries; and 33, for figs, mulberries, &c. The whole of the walls are 12 ft. high, and the trees are, for the most part, trained to a fan shape. The amount of wall space is, as will be seen, very considerable.

Dwarf fruit trees are also grown by the sides of many of the walks, 34 being a row of dwarf plum trees; 35, dwarf apple trees; 36 & 37, pear trees on trellises; and 38, dwarf cherries. The trellis to which the pear trees at 37 are trained is in the form of a low semicircle, 6 ft. wide and 4 ft. high, the trees being planted in the middle, and kept with a single stem till they reach the trellis, when the branches are made to diverge in all directions. By this plan of trellis, the whole surface receives plenty of light, and the trees do not interfere with the view down the garden from the terrace walk.

The compartments nearest the terrace are filled with gooseberries, currants, raspberries, &c., so as to look better from the principal walk. One or two of the smaller inclosed gardens is devoted to strawberries. The remainder of the garden, including the new piece of 8 acres at the bottom (and not shown in our plan), is cropped in the most systematic manner, and kept, as we have already said, in the highest condition. It is entirely managed by Mr. Ingram, her Majesty's chief gardener, who also arranged and superintended the execution of its various parts.

Claremont is the well-known seat of his Majesty the King of Belgium, and was assigned to him by the Crown on his marriage with the Princess Charlotte. It has been occasionally used by the Queen for short periods of retirement from Court life, and is now occupied by the family of the late King of the French. It was here, indeed, that the exiled Louis Philippe found a home, and here he breathed his last only a few months since.

We cannot wonder that our Queen should choose this place as a quiet retreat from the forms and show of a palace residence, as it is eminently adapted to foster the idea of seclusion. Standing on an eminence in the midst of its own ample woods, the prospects from the house and grounds are purely sylvan or rural. There is scarcely a human habitation visible for 30 or 40 miles on the south and west sides, and the neighbouring village of Esher and the high road to Portsmouth are quite concealed on the north and north-east by woods or swells in the ground.

Within the grounds, also, the spirit of privacy seems to reign paramount. A large proportion of them is covered with plantations, kept very dense by a remarkable undergrowth of laurels and rhododendrons, and pierced here and there with narrow, irregular, or winding glades of grass, completely shut out from each other by the masses of evergreens which skirt them, and which interpose, as underwood, between any one of them and all the rest.

Claremont is entered from a road which branches off the great Portsmouth road at the village of Esher, from which last place it is only about a quarter of a mile distant. On getting within the gates, the beautiful slopes of the park on the right, so judiciously planted, give the first favourable impression; and we may here mention that this is considered one of the earliest and best examples of that natural manner of gardening which Kent was chiefly instrumental in creating, and which he had a fine opportunity of exhibiting at this place.

The first object which is reached on advancing up the drive is the farm-yard on the left;—most unhappily situated, and very ineffectually disguised by a few thin and straggling trees. At a short distance from this, too, the kitchen garden, said to have been added by Brown, juts forward on the right, causing the drive to take a sweep round in order to avoid it. There has been little or no attempt to conceal this garden, which, with its numerous and extensive walls, is a most conspicuous and disagreeable intrusion into the park. But for these two objectionable features, the drive to the house would be a beautiful and good one; as,

fter passing the kitchen garden, it ascends rapidly, and begins to reveal
me of the better aspects of the park and the country. The stables
ve, however, been tacked on to the end of the kitchen garden, and are
most full in sight from near the entrance door of the house.

The mansion at Claremont is a large square pile, of no great preten-
ons, and composed chiefly of white brick, designed by Brown, the land-
cape gardener. The main things about it worthy of notice are its posi-
on, and the manner in which the entrance to the offices is masked.
regard to the former, the site is most commanding. The views from
e entrance front, and a part of the south-western side, are of the finest
rder, embracing a number of splendid trees in the valley, and wooded
ills and plains extending away to an immense distance. The ground
lls away from the house on all sides except on a portion of the south-
western, where, after the occurrence of a piece of level lawn, it soon
rises into an eminence, partially clothed with trees, and surmounted by
a kind of observatory.

The four sides of the house are all left open, not being furnished with
any kind of wings or office appurtenances. A clear lawn is thus obtained
all round the house ; the entrance to the offices, which are in the basement of the building, being effected through a tunnel, which opens out
on the face of the hill towards the kitchen garden, and has its mouth
well covered by masses of evergreens, arranged so as to look like groups
on the lawn.

By the side of the entrance porch to the house, and on the lawn to the
north-east, are some very large and noble Cedars of Lebanon, which
blend well with the building, and help to relieve its rawness. Passing
round the house on its south-western side, there is a small old honeysuckle on the lawn, which is religiously preserved as having been a
favourite of the Princess Charlotte. The space immediately around the
house both on this and the next private side strikes one as being very
bare, and hence we are glad to see that Mr. Mallison, the gardener, has
made some recent efforts to furnish a portion of it with good specimen
plants. From the north-west side of the house, the boundary plantations take a very good outline, which only wants to be a little more
broken in order to be perfect.

At a little distance from the house, in the direction of the pleasure
grounds (which all lie on the south-west and western sides), the hill
already mentioned can be ascended, and the top of the prospect tower,
as well as the base of it, will afford the most extraordinary views of the
park and surrounding country. The estate itself includes about 600 acres,
richly clothed with beautiful trees, and the property around is treated
much as if it belonged to Claremont, so well does it harmonize with the
features of the latter, and so little does the division line anywhere appear. Some excellent Scotch firs are situated near this tower, and
many of the rarer pines have been planted in the neighbourhood of it.
On one side of the building is an inscription, put up when Lord Clive
was the owner of this estate, that fixes its designation,—" and Claremont
be the name."

Descending from the mound on which this tower stands, we enter upon
the glades, and among the masses of trees, which are described by Whately,
in his "Observations on Modern Gardening," as among the finest illustrations of what he styles a grove. It is planted for the most part along the
brow of a hill, and sweeps down into a hollow on the south-western side,
where a lake appropriately finishes the scene. As Whately describes it,

F 2

the effect must have been even superior to what it now is ; for at present
it has rather too much the air of being overgrown. No doubt the plants
tions were greatly enlarged and altered by Brown ; and they have no
subsequently been thinned out with quite enough boldness. The sides of
many of the vistas or glades are likewise now too formally preserved.

As a specimen of what the place was seventy or eighty years ago, and of
what deserves to be imitated wherever an opportunity is afforded, Whately's
description is well worth preserving. He says, "A grove is there planted
in a gently curved direction, all along the side of a hill and on the edge
of a wood, which rises above it. Large recesses break it into several
clumps, which hang down the declivity ; some of them approaching, but
none reaching quite to the bottom. These recesses are so deep as to form
great openings in the midst of the grove ; they penetrate almost to the
covert : but the clumps being all equally suspended from the wood, and
a line of open plantation, though sometimes narrow, running constantly
along the top, a continuation of grove is preserved, and the connection
between the parts is never broken. Even a group which, near one of
the extremities, stands out quite detached, is still in style so similar to
the rest as not to lose all relation. Each of these clumps is composed of
several others still more intimately united : each is full of groups, sometimes of no more than two trees, sometimes of four or five, and now and
then in larger clusters : an irregular waving line, issuing from some little
crowd, loses itself in the next ; or a few scattered trees drop in a more
distant succession from one to the other. The intervals, winding here
like a glade, and widening there into broader openings, differ in extent,
in figure, and direction ; but all the groups, the lines, and the intervals,
are collected together into large general clumps, each of which is at the
same time both compact and free, identical and various. The whole is
a place wherein to tarry with secure delight, or saunter with perpetual
amusement."

Except that the whole is not so much broken up into groups, and the
glades are mostly mere narrow openings, and the trees have become much
more grown together into one mass, and the plantations are carried further down the face of the hill, this account will in some measure yet
apply. The undergrowth of laurels and rhododendrons, too, which comes
out to the sides of all the glades, and, in many instances, forms the most
beautiful fringe, is a great additional feature. In the neighbourhood of
the lake the masses of rhododendrons spread down on to the lawn in the
most charming lines, such as could not be improved ; and here, also, the
rhododendrons climb the steep slope of the bank, and clothe it with a
splendid mantle of evergreens, with the most irregular surface, and yet
further broken by a few jutting firs, cedars, &c. When in bloom, about
the end of May, these rhododendrons, and those throughout the entire
place, must be most gorgeous.

An excellent means of observing the comparative merits of laurels and
rhododendrons as undergrowth is furnished in this garden. Although
the laurels have been particularly well treated, having been layered down
to render them bushy, and pruned with great judgment, so as to relieve
them of any formal appearance, they never, as compared with the rhododendrons, grow into any picturesque shapes, always looking too stiff and
regular, and requiring constant and most careful pruning to keep them
from straggling away into the extreme of wildness and bareness. The
rhododendrons, on the other hand, take from the first the most irregular
and broken forms, and every year's growth tends to confirm and vary this

character. They scarcely ever become too straggling, and do not require pruning. At the same time, we must say that the mixture of laurels and rhododendrons at Claremont improves the appearance of both plants, and preserves the plantations from that sameness which rhododendrons or laurels alone would produce; only the laurel is not at all fit for a front plant, where a broken edge next a lawn is required.

Throughout the plantations here, or standing out at points of them on the grass, are many excellent cedars of Lebanon, some well furnished with branches, and others with tall straight stems above 100 ft. in height. The hollies, too, are magnificent, and the silver firs particularly fine. Hemlock spruce is seen here in a splendid state; and many rare trees exist in an unusually large condition. We observed a fine plant of the scarce *Magnolia macrophylla*, not far from the house.

At the top of the great bank of rhododendrons already spoken of, and which has lately had a flight of rustic steps put up through the middle of it very tastefully by Mr. Mallison, is an elegant Gothic temple, called the Mausoleum, and consecrated to the memory of the Princess Charlotte. It is built on the site of a summer-house which was commenced by the Princess just before her untimely death. Around it is a small inclosed garden, planted with junipers, cypresses, and other evergreens of a like character. In the front of it are two large plants of *Cunninghamia lanceolata*, which have stood out above twenty years; but they do not look sufficiently flourishing to warrant their more general introduction into pleasure-grounds.

From the site of this Mausoleum there is a most excellent view down the rhododendron bank and across the lake. Its almost only fault is that it is too confined, being shut in with trees on all sides. The numerous birch trees on the island at one end of the lake here show themselves very favourably.

Not far from the Mausoleum is a small Grecian temple, in front of which is a bowling-green. It is said that the Duke of Newcastle, a former owner of this estate, encouraged his servants to play at skittles on this plot, and that he used to seat himself in a harbour near it smoking his pipe, and entering into their sport with the most kindly relish.

Returning towards the house there is a neat conservatory in the direction of the prospect-tower, where some singularly healthy camellias and citrons are planted out in the beds, and old plants of *Magnolia fuscata* and *anonœfolia* keep the air continually laden with perfume. This house, like every part of the grounds, is beautifully kept, and everything appears orderly and flourishing. The main thing that is wanted in the grounds is the destruction of a large proportion of the trees, which are overcrowding and spoiling each other; though we believe this arises, in part, from a great delicacy of feeling evinced by King Leopold, who would not even *appear* to be injuring the nation's property. Such a process, however, far from being disadvantageous, would be of the highest benefit.

On leaving the pleasure grounds the kitchen garden is entered through the middle of the gardener's house,—a most inconvenient and objectionable arrangement. The greater part of this garden has long been converted into pleasure grounds, the old walls and some of the forcing-houses being almost the only things that remain to remind one that this has ever been a kitchen garden. A small part of it, and a slip on the outside, are still devoted to vegetables; and there is a tolerably large frame ground.

Just within the walls is a small flower garden, laid out for the Princess Charlotte, by whom some of the plants in it are even said to have been planted. There is a basin of water and a fountain in this garden, with some rare exotic plants scattered about it. The magnolias of various kinds are exceedingly rich, and there are some fine specimens of different species of clematis and other climbers on the wall. *Tropæolum pentaphyllum* is here grown out from year to year. The cedars, pines, &c., are excellent.

In looking round the walls, which are rather lofty, the visitor will be struck by the appearance of the large deep recesses which occur in them at regular intervals. These walls were built under the direction of Sir John Vanbrugh; and it does not appear what he designed the recesses for, but most probably it was with an eye to their effect in breaking the lines of the walls.

On the lawns in the various compartments of this garden are many novel and valuable plants, as specimens. We particularly observed the *Thuja aurea*, of which there is a beautiful specimen, and which is of a very compact habit, acquiring a light golden hue at some seasons. The houses here are commonly filled with plants, though vines are grown in some of them. A *Tecoma grandiflora*, which is here remarkably well treated, fills the porch of one of them, and bears a great profusion of its splendid flowers. There is a house filled with healthy young heaths. Another contains a quantity of luxuriant orchids, among which some of the good old species first cultivated in this country, and the terrestrial kinds, seem to be in a particularly thriving state. Many of the best stove plants are grown in another house, of which *Passiflora quadrangularis* partially covers the roof with its handsome leaves and flowers. And there is an extraordinary plant of *Epiphyllum truncatum*, which is unusually spreading.

The pines, for which Claremont has long been famous, are now less cultivated than formerly, and are chiefly in pits in the frame ground. They are conspicuous for being very clean, with broad vigorous-looking leaves, and in the best health. Mr. Mallison grows none but Queens.

Altogether, Claremont is a place which will well reward the visitor who can spare part of a day for seeing it. The fine trees, and the undergrowth, the undulations of the ground, and the richness of the prospects, are all of a superior character.

Chiswick House (the Duke of Devonshire's).—From the reputation for taste which the Duke of Devonshire has acquired, the visitor who is unacquainted with the gardens attached to this elegant villa will no doubt expect to see something beautiful, and we do not think he will be disappointed. This is certainly one of the most satisfactory and delightful places round London, and being only five miles from Hyde Park Corner, and thrown open, with his Grace's usual liberality, to all who attend the July exhibition of the Horticultural Society's Garden (which adjoins it), we shall describe it more at length.

The chief characteristic of the place, like that of Claremont, is seclusion. Although close upon the great world of London, and in the very midst of a populous district, the quietness and privacy of these gardens are complete. They are, however, placed in such a district as to render any but the most limited views from them impossible and undesirable; and hence the whole of their attractions are within themselves. They cannot boast of varied and beautiful undulations of surface either; but there is an air of finish, and richness, and classic refinement about them which quite compensates for the want of natural picturesqueness.

Much of the state in which these gardens are now seen is due to the present Duke. Before he came to the title, the place was a very cramped and meagre one. A great deal of additional land has been acquired, and appropriated to ornamental purposes. In fact, the estate, under the influence of his Grace's enlightened feeling, has been quite transformed. Approaching it from the high road at Turnham Green, what is called the Duke's New Road, by the side of the Horticultural Gardens, has been formed by the present Duke, and has a row of handsome lime trees on either side of it, which have now attained a considerable size. Access is obtained to the place by this route through a pleasant and private avenue, without going round by the narrow and awkward lanes of Chiswick.

Just at the lower corner of the Horticultural Society's Garden, the more private entrance to the place occurs. And here there is a splendid set of gates, which formerly stood at the entrance to Heathfield House, near Turnham Green, and were purchased by his Grace and erected about fifteen years since. At that time, also, a new piece of land was inclosed, so as to yield an open plot of grass within the gates, and the present neat lodge and wing walls constructed. Surmounted by his Grace's arms, the gates are painted white and partially gilt, so as to have an extremely chaste and elegant appearance.

At a short distance within the gates, the avenue of limes changes to one of larger growth, and there is a double row of trees on each side. As the road here passes between the walls of the kitchen and flower garden and those of another property, the extra row of limes is very serviceable, and affords the means of giving another avenue to a walk within the limes on one side. These limes are pruned, and their branches tied down and trained into a flat wall-like shape at the sides, the heads being at present allowed to spread over the centre of the road, which, in a few years, they would no doubt entirely overarch. The trees are pruned and trained to the height of about 18 or 20 ft., and they thus form a close leafy screen on both sides of the road. When the leaves first expand in spring, the mass of tender green which they present is something quite lovely. Where the double row terminates, and the younger trees begin, two stately piers have been placed, so as to justify the contraction of the scene at this point, to form terminating objects for the minor avenues, and to constitute in themselves great ornaments and enrichments to this part of the place.

At the end of the lime avenue, which is straight in this older part, and which is unfortunately without a definite or finishing object, the drive sweeps round suddenly to the right, past the older lodge, and enters the pleasure grounds, where, after winding between open lawns, studded with rare specimen trees, and bordered with masses of plantation, it enters a broad straight carriage sweep, opposite the porch of the house. On the left-hand side of the winding approach, a raised bank beyond the lawn covers the public road outside and the boundary wall, and a formal border extended along the front of this. The shrubs and trees in this border are now, however, experiencing a more natural treatment, and will cover or reveal the bank at intervals without falling into anything like a regular line. There are some good stone pines (*Pinus pinea*) among them, and on the lawn are large plants of the great white-leaved American lime, *Pyrus spectabilis*, &c.

The great straight drive in front of the house has a row of cedar trees, interspersed with sculptured figures on large pedestals, and busts on therms, along each side of it, those of the cedars which are nearest the house being large and lofty, and considerably higher than the house itself, and quite overcanopying the portico. The rest of the cedars are much younger. The view of the portico, which is of the most exquisite proportions and enrichment, thus overshadowed by noble cedars, and the whole surmounted by the dome of the principal saloon, is exceedingly beautiful and impressive ; cedars of Lebanon being among the very best accompaniments of Italian architecture. Very possibly an architect would think the building encumbered by these cedars, and wish them removed ; but we think the picturesque eye of an artist would value them immensely, and consider the picture entirely ruined by their destruction. It is so seldom that trees near houses are at all accordant with the style of architecture, and do not become in every respect a nuisance, that a specimen of this kind, where the house and the trees so admirably correspond, and where both together form such an excellent picture,—the very gloom which the cedars produce serving to throw an air of quietude and privacy around the house and its entrance, and to give greater boldness and character to both its outline and its details on this side,—that this example demands to be particularly pointed out. And a great additional interest is given to the whole subject by the recollection that two of England's greatest statesmen—Fox and Canning—expired in the rooms on either side of this entrance porch. Statues, boldly executed in stone, of Palladio and Inigo Jones, stand at either corner of the entrance front of the house, near the foot of the steps leading up into the porch.

Looking along the cedar avenue from the porch, the public road being hidden by a bank and some low shrubs, the sails of vessels passing up and down the river Thames often make agreeable moving objects in the scene. Several yards behind the cedars, and commencing at some distance from the house, there are double rows of limes on either side of the drive, which are trained in the same manner as those before described, but do not seem so much in place here. On the small lawn at the east side of the porch, too, are some fine plants of *Magnolia grandiflora*, some large fig trees, which bear freely, and a handsome cork tree, among many other things.

In walking round to the west side of the house, we pass an excellent specimen of the Judas tree, and observe a stately *Catalpa* and tulip tree on the lawn to the left. A little in advance of these, and near the margin of the water, is a cluster of common berberry bushes, of great size, and making the most beautiful ornaments to the lawn, especially during autumn, when they are laden with their showy red fruit, so gracefully disposed. The west end of the house, which has a marble statue of the Apollo Belvidere in an elevated niche, is covered, over the basement story, with a noble plant of *Wistaria sinensis*, which stretches round the sides to a great length, and is very delicious when in bloom, as the walk passes within a foot of the front of it, and it can therefore be thoroughly enjoyed. It is a plant which, in order to be fully appreciated, really demands to be brought thus near to the observer.

From this end of the house, and from the longer garden front, the character of the place and its principal parts begin to be seen. The sloping lawn to the west, with the water winding along the bottom of it, very nicely relieves the flatness of the place, and prevents the house from appearing to stand on low ground. On the other side of the water, a broad open glade of lawn, slightly adorned with a few specimens and bushes, carries the eye into a park of 40 acres, well studded with old trees; and this gives an appearance of extent and richness, rendering the boundary plantation in the distance scarcely perceptible, and by no means disagreeably conspicuous. Large masses of old plantations, whose tops are broken into pleasing forms, while their front outline is variedly fringed with evergreens, and relieved by specimens, fill up the rest of the ground on that side of the water, as seen from the western corner of the house; but, by clearing away some of the larger trees towards the southern end, and bringing the lower evergreens more into view, the outline has lately been still further and more boldly broken up and improved.

Across the western lawn in a rather more northerly direction, beyond the capital specimens of *Abies Douglasii, Pinus Cembra,* and other excellent pines, a glimpse of the classic temple, with its Doric porch and its small dome, but half hidden amongst large yews and other trees, is obtained. The manner in which this beautiful temple is half seen half concealed, and the harmonious grouping of the trees and shrubs around it, makes a charming picture from the house and from numerous other points throughout the grounds.

At a short distance to the right of the temple, a peep is just procured of the elegant Palladian bridge over the canal, which is distant and bold enough to form a good object in the scene, and enriches without encumbering it.

Further to the right, and situated on the top of the lawn, near the house, some gorgeous old cedars, the lower branches of which spread down in the most graceful manner, and sweep the grass, constitute one of the noblest features of the place. They are not so large as in some other gardens, either as regards the girth of their stems or their height; but probably they are unequalled in beauty, and stand in a peculiarly appropriate position. A broad gravel walk passes along the garden front of the house, and another broad walk strikes off from this, at a right angle, opposite the centre of the house. The cedars are on either side of this latter walk, their branches spreading out to within 8 or 10 ft. of the gravel, and 50 or 60 yards from the house. There were formerly three of them on each side, but one unluckily died a few years ago. Each of them has a different character; but they are sufficiently alike to blend well together, and those on the top of the western lawn acquire, from their position, and from getting more sun, a most magnificent aspect. Between the cedars and the house, and likewise at the other end, specimens of the Deodar cedar have been planted, and are now from 15 to 20 ft. high. Stone figures of a bear and a boar stand on large pedestals in a line with the front of the cedars, near the house, and there are large stone urns, nearer to the cedars, at each end; thus maintaining the dignity and art-like character of the whole.

A very charming effect is realized on this side of the house by having two of the windows in the basement story formed into mirrors, in one sheet. In these the whole of the lawn and the cedars, &c., are most clearly reflected; and, as the scene is altogether in such a high style of art, there is nothing unworthy or objectionable in this expedient, which is really a very excellent and novel one. One of the large bold upper windows, which is fitly enriched (the house being in the Italian style), and glazed with immense sheets of plate glass, coming opposite the walk of which the cedars compose the side fittings, and a fine porphyry urn being placed on a stand just within the central compartment of this window, the effect of this is also good from the other end of the walk.

The large central walk is terminated by a circular plot of grass, at the back of which, arranged in a half circle, and enshrouded with large evergreen oaks, are some very ancient and mutilated marble figures of Cæsar, Pompey, and Cicero, from Adrian's Villa at Rome, interspersed with ornamented stone seats from the Roman Forum. At either corner there are busts of Homer and Hesiod, and the ends are occupied with large stone figures on pedestals of a lion and lioness, with busts of Virgil and another poet at the other corners. This classic spot is called the Poets' corner. Seated in the midst of it, beneath the shade of the venerable old oaks, and looking out to the lawn, the cedars, and the house, with the tops of the other tall cedars at the entrance side of the house clustering around the dome, it would be difficult to imagine a scene more finished, consistent, and classical.

Standing again at the house, the lawn to the north is seen to be covered with forest trees, some of which are rare kinds of oak, &c., but most of them are common sorts—just sufficiently scattered to allow the grass to grow among them, and yet dense enough to produce a good deal of agreeable shade in summer. As the garden was formerly circumscribed by the fence at the edge of this lawn, these trees were no doubt part of a close plantation, made to cover the boundary, and they have since been only thinned out so as to allow those which remain room for further growth. Among the stems of the trees, however, the arcade which communicates with the flower garden and conservatories is seen, and forms another architectural feature; while in winter, when the leaves are off the trees, a tall pillar, surmounted by a statue of Venus, is visible through the trees to the left of the arcade.

At the northern end of the walk which passes the garden front of the house is a gateway—communicating with another part of the garden—presented by Sir Hans Sloane to the Earl of Burlington. It was erected at Chelsea by the celebrated architect Inigo Jones, and removed here after being given to the Earl of Burlington, an ancestor or family connection of the Duke of Devonshire. The walk leading to this gate is bordered by middle-aged cedars on the side next the lawn, and by yews on the other side. The gateway itself is superbly mantled with ivy, part of which is now trimmed so as to adapt itself to the lines of the entablature and pediment.

From the principal or garden fronts of the house, then, it will be seen that the gardens are decorated with various architectural ornaments, which are nowhere crowded together, and are considerably varied. There is but one temple, one bridge, one tall pillar, one arcade, and one gateway, with sculptured figures, urns, statuary, &c., of different kinds, most judiciously placed. The broad straight walks, cedars, and highly-dressed lawns, all tend to heighten the picture, and to render it more harmonious and artistic. Other decorations of a similar character occur in various parts of the garden, but they do not come into view from this side of the house.

Leaving the house, and passing through the gateway to the east, a sudden turn to the left takes us within the sunk fence which was once the boundary of the place; and along the bank inside that fence many beautiful specimen plants will be observed. There is a large *Rhus cotinus*, which is a most elegant lawn plant, and several handsome magnolias, with a very large *M. macrophylla*, which used to flower freely, but is now gradually dying away. Bronze figures of Achilles and Hercules stand at either end of the plot between the large yew hedge and the sunk fence.

Where the low, flat bridge crosses the sunk fence, there are three arches of ivy, which is trained over light iron supports, and trimmed yearly to keep it in shape. They have a very good appearance in a position of this kind. Between them and the arcade is an octagonal stone basin with a vase and fountain in the centre. It has a variety of jets, so as to be capable of being played in several forms; and in summer this gives another enrichment to the general garden scene.

The arcade is an oblong erection, consisting of a series of arches, with pilasters on the interspaces, and a balustrade running round the whole above the cornice. It has no roof; and simply forms a communication between one part of the garden and another. An extraordinary yew hedge joins up to it on either side, and is 20 ft. in height and 7 ft. in width, being strong enough to allow a man to walk on the summit. It is kept regularly clipped.

Just beyond the arcade lies the flower garden, behind which, on a raised terrace bank, is a handsome old range of glass houses, relieved by porches, and by a semicircular projection in the centre, where the roof rises into a dome, part of which is glazed with stained glass and crowned with a gilt ornament. Considering the period at which it was built, and that it was originally all used, except the central compartment, for forcing houses, this range is a fine specimen of that class of building; though the massiveness of its parts, and its narrowness, place it behind more modern erections.

At either end of this range, still partitioned off, is a small house which retires a little from the front line, and extends back to nearly twice the breadth of the rest, having a porch to face the ends. These two houses are commonly used for stove plants and orchids. The remainder of the divisions have been all destroyed; and the whole presents, including the broader central part, an uninterrupted line of conservatory, with a gravel walk from end to end. The length of the entire range is 310 ft., and its ordinary breadth 21 ft. A stone stage, in two steps, extends along the front of the house, in all but the middle portion, and is covered with Pelargoniums and Azaleas in their season, and with chrysanthemums late in the autumn; a more mixed collection of flowering plants keeping it gay at other periods of the year. The pelargoniums and the chrysanthemums are here particularly well cultivated, especially the latter, of which there is a first-rate collection. As the plants are grown to an immense size, and many hundreds of them are prepared for the conservatory, they produce a magnificent display when in bloom.

Between the gravel walk of the conservatory and the back wall, there is a bed of earth, chiefly filled with camellias of various sorts, and a few varieties of *Rhododendron arboreum*. Camellias are likewise trained to the back wall. The whole of the plants, of which there are a great many different kinds, are in the most vigorous health, and flower prodigiously. During the months of March and April, they present a gorgeous appearance.

A number of light pillars by the side of the walk are covered with Acacias, Passion-flowers, Tacsonia, and a variety of climbing plants. In the central part of the conservatory, too, there is a Wistaria and a Banksian rose trained round the dome; and in the beds there are magnificent plants of *Camellia reticulata*, which bears many hundreds of its glorious flowers annually, and *Rhododendron metropolitanum*, one of the very best of the crimson-flowered hybrids, with very large spotted blossoms, and a particularly dense and vigorous habit. Beneath the centre of the dome is generally placed a cluster of some rarer things. A collection of Mr. Smith's best yellow rhododendrons, of which his Grace purchased many large plants, display their flowers here for a couple of months in the summer, and a group of Azaleas, or large *Rhododendron formosum*, the latter of which has immense white sweet-scented blossoms, occupy this compartment at other seasons ; while some of the best chrysanthemums are assigned to it in the autumn.

At the back of the central part of the conservatory is a small room, in which is kept a drawing, by Bartholomew, of the great water lily (*Victoria regia*), made before the plant was introduced to this country. From this point there is a vista view, through a glass door at the back, down a long grass walk which passes through the middle of the kitchen garden to the gardens of the Horticultural Society. It has a very pretty effect from the conservatory, and by it his Grace and his friends can go to a corresponding walk in the Society's gardens without leaving his own estate. For a short distance, until it reaches the kitchen-garden gates, this walk has to pass through the middle of the frame ground, from which, however, it is effectually screened by a tall rustic fence, covered with ivy, and fronted with a border of shrubs and flowers. And as rows of some showy flower are generally put along the sides of the walk through the kitchen garden, the effect of the vista is much improved thereby.

From the opposite side of the conservatory, another vista passes through the flower garden, and down a grass glade to a boundary walk. Through the centre of the flower garden, this view is flanked by a row of standard *Robinia inermis* on each side, and these, being kept pruned into a roundish head, are, when in leaf, a most elegant and appropriate feature in the scene. Nothing could exceed the gracefulness of their appearance.

At the eastern end of the glass range, the small house already mentioned is occupied usually by orchids, ferns, &c. There are many healthy plants of the former, and one of the earliest specimens of *Clerodendron splendens*; though these are sometimes placed in a pit in the frame ground, where, also, large quantities of roses and other flowers are forced, and the Pelargoniums, &c., which supply both the conservatory and flower garden, are cultivated in houses and frames.

Along the front of the conservatory, a small border, partially covered with masses of tufa, supplies a place for growing the prettier and more curious kinds of alpine and herbaceous plants, with a few of such trailing shrubs as *Cotoneaster microphylla*, *Alyssum sempervirens*, &c. This border is edged with a double row of *Gentiana acaulis*, which, by being watered every evening regularly through the summer, when the weather is not actually wet, is retained in the best health, and blooms abundantly.

Standing on the terrace bank, opposite the centre door of the conservatory, an excellent view of the flower garden is gained. And, if this be seen in the months of July or August, when all the beds are well filled with flowers, there is nothing of the kind in the neighbourhood of London at all equal to it. The general shape of the garden is a semicircle, of which the range of glass and the terrace bank form the base.

This bank is thrown out in the centre, in accordance with the projection of the conservatory, and there is a broad flight of steps from the middle of it, supported by large handsome vases on pedestals, with a few busts on therms at a little distance from these. Besides the rows of Robinias before named, there are other parallel rows of standard roses by the sides of a walk which divides each half of the flower garden, and various specimens are placed about in other parts. A beautiful cork tree, a large *Salisburia*, and some fine scarlet thorns, may be specially mentioned. At the corner near the arcade, too, is a cluster of good climbing roses, on poles, and a remarkable standard rose, with a clear stem nearly 18 ft. in height, and a drooping head.

A semicircular gravel walk defines the flower garden on the southern side, and some large and ancient urns occur at intervals along the outer margin of this walk. Behind them, the border is filled with different kinds of plants in lines, to form a regular boundary fringe to the whole garden. These plants are arranged and varied so as to have some of them in bloom at most periods of the spring, summer, and autumn, and to produce a strip of flowers of one conspicuous colour. In the front rows are *Iberis sempervirens* and *Alyssum saxatile*. Then there is a broad band of China roses, which bloom for a very long period. Behind these is a row of common white lilies, and, still further back, a row of holly-hocks. The border is backed by festoons of climbing roses, with a planta-tion, chiefly of evergreens, to finish and support the whole.

Within the flower garden, the beds are arranged in regular figures, divided into several compartments on each side, so as to suit the general form of the plot. A few of these compartments have the beds cut out in the grass, with broad grass margins; but the bulk of them are separated by gravel walks, with box edgings. Some of the larger and central beds in the compartments are raised a foot or two above the rest, to relieve the flatness which would otherwise result from having so large a surface covered with flowers. The system of putting one sort of plant, with flowers of a distinct and decided colour, in each of the beds, is the one adopted for filling this garden, and answers most effectively. Indeed, in so large a space, any other plan would be productive only of confusion; for when the garden was furnished with mixed herbaceous plants, several years ago, it had an exceedingly tame and common appearance. A few small sculptured figures, on pedestals, and some plain vases, filled with scarlet pelargoniums and other summer plants, form agreeable breaks and raised points in the garden during summer. Pansies are a good deal used for covering the beds during winter and spring; but, as the flower garden is so large, and in quite a detached portion of the pleasure grounds, no systematic attempt is deemed necessary for supply-ing it with evergreen furniture in the winter. This flower garden, with its accompanying range of glass houses, shrubberies, &c., is part of the additions made to the place by the spirit and taste of the present Duke.

Leaving the flower garden at its western end, a walk in continuation of that on the upper terrace conducts us, by the side of a laurel-covered wall, to the Rosary. It will be noted that the top of the wall thus passed is covered with the common fleur-de-lis (*Iris Germanica*), which is planted in a narrow gutter, prepared by raising up two courses of bricks at either edge of the wall, and filled with soil. The whole of the kitchen-garden walls are similarly crowned; and the plants seem to thrive well, and bloom abundantly. Before reaching the Rosary, we notice a specimen of the *Ruscus racemosus*, a neat little evergreen shrub, very rarely seen in gardens, but lively in winter from having large red berries.

The Rosary is a small circular plot, partially inclosed with large evergreens, and surrounded with a sweet-briar hedge. It is composed of beds all radiating from a central one to the surrounding walk, and being of various widths. The divisions of these beds are gravel walks, with box edgings. In the centre is a tall pillar, before alluded to, surmounted by a statue of the Venus de Medicis.

Near the Rosary, at the end of a long broad walk which runs parallel with the sunk fence opposite the arcade, is a spirited stone group of figures on a pedestal, by Schermaker, representing Cain in the act of destroying Abel. At the back of the Rosary, near a door which communicates with the kitchen garden, is a very beautiful cork tree ; and, on the adjoining lawn, there is an elegant mass of ivy, flowing gracefully from a head of it which is supported by the broken trunk of a decayed tree. Near this, too, is a most superb specimen of the charming snowdrop tree, spreading around its drooping branches with such regularity that the interior, about the stem, forms a complete natural bower.

An opening through the neighbouring yew hedge leads into a long straight walk, called Napoleon's Walk, bordered on either side by a tall yew hedge, which is kept carefully trimmed. A small temple or summerhouse is placed at the lower end of this walk ; and in the back wall of the building is a central niche, containing a fine marble bust of Napoleon Bonaparte.

At the upper end of Napoleon's Walk, a path to the west carries us along the back of the Poets' corner, and round the whole western side of the place. Just after entering it, however, we see on the right a figure illustrative of the bringing home of the "lost sheep," and soon afterwards the temple comes into view on the left, and shows itself very advantageously. Advancing towards this temple, it is found to stand near the lower or flat side of a hollow, which is partially surrounded with a bank, formed into a series of terraces, on the platforms of which bay trees and cypresses are placed. The bays were much injured by the frost of 1837–8, which has greatly diminished their beauty. There is a circular basin in the centre of the hollow, filled with aquatic plants, and myriads of gold and silver fish ; and a tall obelisk stands in the middle of it. On the other front of the temple, which is by the margin of the canal, a narrow vista is formed through the trees on the opposite side of the water, to reveal an obelisk which there terminates both this and a similar narrow vista which is seen from the front of the house. Behind the obelisk is an open iron gate, with an arched canopy.

Returning to the walk from which we entered this portion of the grounds, and pursuing it in a westerly direction, it curves gently through masses of rhododendrons and other American plants, varied by occasional specimens of noble hollies and other evergreens, and passing round a specimen rhododendron fully 30 ft. in diameter, until it reaches an open glade of lawn, and crosses the canal by the Palladian bridge already noticed. The sides of this walk were originally occupied by a common-place dressed border, filled with miserable-looking shrubs and herbaceous plants. These borders are now grassed over, and all the commoner things removed, and the shrubs stand forward or retire, in groups or singly, in the most irregular manner. Being nearly all evergreens, and mostly rhododendrons, broken here and there with large box trees, hollies, Portugal laurels, cedars, &c., and retiring into the wood on the right for a considerable distance in some parts, this walk is rendered most interesting in winter, and exceedingly attractive when the rhododendrons are in bloom, and retired and shady at all times. Mahonias, kalmias, periwinkles, &c., occur now and then in masses, to supply a lower growth, and Azaleas are mingled through some of the clumps, to secure variety of foliage, and enrich the effect in summer by their brilliant flowers. Where the groups fall back into the rougher and undressed ground of the wood, such minor plants as foxgloves, wild hyacinths, *Saxifraga crassifolia*, wood anemones, &c., are not thought too insignificant to be cultivated as accompaniments; though of course they are merely inserted, and left to nature. When the shrubs shall have made a few years' additional growth, and acquired rather more broken and ragged shapes, this shrubbery walk will be one of the most perfect and delightful which it is possible to form.

Near the bridge some beautiful masses of evergreens border the lawn on the left, and there is here a curious yew tree, trimmed up annually into a slender spiry shape, from 40 to 50 ft. in height. Standing on the bridge, a full view of the canal is obtained in both directions, without either of its ends being seen. Some large weeping willows by the side of the water here show themselves to advantage. In the lower part of the canal, where the water widens out considerably, and where it flows through the park and meadows, it is left in a wilder state, sedgy weeds being allowed to grow at pleasure along its margins. A tangled mass of shrubs and trees on an island at the lower end gives a happy finish to this rougher portion.

Within the pleasure grounds, the weeds in the water, except a few patches of water lilies and the better kinds of aquatics, are kept down by a yearly mowing. Looking along this part of the canal from the bridge, its principal defect is that the bays and waviness of line along its margins are too artificial. In a natural river, of which alone this water can be considered an imitation, so many and such formal minor variations of line would certainly never be witnessed. But, relieved of this, the effect of the water and its accompaniments is good, in general, and is particularly beautiful as regarded from the mound at the other end.

One great point, for a place situated in such a district, is that from the bridge the view is only bounded by the park, fields, and plantations within the property, and that nowhere does anything having the appearance of a boundary present itself, nor do the outside plantations press unduly forward in any part; and this is the more observable when we perceive the distance at which the bridge is placed from the house.

On the top of a grassy slope northwards from the bridge is a small building, formerly used as a menagerie, where a variety of rare birds, which have since been removed to Chatsworth, were once kept. Here, also, was lodged a fine elephant, which died many years ago, and which was so docile that it would fetch water in a pail from the canal, and perform other equally serviceable feats, at the bidding of its keeper. Few birds are now preserved on the water, except a quantity of that once "*rara avis*," the black swan, which here breeds very freely.

From the bridge the walk continues along the edge of the park, and is skirted by a very irregular margin of turf, on which the shrubs lie in a broken fringe, there being still a large number of evergreens among them, and the ground falling away from the walk a good deal on the left-hand side. A small detour has, however, been lately made, carrying the walk further into the park, so as to embrace a magnificent oriental plane tree within the pleasure grounds. In this new part a variety of rare and valuable plants have been inserted; and when they are large enough to allow of the more common undergrowth being removed, they will no doubt present some excellent specimens. There are, already, two or three good examples of the Judas tree ; and in the park, which contains many fine elms and thorns, there is a curious instance, near the new walk, of a birch tree growing out of a cherry. The latter tree is now somewhat overgrown and decayed, but the two together form a most picturesque object.

After reaching the line of the old walk again, we come to the broad glade of grass which is seen from the house, and on the first corner of this is a good example of the *Mespilus canadensis*, which, whether sheeted with its snowy white blossoms in spring, or its deep rich red foliage in autumn, is a most valuable lawn plant, and is conspicuous for a great distance. The sides of this large glade, which were quite straight till very recently, and had dug borders of the plainest description, have now been judiciously varied and furnished with appropriate evergreen and other shrubs and low trees, some of which are thrown into small masses of one sort, to give greater character when they are in bloom.

Continuing along the walk, which remains of a very similar character, we arrive at the obelisk, from which two grass vistas pass off through the lofty woods, one terminating in the temple before described, and the other revealing a small portion of the house, with a side view of its porch and accompanying cedars. The walk then ascends, beneath a number of evergreen oaks, to the summit of a lengthy bank or mound, along which it passes for a considerable distance. A peep of the great pagoda at Kew is here obtained *. The sides of the walk, of which the formal borders are happily now destroyed, are furnished with the most beautiful and picturesque evergreens, and the slope of the bank, between this walk and the outside road, is principally clothed with lilacs, which, extending a great part of the way from the obelisk to the entrance lodge, have a most festive air in the flowering season. Views of the Thames, and of Mortlake, Barnes, and the woody district between Kew and Putney, are procured from many parts of this mound, without exposing the observer to the public gaze. But the country around is too flat and tame to form a good landscape.

As we near the end of the mound, however, we come suddenly on an opening which has been made in the plantation to the left, and which exhibits the lawns, cedars, temple, &c., in a most attractive point of view. At the extreme end of the mound, too, where it comes nearly into a line with the water, it has been raised six or eight feet into a knoll, which is clothed with laurels and other evergreens, from the midst of which, over the tops of some picturesque low trees, nicely mantled with ivy, the most effective scene in the whole gardens has been secured. Looking down the canal, which does not here show such wavy margins, the bridge is an admirable object, and the masses of trees, the temple, the beautiful lawns, and the specimens on them, with the house itself, produce the most delightful and harmonious combinations, particularly when the summer or early autumn sun is declining in the west, and the crimson and gold or softer tints of the clouds are reflected full along the line of water. But the cedars, as seen from here, are the most striking, as they stand on the top of a sloping lawn, out of which their gracefully curved branches seem

---

* This mound was no doubt formed from the material obtained in making the canal; and tradition says that the Earl of Burlington had the whole of this work executed during an inclement winter, and at a period of commercial depression, with a view of furnishing employment to the suffering poor of the neighbourhood.

almost to grow, so very close do they lie to the ground, being, in fact, nearly half buried in the mossy grass.

Descending from the mound, we see the southern termination of the water. After passing under a low bridge, over which the walk is carried, and which is broad enough to allow a strip of grass and shrubs upon it, on either side of the walk, the water expands and surrounds an island, covered with periwinkle, in the centre of which is a very large willow. A plain rustic bridge, half enshrouded by willows and other trees, constitutes the terminating object to the water scene, although the water actually goes beyond the bridge, amongst a dense thicket of branches, through an arch beneath the public road. A few years ago the whole of this portion of the pleasure grounds, south of the house, was a dense ugly thicket of trees and shrubs, and the water altogether stagnant. Now, however, the plantations have been turned into a pleasant lawn, and, by a very little labour, the tidal water from the Thames is brought into the canal, so that it can be frequently changed, and is preserved fresh and pure, and can be raised to any desired height. This and nearly all the other improvements which we have pointed out have been effected from time to time by Mr. Charles Edmonds, his Grace's present gardener, who, from the kind encouragement and appreciation he receives, is enabled every year to carry forward some desirable change or other, and who, we must add, has manifested a very proper regard to the genius and character of the place.

The gardens of Chiswick House are not an example of any pure style of landscape arrangement. They do not belong exclusively to any recognised period or system of art. Fortunately, however, their prevailing character conforms well with the requirements of an Italian villa, and the numerous architectural objects disposed about the place preserve an air of consistency without ostentation. The grounds are mainly made up of a few larger scenes, which are generally harmonious throughout, and are viewed in many different aspects; while there are, as there should be, a number of independent or partially isolated episodes, in which there is much of change, without any violation of the connectedness and propriety of the whole. A great deal of the stiffness which once characterised the place, except in so far as this is essential to preserve its dignity, is wearing away or has been discarded. And every year little defects that exist, and for which it is often most difficult to find an instant remedy, are in process of being rectified. But nothing is more perplexing than to have to correct errors in a general plan, especially when the main features of that plan have acquired the standing or growth of a full century.

Corney, another small property, formerly belonging to the Earl of Macartney, and situated by the side of the Thames, a little above Chiswick Church, belongs to the Duke of Devonshire, and is used as a bathing place. On the lawn, near where the house once stood, are magnificent specimens of the tulip tree, and there are very fine plants of various thorns, of *Pyrus spectabilis*, and of *Liquidambar styraciflua*. The masses of Portugal laurels are also unusually large. On the terrace, too, by the river side, are some handsome plants of the *Pinus pinea*, the seeds of which were collected by his Grace on Mount Ætna.

At the *Grove*, which also belongs to the Duke of Devonshire, and is still higher up the river, near Strand on the Green, there are in the park some extraordinary Spanish chestnut trees, the magnitude and grandeur of which are probably nowhere surpassed. The girth of three of them, at one foot from the ground is respectively 22 ft. 2 in., 24 ft.

4 in., and 26 ft. 2 in. They are perfectly sound, to all appearance, with a clear straight trunk, and most spreading and well-balanced heads. Many others exist besides those of which the dimensions are thus given and are almost equally large. When in full foliage, and covered either with flowers or fruit, they are truly glorious objects; for very few things in nature can equal a majestic old tree, whether in picturesque decrepitude and ruin, or, as in this case, in the full richness and luxuriance of its meridian strength*.

Syon House, the seat of the *Duke of Northumberland*, is about two miles higher up the river than Chiswick, and is between Brentford and Isleworth, nearly opposite Kew Gardens. It is at present occupied by the Dowager Duchess. The gardens have been much celebrated as containing an extensive collection of large hardy exotic trees, and a splendid range of plant houses, with a bold mass of rockery in front, and a well-arranged kitchen garden, comprising many forcing houses, which are built chiefly of iron, and, at the time they were erected, combined every known contrivance that could render them perfect.

At the present time the only one of these features that has undergone much alteration is the kitchen-garden department, which, not being so much required, has been allowed to fall somewhat into the shade. Some of the forcing houses, indeed, are now devoted to plant culture; and two very interesting new houses have been erected in this department—the one for the culture of tropical fruits, and the other for growing the large water lily (*Victoria regia*).

The kitchen garden covers between three and four acres, with an extensive range of glass houses in it. Its shape is a nearly regular parallelogram, but the ends are not at right angles to the sides. The forcing houses, which are placed nearly across the middle, stand somewhat obliquely to the sides, and have almost a full south aspect. The roofs, fronts, and ends are composed mainly of iron, the bars of the sashes being of copper. Although built at a time when metal roofs were little known, and much distrusted by some, they have always been found to stand satisfactorily. They were originally all heated by common flues, and were built by Messrs. Richards and Jones, of Birmingham. Comparatively little forcing is now done in them; but we observed a quantity of very excellent greenhouse plants occupying the pit of one of them, and some similarly good stove plants in another. Mr. Ivison, the gardener here, has evidently fallen into the right method of cultivating these; for only ornamental sorts seem to be kept, and each plant is treated individually, according to its character and habits, and made into a specimen.

The lily house at the end of this range, which has been enlarged and altered expressly for this plant, is a span-roofed erection, with a porch and second door to prevent the external air from acting on the plant. It contains a slate tank, 21 ft. square, which is occupied principally by the Victoria. The plant flowered here very shortly after that at Chatsworth, and continued to bloom and bear seed most profusely. It was planted out near the centre of the cistern, and the water in the tank is kept heated, while the atmosphere of the house is maintained at a high temperature. A small water wheel, over which a supply of water is continually flowing, keeps the water in the tank always fresh and constantly

---

* In passing from Chiswick to the Grove, the wall which forms the boundary of his Grace's gardens and park will be seen to have a neat coping of ivy, which, by being kept regularly trimmed, to the depth of about 18 in., gives a nice finish to the wall, and relieves its apparent harshness and heaviness.

in motion. When we saw the plant last autumn it had fifteen full-grown leaves on it, which were a good deal curved upwards at the edges, as in its native state, and several younger leaves were appearing. These latter have something of the appearance of a light-coloured hedgehog or an indented Melocactus, being curiously folded up, and presenting only their prickly under surface to view. Several other aquatics, chiefly Nelumbiums, are grown at the sides and towards the corners of the tank, but are not allowed in any way to interfere with the Victoria.

In a back corner of the kitchen garden, adjoining the lane that leads from Brentford through Syon Park, is the large tropical house. This is a lofty structure, with an upright back wall, and a curvilinear iron roof. It has a glass division in the centre, and contains a collection of tropical fruits which is probably quite unique in this country. Many of the plants are very large, and as they are kept in a rather high temperature, with an abundance of moisture, all of them appear healthy. Several things have, we believe, fruited here which have not borne fruit anywhere else in Britain; and many plants which here fruit profusely are scarcely ever seen to fruit in general collections. Indeed, it is pretty well known that this tribe of plants must have a peculiarly high temperature and much moisture, and plenty of room to grow in, ere they can be expected to succeed.

Some of the most striking plants in this house are the Mangosteens; the Nutmeg, which was in fruit last autumn; *Carica papaya*, which was flowering; the Bread-Fruit trees, of which plants have flowered, though not at a time when they could be impregnated; the *Passiflora quadrangularis*, bearing an immense quantity of handsome fruit; the Snake Gourd, which had fruit from 6 to 7 ft. long hanging from the roof; the *Vanilla*, with large clusters of its long slender fruits, and the Rice plant. *Hoya imperialis*, a noble climber, was also growing and flowering in the richest manner; and a large *Platycerium grande*, fastened to a board, and hung against the back wall, forms a remarkable specimen. We have, however, necessarily mentioned only a few of the interesting objects in this house, since every plant in it will be more or less attractive to those who know them, or who wish to become acquainted with those fruits of the tropics which are too often heard of only by name, or as coming over in some confection.

An unusually large and bushy bay tree stands on each side of that door in the kitchen garden which leads to the pleasure grounds; and passing through this door and a screen of evergreens formed to shut out the kitchen garden, we are soon by the side of a piece of water, which extends a considerable distance eastward, and on either side of which there is a walk, sometimes following the course of the water, and in other parts leaving it altogether for a time. The whole of this space is kept up as pleasure grounds, and includes a small flower garden, with a statue of Venus on a tall pillar, and various masses of the rarer kinds of rhododendrons and American plants. In rhododendrons, of the best sorts, the place seems particularly rich; though it is unfortunate that here, as elsewhere, the splendid varieties of *R. arboreum* and the hybrids from it nearly always have their flowers more or less injured by frost, on account of blooming so early. Of all the choicer kinds, therefore, those with whitish flowers, which generally come into bloom after even the common ones have ceased flowering, are the most to be depended on in respect to the production of their flowers.

Throughout this part of the pleasure grounds, too, are scattered the numerous valuable specimens of exotic trees; some of them standing on the lawn by themselves, others growing by the margins of the water, and many situated in clumps of other trees, with which their branches have is a few cases become permanently mingled.   Here are some extraordinary specimens of different kinds of Oak, Acers, Magnolias, Robinias, Hickories, Gymnocladus, Ailanthus, Purple Beech, Liquidambar, Deciduous Cypress, &c.   And there is a remarkably fine *Laurus sassafras* and *Ilex opaca*, and many plants of this dwarfer class.   The deciduous cypresses, especially, of which there is a great number in the neighbourhood of the water, are exceedingly healthy, tall, and beautiful.   Proximity to the water seems to suit them extremely well, and to impart to them superior luxuriance.   As we have comparatively few water-side trees, and the character of this is in the highest degree elegant, the leaves being so delicately formed and of such a tender green, it is an invaluable plant for positions of the kind mentioned.   The cut-leaved alder, likewise, is a good tree for the edges of lakes or rivers, and is frequent here by the side of the water, though the specimens are not remarkable for size.

It is gratifying to learn that his Grace, who possesses such a number of fine hardy trees, is a great admirer of them, and that the rarer kinds are all being labelled, and, as far as possible, disencumbered from the pressure of commoner things, which were in many instances spoiling them ; while the collection is speedily to be perfected by the addition, in suitable spots, of all the newer kinds, and of such older ones as are not already to be found there.   In the coniferous tribe, especially, there is, we should think, a dearth of good examples.

In passing round these pleasure grounds, with so many noble trees to adorn them, and such a long canal of water winding through them, there are, of course, many agreeable little scenes, and some beautiful combinations.   No *great* effects appear, however, to have been attained, or even sought.   Towards that end of the water which is nearest the house there is a light bridge, which is crossed in going from the kitchen garden to the conservatories, and from which, perhaps, one of the best views of the water may be had.

A short walk westward from this bridge brings us to the range of ornamental houses, which, when they were erected, ranked among the highest and best specimens of plant houses in Europe.   Regarded as buildings for exterior show, they still necessarily retain their claims to attention, and possess much merit.   But now that all *ranges* of glass are becoming exploded as plant structures, and the cheapness of glass, as well as the advancement in taste, are leading to the adoption of a more natural shape for such buildings, and one better calculated to produce a varied and effective internal arrangement, the conservatories at Syon have been robbed of much of their *eclât ;* particularly as far larger houses are rendered familiar by the erection of those at Chatsworth, Kew ,the Regent's Park Botanic Gardens, &c.

SYON PLANT HOUSES.

In general shape the plant houses at Syon take the form of a **crescent,** which is a decided improvement on the old straight ranges. The **centre** of the building, which is broadest, rises into a lofty dome, and **the two** end houses are also broader and higher than the intermediate **parts.** The whole of the framework of the roof being formed of light iron **bars,** and the ends and centre having stone pillars and cornices, while the en- tire range stands on a well-finished and **raised** stone basement, adorned with handsome **vases** and urns at either end, the effect of the struc- ture is one of great neatness, and elegance, **and** richness. Everything about it looks **good and** substantial, yet light and fitted for its **object.** And if the length of the range did not **demand** that, for the sake of proportion, it should be

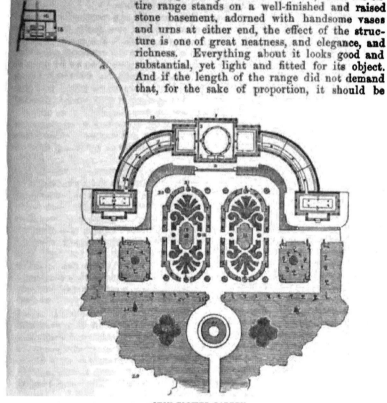

SYON FLOWER GARDEN.

References to Syon Conserva- tories.

The centre division has 17 four-inch cast-iron pipes below the paths and all round.
1. The steam from the main.
2. Condensed water outlet.

The two square divisions, ad- joining the centre one, have 14 four-inch pipes round three sides of each.
3. Steam entrance.
4. Vapour valves, for steaming the house.
5. Condensed water outlet.
6. Steam entrance.

The other curved divisions have five pipes in front, and four at the back of each divi- sion.
7. Vapour valves.

8. Condensed water outlet.

The end divisions, forming the extreme wings of the range, have eight pipes all round.
9. Steam entrance.
10. Vapour valves.
11. Condensed water outlet.
12. Main.
13. Main from the boiler con- ducted in the wall.
14. Boiler house.
15. Boilers.
16. Coal shed.
17. Chimney, divided into four flues, to cut the column of smoke.

Flower Garden.
18. Compartments of beds (for low flowers), edged with box upon gravel, and circum-

scribed by a grass verge, planted with dwarf standard roses.
19. Large vase and pedestal, upon a grass plot.
20. Small vases, on circular grass plots.
21. Small junipers.
22. Irish yew.
23. Cypress.
24. Auracaria imbricata.
25. Yucca gloriosa.
26. Hybrid rhododendrons.
27. Fountain.
28. Standard roses.
29. Rock, &c.
Note.—The plan of the flower garden and its accompani- ments has undergone some little modification since this sketch was taken.

kept as high as it is, the various houses would be by no means adapted for growing and preserving plants. The two end portions of the building, which has many glass partitions, are of a somewhat square figure, and are used as conservatories, for containing such large plants as orange-trees, camellias, brugmansias, &c., with a few showy flowers set among them to create a little gaiety. They are without stages, and the plants stand about in groups on a paved floor.

The shape of these houses renders them capable of a very effective and artistic internal arrangement; and when we once saw them, the plants in them had been disposed with great taste and skill, but their position appears to be changed several times in a year. On the occasion of which we speak the plants were nicely broken up into groups, so as in part to cover the walls of the building, and to allow space for walking about among the groups on the floor. The plants were of varying heights, not brought together in the common-place conical or pyramidal masses, but picturesquely mingled, as if they were in the shrubbery. A charming marble statue stands, within the building, opposite the entrance to each of these wings, the subjects being Activity and Repose. The latter is by Gibson. The white marble is beautifully relieved by being backed with clusters of evergreen shrubs.

Next to the two end houses are narrow greenhouses, in which the plants are arranged on stages, a walk passing through the building near the front. Adjoining these greenhouses there is a stove on either side of the central house, and the larger middle space, which has the dome to it, is devoted to palms and bananas, and other large tropical plants. This central compartment is altogether the most attractive and conspicuous. It contains many fine palms, especially the *Phœnix sylvestris* and *Caryota urens*, which were both flowering last autumn; and the bananas and the various scitamineous plants are most luxuriant. There are likewise some excellent melastomaceous and general stove plants; this collection being particularly rich in tropical species, and containing numerous objects which, within the last few years, were flowered here for the first time. An enormous plant of *Cereus hexangularis* will be noticed in the front of this stove; and the arrangement of the plants in this compartment is such as to afford some good grouping and artistic combinations.

In the front of this range of plant houses is a somewhat triangular flower garden, the shape of which seems rather appropriate to a building in the form of a crescent; there is also a basin and fountain, with a group of dolphins forming the pedestal of the jet. There are rows of standard roses by the sides of the walks, and the beds, which stand on grass, are each furnished with only one species of plant. A walk strikes off from the fountain in the direction of the house.

On the lawn at either side of the flower garden, where the area in front of the houses is extended into something like an oblong figure, there are several good specimens of the dwarfer and rarer shrubby and half-shrubby plants. We noted *Aralia spinosa*, which was just coming into bloom last autumn, as a lawn plant of great character; and *Mahonia fascicularis* seemed to stand out well as a hardy bush.

The method here adopted for inclosing the flower garden, and separating it from the rest of the pleasure grounds, is peculiar, and was frequently commended by the late Mr. Loudon in his various works. The object is effected by a lofty screen of rock-work, which is of the boldest and most varied kind, being formed of huge blocks of stone, and rising to the height of nearly 50 ft. in some parts. The trees and shrubs, which were at first employed to diversify and enrich it, are now, however, over-

growing and concealing it, as they always will do with any such decorations, unless they are kept continually thinned out.

In the character of the material employed, and the general grouping
of the stones, and the details of the execution, this rockery is doubtless
worthy of its fame. The most irregular front outline has been secured,
and the rocks at the base are either half buried in the soil, just jutting up above the surface, or standing up more prominently, in the most
natural and pleasing manner. The whole of the available parts are likewise clothed with appropriate vegetation, though many of the smaller
alpines appear to have been smothered by the crowding of the shrubs
and trees.

It is, however, a matter of the gravest doubt whether any such object
as a rockery is at all admissible into so highly dressed a scene. Everything else in this neighbourhood is in the most finished style of art. The
range of glass, the formal flower garden, the vases, the fountain, the walks,
the lawn, and the plants, are all indicative of the greatest cultivation and
refinement. Assuredly, therefore, a rockery is not a consistent framework
for such a picture, however happily it may in itself be conceived and
carried out. And if this be correct—for the question is one of such
general consequence that we felt called upon to raise it—the manner in
which the rocks are gradually becoming covered, so as to look more like
a mere mass of plantation, is not so much to be regretted. Be this as it
may, the screen is certainly a most effectual one, for, on entering a small
concealed tunnel in the rockery, we were surprised to find ourselves all
at once upon a gate which opens into the court attached to the stables.

Near the house there are some exceedingly beautiful cedars, which
group well together, and produce a splendid effect, as seen from the river
or from Kew Gardens. One of them is considered by Mr. Loudon to be
the finest anywhere around London, and is of a great height, with a tall
straight trunk of considerable girth. From this front of the house the
park, studded with a few varied groups of trees, stretches down to the
river, and all the woods of Kew Gardens, and of the Little Park at Richmond, lie beyond, making a thoroughly sylvan line of horizon. A shrubbery walk extends westward to a small temple by the side of the river,
near Isleworth Church.

On the northern side of the house, which is a plain heavy structure
in the Gothic style, with battlements round the edge of the roof, there
is a small bare lawn, having a sunk fence to separate it from the park,
and a few bushes along the inside to cover the fence. At either end of
this line of fence a small square lodge is placed, though by no means
harmonizing with the style of the house. A public footpath exists
through the park on this side of the house, and is discharged from the
estate at the Isleworth end, by means of large upright revolving iron
gates, which answer the purpose of turnstiles, but at the same time form
a fitting part of the large general gateway.

The drive through the park towards the lodge in the Hounslow Road
crosses a small strip of water by a raised iron bridge, in a part where it
takes a considerable curve, and the extreme slenderness of this bridge,
its want of architectural character, the sudden rise in the road to get
over it, its occurrence at such a sharp turn in the drive, and the absence
of all support or concealment from trees or bushes on the side most
needing it, render it one of the most awkward things imaginable. Between the bridge and the house, there is a short and good double avenue
of limes. Near the side of the water are admirable groups of deciduous

cypress ; and in other parts of the park the old thorns are truly splendid, having acquired quite the character of trees. Groups composed entirely of the common acacia exist on the westerly side of the park, and are highly picturesque. There are also some extremely beautiful low spreading horse-chestnuts and noble hop-hornbeams between the bridge and the entrance lodge, as well as in other parts. The short piece of drive, and its park-like accompaniments, from the entrance lodge to the bridge, are, as seen in going towards the house, of the best description possible on so flat a surface. The whole of the plant houses, rockery, kitchen garden, &c., were designed by Mr. Forrest.

Bedford Lodge, the residence of the *Dowager Duchess of Bedford*, is situated at Camden Hill, Kensington, in the immediate neighbourhood of Holland House. It affords a very interesting illustration of how much may be done in a small suburban place, which has many disadvantages of position, by carefully working in all those features of the neighbourhood which happen to be favourable, and by a well-considered arrangement of the space actually belonging to the estate. Although containing little more than four acres of land, lying so near the thickly populated district of Kensington, and having a public lane and road on two sides of it, with another villa and garden adjoining it on the east, and an atmosphere which is, of course, an almost exclusively London one, Mr. Caie, who has been for many years the gardener here, has contrived to make it into a most delightful summer place, with a great deal of variety in it, and some very artistic effects.

With the lawn on the southern side of the house, where an orchard formerly existed, we have been particularly pleased. It is a small oblong area, with a nearly regular outside boundary, and a walk all round it. The trees in Lord Holland's Park shut it in from the west, and those of an adjoining garden cover it on the east. The ground falls pretty regularly to the south, and sufficiently so to enable a person standing under the veranda or on the lawn at the house to see over the bushes and trees on the southern boundary, which are almost enough to blot out the houses in Kensington, and catch some older trees at a little distance and the Surrey hills in the extreme distance.

Of this simple space, however, the utmost possible has been made, by varying the outline of the surrounding plantation so as to produce a number of bays and projections on the lawn ; by diversifying the heights and characters of the trees so that there shall be contrast as well as harmony of tint and succession of flowers, and that every break in the plantations not belonging to the place shall be scrupulously preserved, while projecting trees in those plantations are supported and brought forward with the aid of similar trees inside ; and by the introduction of two or three detached masses of mixed shrubs and low trees and occasional specimen plants on the lawn, so as to secure length of glades, and great change of aspect in walking round the place.

From the walk, too, although it nowhere comes into sight as the lawn is viewed from the house, there are numerous and well-arranged openings on to the lawn, producing the greatest possible variety of view as we pass round the place ; and resting points are here and there provided for the eye in the shape of summer-houses or arbours, with a few flower-beds attached, or collections of some interesting tribe of plants, so that, in effect, the walk seems much longer and the whole lawn far larger than it is. A better specimen of how to treat a small lawn could, in fact, hardly be found. And Mr. Caie manages to render his masses of plantation more riking in summer by the use of tall-growing ferns, *Heracleum giganteum*, rhubarb, and similar plants with large leaves, scattered about among them.

On that part of this lawn which is nearest the house a few flower-beds are grouped together, and interspersed with two or three ornamental wire trellises for climbers, and flat wire baskets; while summer climbing plants are also trained on festoons, attached to two trees which happen to stand in the lawn at this point. Mr. Caie claims (we believe justly) to be the author of that system of filling flower-beds which assigns one sort to each bed, and disposes the sorts in contiguous beds according to the harmony of their colours. This was certainly an immense advance, in the way of art, on the old promiscuous manner of furnishing beds, and is very well exemplified by those on the lawn now referred to. Standing on the grass, and not too thickly grouped together, the plants become, when they are fully grown, quite blended with the grass at their edges, so that they are simply a mass of colour rising very softly out of the lawn, with the neutral tint of which and of their foliage the various colours mingle so agreeably, that the eye is pleased with the variegation yet combination of the whole, while none of the parts arrest the attention too much, or interfere materially with the repose of the lawn. This, which is unquestionably a delicate point to attain, is here beautifully accomplished; and we were much gratified, in particular, with the effect of these beds, as witnessed from a lower level at the bottom of the garden. Regarded from this point, the various outlines of the groups seemed much more merged into the grass, the colours were brought into more decided masses, and the general harmony of the tints was much more manifest; suggesting the idea whether, especially on a sloping surface, it is not desirable to obtain a view of a flower garden or group of flower-beds from some point where the ground is much lower, as well as from the more common terrace-bank or raised floor of a house. In the latter case, it is true, the outline of the individual beds, the general pattern of the parterre, and the form of the plants composing the masses, are more distinctly shown; but it is very doubtful whether the full effect of a felicitous arrangement of *colours*, and that charming *tout ensemble* which results from the comparative interfusion of the various parts, is not at least greatly weakened by having to take a sort of bird's-eye view of the plot from any raised point of observation.

At the top of the principal lawn, and nearly parallel with the garden front of the house, but forming the centre of a little side scene of its own, is a neat wooden greenhouse, in three divisions, which is kept filled with showy Pelargoniums and other flowering plants during the early summer months, which is the period at which her Grace resides here. The garden sheds are at the back of this greenhouse, but so well covered from view that their existence would hardly be suspected. Another small greenhouse, for rearing and bringing the plants forward, occurs in the frame ground, which is a narrow slip at the west side of the garden. And in order to make the most of the space, and disguise the real nature of the erection, as it is not a show house, an arbour is formed against it at the side next the pleasure garden.

The small frame ground just noticed, although much shaded by trees, and containing only a few pits and frames, is the great laboratory of the garden; for here alone those myriads of flowers which decorate the place in the summer are prepared. Almost all the plants required for the flower garden are kept, of necessity, in the cutting pots during the winter,

G

and potted and hardened off in sets at as early a period as possible in the spring, being planted out somewhat sooner than usual in order to fill the beds the moment it is at all practicable. Such things as the more hardy Verbenas are, however, struck by thousands in small frames filled with soil, in which the cuttings are very thickly planted in sufficient time to be thoroughly rooted before frost commences. In the bottom of the frame a good quantity of drainage materials is first placed, and then 5 or 6 in. of common earth. Over this a layer of fine peat is put to the thickness of about 2 in., and in that the cuttings are inserted in rows about 2 in. apart and 1½ in. between each cutting. When they are well rooted, water is gradually withheld from them, and as they get scarcely any sun, they are merely furnished with air in dry weather, and covered up duly in severe frosts, no water at all being allowed them throughout the actual winter. In the spring they are shifted at once to the flower-beds, with a small mass of earth to each, and hardly any of them ever fail. It is quite wonderful to see how well they look, and how easily they are managed. On witnessing this wholesale propagation we can no longer doubt that such things may be grown for the million. The great enemy of all such plants in winter is dampness ; but as they are never watered, and damp air is not admitted, and the frame is raised on a dry foundation, they can never be in danger from this source.

At the west end of the house is the principal flower garden, which is nearly of a square figure, and is divided into compartments by walks which pass across the centre of it from each of the four corners. In the middle is a marble basin and fountain, over which is a bower of trellis work covered with climbers, and rows of standard roses are placed at the sides of the principal walks. On the north side is a wall, which separates the garden from the outside road, and is covered with the more ornamental and delicate kinds of climbing roses, honeysuckles, Wistaria, &c., with the graceful *Maurandya, Ecremocarpus scaber, Lophospermum,* and other purely summer climbers. A narrow border in front of this wall is filled with various showy flowers, in patches of one sort, harmonized as to colour. And on the other side of the walk which fronts this border is a low terrace wall, along which, at regular intervals, different kinds of ornamental vases are placed, and occupied with Pelargoniums or various other conspicuous plants. The wall beneath these vases is mostly covered with one kind of *Tropæolum,* or other free growing and liberal flowering climber. At either end of this low wall a wire basket, filled with some one dwarf plant, is placed ; and from the sides of this wires are run up to a common centre, from 4 to 5 ft. high, for supporting wreaths of climbers.

In the compartment nearest the house, besides a series of beds ranged round a circle in the centre, there is a series of circular beds along the two principal margins, defined by box edgings, and each of them surrounded by a very narrow walk, a small border extending along the sides of them, and two parallel walks defining this on the other side. The circular beds are slightly raised, and filled with Verbenas of different sorts, having only one colour to each bed, while the side beds contain the beautiful little *Campanula carpathica.* The arrangement is an exceedingly pretty and effective one.

The western and larger compartment of this garden contains a great multitude of beds, all separated by little walks and box edgings, and devoted to herbaceous plants, chiefly of taller kinds, dahlias, &c. The southern compartment, which has larger beds, is for the more decided summer flowers; and the northern compartment is a rosary, in which the summer and autumn roses are so mixed as to yield a pretty certain and continuous supply of bloom.

By the sides of the principal walks there are borders for mixed plants, in which the aim, as it is in the beds also, is to keep up a succession of bloom for the early spring and summer months. We observed that the Alyssums and plants allied to them were much used in these borders, especially *Iberis sempervirens*, which appears to bear any amount of cutting, and is a most valuable border plant. A double white *Achillea* was also very beautiful, as was *Silene tomentosa*, and *Œnothera prostrata*. Throughout the garden, however, there is an immense variety of pretty herbaceous and bedding plants; for, perhaps, the practice of seeking to obtain a succession of flowers from March to August is nowhere more earnestly or more successfully adopted, and everything likely to minister to that object is eagerly obtained and diligently preserved.

Considering how few plants there are which are sufficiently dwarf, free growing and flowering, and easily propagated, to be fit for bedding purposes, and how one meets, in ordinary places, with much the same kind of plants occurring everywhere, we were much pleased to see, in this collection, how many little known and less used sorts are applicable to the object. Indeed, were this not the case, the system of massing plants in flower gardens would probably soon wear out, on account of the universal sameness it would produce. But with variations in the mode of combining colours in beds, such as a little ingenuity will in time supply, and the bringing to light of those large stores of suitable plants which are yet available, there is no reason at present to apprehend such a result. We often now meet with examples in which beds are fringed with plants of a different colour and character to those in the centre; and probably much may yet be done by introducing a variety of plants in patches, with due regard to their habits and the arrangement of their colours, in different parts of each bed in a parterre, thus producing a more chequered but not less harmonious assemblage. Or concentric rows of separate colours may be used for filling beds, according to the manner in which the French and other bouquets are now so tastefully made. It would be by no means essential to the execution of either of these plans—the mention of which naturally arises out of our description of the flower gardens and bedding plants at Bedford Lodge—that the branches of the several plants should be kept quite distinct. If the colours were harmonious, a little intermixture of them at the edges would rather be desirable, as no bed of flowers ever looks well, at least on grass, when the edges are too hardly defined.

There is a little rockwork in a corner of the flower garden adjoining the entrance sweep, where a few pretty alpines are cultivated. Fortunately, as the house lies so near the road, there is only room for little beyond a court at the entrance door, and as this is planted off from the flower garden, the place is thus kept quite private till it is seen and entered from the house. An arrangement of this sort is of immense value in a small place, as it prevents it from being intruded upon by strangers, and serves for private use, and for contributing to the general effect all that space which is so often lost by the ambition of having a long drive, to reveal the greater part of the grounds. All the offices of the house are situated on this entrance side of the house likewise, and at the eastern end, the coach house and stables being at the loft-hand side of the court as you enter the gates. By this plan the entire south or garden front

G 2

and the western end are kept for the use of the family, and the garden is not bared to the servants' windows.

Compactness and seclusion, though in the midst of a town district, are thus the characteristics of this pleasing villa garden; and yet, happily, it is not destitute of a good view into the distant country. From the great variety and change in its parts, and from these parts being pretty much hidden from each other, or only partially revealed, it is well fitted for entertaining those large summer parties which residence in the neighbourhood of the metropolis generally brings together. But as it is essentially a summer place, those who expect to see anything very attractive in it after August, or a little later, will be sure to be more or less disappointed.

Wimbledon Park, the present residence of the *Duke of Somerset*, but once the property of Earl Spencer, is in one of those admirable situations which are rarely met with so near town. The house, which is an unpretending structure, is situated a little to the east of Wimbledon Church, and it and the gardens command some of the best home views and distant prospects which are to be found around London.

A walk round the pleasure grounds here, on a favourable day, will furnish a multitude of most charming landscapes, especially to the north-west and south-east. It is said that no less than thirty churches can be seen from different points in the grounds; and though such a circumstance is not in general to be taken as an absolute criterion of merit, yet in this case it affords a good indication of the style of the scenery; for, being only ten miles from London, churches are of course the centres of population, and the numerous detached villas and clusters of houses which are dotted about through this richly-wooded scene, at once afford an evidence of habitation and of social life, while they picturesquely vary the aspect of the country. Nothing can be more effective in a landscape that is sufficiently rich in trees than the groups of dwelling-houses or isolated villas which jut out here and there over the face of a district around the village church, provided these do not come too near the eye, or take a too prominent position, and that the scene is broad enough to keep them duly subdued. And when, as in this instance, the surface of the country is greatly varied, being thrown up into occasional swells or ridges of hills, or expanding into a wide and winding plain—the buildings now occupying the face of some of the hills, and now being gathered together in a valley, or peering out from a tuft of noble trees in either position—the entire scene becomes greatly enriched by such objects.

On the north-western side of the garden, a short terrace walk, at the edge of a steep bank, overlooks some of the chief features of the park. With a few tufts of thorns as a foreground, and a screen of larger trees to support and confine the view, there is here presented a rough and broken bank sloping away into a hollow beneath, in which last a portion of the large lake is visible.

The park then rises into another bank, studded liberally with trees, on a portion of the other side of the hollow, while, further to the right, the valley expands, and stretches away into the flat country of Middlesex, the hills behind Kensington, and those at a greater distance, filling up the scene to the extreme right. This landscape has almost every feature which could be desired. There is a good foreground, with the land sloping away rather quickly, just below the point of observation. This foreground and the slopes on either side are well timbered. Water is seen in the contiguous hollow, in a sufficiently broad gleam to appear extensive, but so indefinitely, and so shrouded up with trees at the sides of the view, that much is left for the imagination to fill up in reference to its actual outlines and extent. A beautiful grassy slope, richly adorned with old oak and other trees, and crowned with a broad but not unbroken mass of plantation, occupies part of the opposite side of the valley; while round the end of this swell, and between it and a more distant range of low hills, the valley stretches away into an almost boundless plain, the horizon of which, however, is not entirely flat or tame, and remoter hills, of bolder character, are discernible far behind those in the middle distance. For the greater part of two miles the valley is such as to appear to belong to the estate, and when it reaches Putney, and extends towards Kensington, villas and churches, and portions of more densely-peopled tracts, mingle with the ample wooding of these fertile borders of the Thames, and enliven without encumbering or marring the scene.

The gardens here contain little in themselves to interest the cultivator. They are, however, very neatly kept. Some of the flower-beds on the lawn have a quaint old bordering of Turkey oak, which is kept to within a foot of the ground by constant pruning. A small temple at the west side of the place yields a good view to the north-east, embracing the splendid trees and varied surface about Tooting and Streatham, and part of the Norwood ridge of hills. A large and ancient sarcophagus of porphyry is placed in this temple. Mr. Thompson is the gardener here.

The park, which was once an adjunct of this house, and which comprised about 1200 acres, being beautifully undulated and well wooded, and having a large lake in the low ground at the bottom of Wimbledon Hill, is now, unhappily, in process of being entirely changed, many parts of it having been sold for villa purposes, and several of these residences being actually built. New roads have been formed through it, and other portions are being gradually brought into the market; so that in time it will no doubt be almost wholly cut up; and its noble trees and ample lawns be sacrificed before the requirements of the vast London population.

Kenwood, the seat of the *Earl of Mansfield.*—This place has the great advantage of being situated between the picturesque hills of Highgate and Hampstead, embracing some of the intermediate heights, and nearly the whole of the beautiful intervening hollows, with their softly-rounded and various undulations. From this circumstance, and because it commands excellent views of Highgate Hill and church, the grounds would necessarily be pleasing. But they are further and more markedly distinguished by their extraordinary masses of wood, which are principally made up of oak. These, occurring over the face of the various swells on the southern side, and also on some parts towards the northern boundary, and being so very dense as to grow together into broad masses, the upper surface of which is only relieved by the changes in the ground itself, and by the slightly-different heights or tufting branches of individual trees, compose, altogether, a unique and highly sylvan landscape, which acquires much interest, beyond its own intrinsic attractiveness, from being so close to London.

The abundance of oak trees throughout this estate is supposed to have imparted to it the name by which it is now known—*kern*, which has been corrupted to *ken*, being the old British word for an acorn. The oak woods are also considered to be of spontaneous growth, and are therefore doubly pleasing. Mr. Loudon once thought they were composed of the *Quercus sessiliflora* alone; but they have since been found to comprise a great deal of the *Q. pedunculata*, and a number of varieties apparently intermediate between the two.

There are two carriage entrances to Kenwood, neither of which is long. The one nearest Highgate is shortest, and without any peculiar character, except that the belt of oaks forms a very fine fringe to the lawn opposite the house. The other approach, from the Hampstead side, is of a widely different sort, and exhibits a master-piece of good treatment. Here the road is cut through a high bank, the face of which is left, for the most part, in a rough and broken state. The banks, however, by no means follow the line of the road, but are thrown back many yards in some places and jut forward in others. They are partially clothed with a little wild vegetation, having a few tufts of such things as the common broom clinging here and there to little masses of projecting soil. Beyond these banks the ground falls away into a rough hollow. The whole drive is much darkened and overshadowed by a canopy of picturesque trees, principally oaks; and the ground beneath these is carpeted with ferns and the wilder forms of low native plants that are usually found in natural woods.

Even here, notwithstanding the great extent of the place, and the possibility of obtaining a road of a mile or more in length, one cannot but rejoice that the drives are so short. It leaves so much to be seen after the private grounds are entered, and accords better with a mansion that has not palatial magnificence to boast of. In approaching the house at Kenwood expectation is not at all excited. A large estate is not looked for. And hence, when the private front of the house is reached, the stranger is seized with astonishment and admiration.

Passing at once to the terrace walk on the south side of the house, a scene of grandeur and variety is presented, which, though in the very precincts of London, is seldom rivalled in even country places. We here stand in the midst of a large amphitheatre of woods. Not, however, that there is any great elevation or sameness in the hills which environ this spot. The two hills of Highgate and Hampstead, which are the highest, shut it in to the east and west; but on the south the ground is broken into lower and softer swells, and the valley beneath finds a contracted exit at either end of this central group.

So thoroughly is this place embosomed in woods, that there almost seems to be too much timber; and nothing in the way of distance enters into the composition. A few breaks through the leafy screen into the country beyond are among the first things which are longed for; but it must be remembered that the summits of the trees, more than even the surface of the ground, are beautifully rounded and varied; that the plantations are separated from the house by a valley; that there is little beyond a flat, tame district behind them; and that any openings would seriously prejudice, if not entirely destroy, the secluded and sylvan character of the place.

From the terrace walk, a large sheet of water, which loses itself among the trees in the hollow, forms a conspicuous object. The walk itself is 20 ft. broad, and a good deal raised. At the eastern end of it, on the lawn, is a very peculiar plant of the black spruce. Many of the branches, having spread down to the ground during their growth, have there struck root and thrown up new stems, so that the old tree has now a cluster of younger ones around it, of different ages and heights.

At the western end of the terrace, after the walk quits the front of the house, it enters an avenue of limes, after it emerges from which it begins to curve to the right and the left, and, by the left-hand route, is gradually narrowed to more ordinary dimensions.

Just beyond the lime avenue, a number of nice specimens of the better kinds of exotic trees occur at the sides of the walks, on the lawn, and are of a younger growth. There is a beautiful plant of the fern-leaved beech, which is an elegant tree for lawns. Taking the walk to the right, and following along a narrow strip of pleasure grounds, with the park, and the woods, and different views of Highgate Hill and church all the way on the left, we continue by a most delightful route along the northern boundary of the place, and climb two or three superior elevations, all revealing fresh aspects of the home estate and of the neighbouring hills. From one of these eminences, called Tyndal Mount, because, we believe, it formerly composed part of the estate of Chief Justice Tyndal, there are, especially, some enchanting views of the place; and near this point, on opening a door in the outer wall (which is not thought to be so close at hand), a prospect is suddenly obtained across the bare heath of Hampstead into a good part of Hertfordshire; affording a strong contrast, in the breadth of the landscape and the bareness of the foreground, to the rich and comparatively limited scene within the place.

Crossing the valley, we observed that the surface of the path, not here required to be of a polished or finished character, is coated over with a thin covering of burnt clay, which is recommended as a good material for putting a smooth face on walks across parks, where gravel would not be desirable. We then enter some of the woods which are seen from the front of the house, and in which there are numerous winding walks, penetrating among the trees, and enveloped in the densest shade. An excellent undergrowth of rhododendrons occurs through the greater part of these woods at intervals; and there are a few groups of most remarkable old rhododendrons, which have become, through age, quite like little trees, of the most picturesque form. Amongst their broken and wild stems, the walk often winds, and large, bare, tree-like branches from them actually overarch the path in some places.

The main line of walk keeps just within the southern margin of the plantation; and through the rugged stems of the trees, and across the undulated meadows to the south, a great many broad views of London are obtained. It is, indeed, quite a matter of taste to pass round this little-used walk, in order to discover the true position of the property, and appreciate more thoroughly the richness and repose it exhibits; that, after looking awhile through these "loopholes of retreat" on the great world of London, the retirement and shade and highly rural character of the grounds, may be returned to with greater relish.

Within these woods, it is most interesting to mark the relative heights and dimensions of the different kinds of trees which are of the same age; for, although oaks form the chief ingredient, there is a good sprinkling of other kinds. Many persons will be astonished to learn that the cedar of Lebanon has fairly outstripped all competitors, and evinced a rapidity of growth which not even the larch can equal. There is one cedar here above 100 ft. high, with a clear stem nearly to the summit; and many more are of almost equal height. This quickness of growth in the cedar, and the great height to which it attains as a plantation tree, when standing in a dense mass of wood, recommend it as very useful where tall evergreen trees are wanted, and as a valuable occasional substitute for the Scotch fir and the spruce. From the extreme beauty which the flat heads of older specimens usually attain, it is most effective in regard to the upper outline of a wood.

Next to the cedar in point of growing fast is the common larch, of which there are some first-rate examples here, and then the Spanish chestnut. The tops of these three trees tower above all the rest, and their trunks exhibit a proportionately greater increase of bulk.

Striking across the middle of the wood, towards the house, we pass the lake on the right, which is formed out of one of a series of pools that extend through the meadows towards London, and, a little to the left, we come upon a small new American garden, lately taken in from the park, and containing a variety of rhododendrons, kalmias, ledums, &c., in beds, many of which are edged with the common heath or lyng. There are two lines of standard rhododendrons through the middle of the plot, forming a sort of small avenue. The whole garden is in a retired corner, not seen until it is entered. The main walk afterwards recrosses the hollow, and joins into the terrace walk at the end of the lime avenue. Another walk passes round the eastern side of the lake, and enters upon the terrace at its eastern end.

In all the walks which either traverse or skirt the place, the leading object has clearly been to show the grounds to most advantage and in every variety of aspect. Hence, with the exception of the paths through the woods, which are most effective in the way of producing a deeper retirement and shade, the scenery is all kept open from the inner side of the walks, and only a few specimen plants sparingly introduced to furnish little breaks and foregrounds here and there, and to obviate anything like tameness. The openness of the interior views is further preserved by the use of light wire fences everywhere, to separate the pleasure grounds from the park ; and so inconspicuous are these fences in themselves, or so well placed as to the levels of the ground, or partially screened by a few plants, that the grass in the pleasure grounds and that of the park merge into each other imperceptibly, and all the appearance of ample lawns is obtained without there ever occurring more than a narrow strip of mown grass. It should be noted, too, that although the walks are of great length, and little beyond the estate itself ever comes into view, the scenes do not degenerate into sameness ; but, from the great variety of undulations and woods, the trees and the ground take fresh shapes continually, and the latter part of the walk round the whole is enjoyed with almost as much zest, and fully as much appreciation, as the first survey obtained from the great terrace.

At the west end of the house, on a lawn so far detached that it is surrounded with trees on every side except that next the house itself, is the flower garden ; which is not laid out as a regular parterre, but consists of a number of beds scattered over a spacious flat lawn, and some of them filled with flowers alone, while others are occupied by mixed shrubs, with a variety of specimen plants interspersed. This is the most unsatisfactory part of the place. There is a want of art and of a distinctive character in the arrangement of everything in it, and it is sadly too much inclosed and overshadowed by high trees.

The beds of shrubs are so placed that the whole of the plot cannot be seen at once ; and the specimen plants contribute to the same end. Among the latter are a beautiful *Araucaria imbricata*, some fine standard rhododendrons, a large *Sophora japonica* and *Liquidambar styraciflua*, a good

Buxus balearica, several handsome standard Persian lilacs, &c. The flower-beds are mostly edged with some low kind of shrub or plant that is kept dwarf ; and these are sometimes treated with great quaintness. Two low hedges of *Kerria japonica*, for example, which are clipped to about 18 in. in height and a foot in breadth, cross each other at right angles in a circular flower-bed near the house. Others of the beds are bordered with dwarf oak, with *Gaultheria, Cotoneaster,* &c. ; and some are more naturally surrounded by a fringe of appropriate herbaceous plants, which contrast in colour with those which compose the centre of the beds. At the corner of this flower garden, near the entrance front of the house, is a very elegant specimen of *Crategus multiflora*, conspicuous for its dwarfness and dense habit of growth, and admirably fitted for a lawn specimen.

Between the entrance front and the kitchen garden, which lies on the east side of the house, there is a walk through the oak wood, lined with rhododendrons, a great many of which have been trained up as standards, and will ultimately have a good effect. The kitchen garden is a long narrow piece of ground by the side of the road towards Highgate, and having a varied surface. It contains a few old forcing houses. We noticed in it and in the frame ground a very excellent stock of different herbaceous and summer bedding plants, which are here propagated and managed with great neatness and success. The better kinds of rhododendrons are also extensively reared for planting out in the pleasure grounds ; a practice that is very commendable, as tending to enrich and adorn the place at a light expense. A small wooden pit, in which to keep the grafted rhododendrons and similar plants that require a little protection for the first year, has lately been erected. Mr. Cockburn, the experienced gardener here, has had the charge of the place for a great many years, and manages everything most creditably.

Holland House is the London residence of *Lord Holland*, and stands about midway between the Kensington and Uxbridge roads, a little to the west of the more densely populated parts of Kensington. The house is well known as a fine example of the ancient English mansion, and is rendered classic by having once been in possession of Addison, the essayist and poet, who wrote his *Spectators* in the library here, while the early days of Charles Fox were also spent in this home of his ancestors and family. A public path passed very near the south front of the house till about two or three years since, when it was happily diverted, and his lordship formed another for public use by the side of the park.

In some parts of the gardens here there is much of that quaintness which one would expect to find in connection with so old a mansion, and which becomes an appropriate and characteristic feature in such a position. The flower garden, for example, is laid out with that intricacy and minuteness of pattern so common to ancient parterres, and all the beds are edged with box. At the corners of the beds, in some parts of the figure, the box is allowed to grow larger, and is clipped into the shape of a ball. In other parts, dwarf evergreen oaks, not more than a yard in height, are similarly clipped into globular shapes. The pattern, again, is so minute in other portions that the beds, being too small to admit flowers, are filled with sand of different colours. Others of the beds represent the initial letter of his lordship's title, in the quaint old English character. And near an arbour in the wall which bounds the garden towards the north, and which arbour is dedicated in an inscription by the late Lord Holland to the poet Rogers, who spent much of his time

G 3

here, there are two beds in the shape of foxes, in allusion to the family name of Fox; and a lotus fountain adjoins these beds. A fine bust of Napoleon, by Canova, partially screened with evergreens, forms the centre of a compartment by itself, at the lower end of the flower garden. A long scroll of beds, filled with Verbenas (one variety being placed in each bed), ranged along the side of the principal walk down this garden, looked very well when we saw them last year. The flowers used in all the beds are judiciously kept of the dwarfest character, that the precise figure of the beds may be preserved, and that the box edgings may remain conspicuous. The dahlia is believed to have been first introduced to this garden by the late Lord Holland.

The interest of this garden arises almost wholly from its age, and from its correspondence with the antiquity of the mansion. It is deficient in not having a regular general shape, in not being arranged with sufficient order and symmetry, in having the lower portion of it partly but not wholly detached, and not properly united with the rest, and in not being architecturally connected with the house. A plain brick wall, chiefly covered with peach trees, also forms its northern boundary; though the removal or alteration of this will, no doubt, in time rank among the improvements which the present Lord Holland is effecting.

A very nice finish is given to the lower end of the flower garden, by a series of light arches, covered with ivy, intermingled with Virginian creeper; and along the western front of these arches is a small terrace flower garden, of a much more artistic kind than its larger neighbour. It is a narrow strip of beds, laid out symmetrically, and bordered with low walls, having vases on them at regular intervals. Being backed by the formal (yet not close) series of arches just mentioned, and having a small open lawn, furnished with specimen evergreens, in the front, this is a very pleasing and finished little scene.

At the southern end of this terrace, on the site of what was formerly the stables, some extensive and remarkable improvements have recently been made, and are yet, we believe, in progress. If carried out and completed with the same spirit which has already been evinced, and if the accompaniments be well adapted to them, these alterations will make very striking and important features in the place. Partly out of the old stables, a handsome summer ball-room has been constructed, with very complete culinary offices attached; and a flight of steps from the former leads up to a smoking room, which is roofed in, but open at the sides, while a continuation of the steps carries us on to a balustraded roof, where there is ample space for enjoying the summer evening air. From this roof an open terrace is in part completed in the direction of the house, and is, we are told, to be connected, on a series of platforms, with occasional flights of steps, the whole supported by arches, till it joins the new terrace in front of the mansion. A continuous terrace will thus be obtained, to the exclusion of all the inferior offices and of the back road to them, from the principal terrace front of the house to the ball room, &c., making a very unique and agreeable arrangement. The new building is in the Roman style, formed chiefly of red brick, with stone or terracotta ornaments. It is adorned with a low tower on the northern side, and the staircase, ball room, smoking room, &c., are tastefully though not elaborately decorated with figures, vases, and other appropriate ornaments of a quiet character.

On the southern side of this building, however, and beneath the broad terrace platform leading from the roof of the smoking room, is an area intended for orange trees, and having a glazed end. The orange trees are to range along either side of it, so as to leave the centre well open for promenading. And between the brick pilasters which form the sides of this area, there are openings into an eastern and western green-house, which have roofs sloping away from the walls of the central space. An orangery and greenhouses will therefore exist under the same roof as the ball room, &c., and the whole will be duly connected. A more delightful arrangement than the whole of these erections will afford for spring and summer parties can hardly be imagined.

Some first-rate orange trees have been brought from France, many of them having been purchased from the collection of the late Madame Adelaide, for furnishing the orangery. They are among the largest, and most healthy, and best-shaped plants in the country. An old stone basin, of a circular figure, stands in the immediate neighbourhood of the new buildings, and is filled with the common water-lily, which, being in great luxuriance, has a pretty effect in summer. The kitchen garden, which once occupied the ground adjoining the new orangery, &c., has been removed farther to the west; and the remains of it yet existing will doubtless in time be also cleared away.

Close to the ball room, on the western side, we enter the more varied and less formal pleasure-grounds, which are said to have been originally laid out by Mr. Hamilton, the celebrated designer of his own gardens at Pain's Hill, in Surrey: and here we come immediately on a feature which appears to be unique, and is certainly very beautiful. From the Kensington to the Uxbridge Road, there seems to have once been an old lane bordered by lofty trees and bushes, and taking a slightly-winding direction. This is now converted into a grass glade or drive. There is a charming naturalness and absence of everything like regularity in the arrangement of the trees and shrubs by the sides of this glade; and it is also just sufficiently curved in parts to produce indefiniteness and variety without giving the least intimation of the interference of art. Being so completely overshadowed with trees, while at the same time it is broad enough to prevent these from killing the grass, it constitutes a delicious summer walk or leisurely drive; and is straight enough to be used while reading a book, without the inconvenience of having continually to look to one's steps, while it is not so straight as to seem artificial. The thorough seclusion and quiet which it supplies, in a place so close to London, is an additional recommendation. The last time Fox was in these gardens, he is stated to have expatiated long on the beauty of this glade.

In this lower part of the gardens there is a pleasant bower formed around an old ivy-clad trunk of a tree, a number of props placed round it being also covered with ivy. At the bottom of a walk which extends in a straight line from the north front of the mansion, a view up the walk, revealing a few steps opposite the flower garden, and the branches of some cedars lying down on the grass banks at the sides of these, is very effective. This little scene is observed from an alcove at the end of the walk. There is a very fine cedar in this part of the grounds, and a noble elm up nearer the flower garden.

From the north front of the house an extensive prospect is gained across a swelling lawn and park, and many beautifully-wooded eminences enter into this landscape. But it is becoming much disfigured by the erection of large masses of houses in the nearer view, just beyond the park; and as the belt of plantation which surrounds the park on this side is on very low ground, as compared with the house and the outside country, this, which was unquestionably an advantage before the neighbourhood became so much built over, as it enabled any one at the house to see over the broken tops of the trees into an agreeable rural district, has now been found to be a defect. The remedy that has been most skilfully provided is the planting of another mass of trees and shrubs all along the higher ground of the park, nearer the house; and although this young plantation looks very stiff and out of place at present, yet, when it grows up sufficiently, the trees will be thinned out and thrown into groups, so as to cover all the objects that want concealing, and still reveal Harrow Hill, and some of the better parts of the exterior landscape.

On the highest swell of the north lawn is a group of most venerable cedars, supposed to be among the earliest introductions to this country; but their exposed situation has most unfortunately subjected them to several accidents from storms, and they have lost many of their branches: they have still, however, a very characteristic and noble air. The eastern side of this lawn is furnished with numerous stately elms, which are formed into an avenue along the boundary.

At the northern end of the straight walk along the garden front of the house is an alcove, containing a statue of Charles Fox. Although this building is wholly of brick, yet, as it is of a tolerably tasteful form, and is covered with trellis work, it has a sufficiently good appearance. Between it and the mansion is a very handsome screen, forming one side of the entrance court. It is composed partly of stone and ornamental iron railing; but a new portion has been added, with alternate square or lozenge-shaped apertures and ornaments of Staffordshire ware, with different figures and devices impressed upon each. A lower terrace wall of the same material has been carried along the southern front of the mansion, on the site of the old public path, and there are vases filled with flowers on each of the piers. When we saw them they were all full of large scarlet Pelargoniums. The walls are exceedingly rich and suitable. They were prepared and put up by Messrs. Copeland and Garrett, of London. The stone portion of this screen, with its gateway, is by Inigo Jones.

There is now a fine bold area on the south side of the mansion, inclosed within the terrace wall. It is paved with stone in the immediate neighbourhood of the building, and there are a few curious old exotic plants growing out of the pavement here and there against the walls of the house. The rest of the area is laid down in grass, with a broad walk around it, and a fountain (the basin of which is of cast iron) in the centre. From this terrace the southern park is seen to be a very plain piece of grass, with some lines of elm trees down either side of it, and similar trees extending partly along the side next the Kensington Road. The site of the house is, however, fortunately high enough to afford views over the tops of the houses in the front of it, and across various tufts of trees in the neighbourhood, to the Surrey hills. The entrance to the place is by a neat gateway from the Kensington Road, up an avenue of elms. Mr. Scobie is Lord Holland's present gardener.

The Manor House, at Fulham, is the seat of the *Bishop of London*, and is a small but neatly-kept place, in so flat a district that the views are confined to its own grounds. Nearly everything in the gardens here is good of its kind, though there is nothing conspicuously so. The kitchen garden is well cropped, and has excellent fruit trees, of nearly

every class, on its walls. There are three forcing-houses here, heated
with hot water, by the father of the present Mr. Weeks, of Chelsea.
They are used as vineries, but a few plants are grown on a stage in the
central one, and when they were visited last autumn, some pines were
also placed in a pit belonging to one of them.

In the vineries, Mr. Hay, the gardener, adopts the plan of growing
two crops of grapes from one house every season, and has experienced a
very satisfactory amount of success. The plan pursued is to train the
earliest vines to upright trellises, which are nearly as high as the roof of
the house. When the grapes on these are sufficiently coloured to be
able to dispense with a portion of the light, the other set of vines,
growing in the outside borders, and previously trained to the exterior of
the rafters, is introduced and fastened up to the rafters, and the two
crops then receive the same treatment. The first crop is brought
on as early as possible, being generally cleared off by about April;
and the second crop is of course an autumn one. The latter consists
mainly of black Hamburgh and black West's St. Peter's grapes; but
there are a few of the white sweetwater and muscat of Alexandria kinds.

Pines, of which no great quantity is grown, are very well cultivated
here, in pits, and appear most healthy. Some cucumber plants were
likewise growing very favourably, last autumn, in a small pit.

In the pleasure grounds, at the garden front of the house, there is a
good open lawn, bordered with a few beds of flowers; and a walk to the
kitchen garden has also some flower-beds on the grass at each side of it,
with two rows of standard roses. There is likewise a small American
garden, well filled, with *Magnolia purpurea* and *cordata*, &c., growing out
of the masses of rhododendrons, and greatly enlivening and varying
their appearance in summer. The beds in this garden are so small, and
the plants have grown so spreading, that many of the latter have to be
cut into a complete hedge by the sides of the walks.

But the great thing in the place is the specimens of old exotic trees
on the lawn. Out of many others, the noble tree of the black American
hickory, some of the outer branches of which are beginning to decay,
appeared the most striking. There are, besides, an excellent cork tree,
a very fine old evergreen oak, an ancient but not handsome cedar, a
beautiful *Crataegus orientalis*, with its branches sweeping the grass, some
capital specimens with the character of low shrubs, and nice plants of the
Deodar cedar, and *Pinus laricio.* Loudon mentions a *Kolreuteria pani-
culata*, a standard Judas tree, and a *Pinus pinaster*, as further conspicuous
for size and beauty. These grounds have been noted for their exotic
trees for more than a century.

Lord Kilmorey has a small seat at *Isleworth*, on the banks of the
Thames, a visit to which will be sure to afford much pleasure. It has
the rare merit of having everything about it cultivated in the very best
manner. Even the park, which does not contain more than 14 acres, is
so neatly kept as to look almost like a lawn. It is fed entirely by sheep,
and is divided into several portions by low wire fences, for the purpose
of changing the pasturage without the use of moveable hurdles. The
whole of the sheeps' dung is regularly picked off, and manure applied
equally over the surface in winter. This avoids all tufts and patches
in the grass, which, when we saw it, was eaten as close as if it were mown.
One hundred sheep and the same number of lambs are annually fattened
from this pasture. We noticed that the wire fences were provided here
and there with a flat iron step, about 18 in. from the ground, sup-

ported by a strong iron rod, which prevents the fences from being injured by having to be climbed over.

There are many good and beautiful specimens of trees in the park; and, as we proceed along the drive towards the house, we get all the benefit of a glorious avenue of cedars in the adjoining estate of Mrs. Byng. Opposite the entrance-door of the house is a large circular basin, in artificial stone, with the fountain in the centre issuing from a simple jet. This has a cool and refreshing influence about the entrance in summer.

On the south or garden front of the house, the first object we come to is a small orangery, where the orange trees are particularly healthy, and are mingled with some first-rate specimens of greenhouse plants. *Pimelea decussata* is here unusually fine, and plants of *Rhipipodendron plicatile* are most remarkable for size and character. A few flower-beds enliven the lawn in front of the. conservatory.

From the actual front of the house, we see the principal part of the lawn on this side, and get views across the river into the flat country on the opposite shore, with a better and richer landscape towards Richmond Hill. The lawn itself is exceedingly well treated. Some small groups of flower-beds near the house just serve to enrich it in summer without interfering with its breadth. A basin and elegant tazza, with fountain, occur in the centre, and this is supplied by a small Artesian well. Specimen plants, chiefly evergreens, and small groups, are sprinkled over the rest of the lawn, though chiefly on the parts farthest from the house, and the sides are inclosed with larger trees, which form a kind of frame to this lawn scene. Nowhere, however, do the plants occur too numerously, or break up the grass too much. There are many nice young plants of the rarer pines and firs among them, with Deodars, *Cryptomeria japonica*, *Taxodium sempervirens*, standard Rhododendrons, and a very beautiful *Cupressus macrocarpa*. Although the lawn is severed from the river by a public lane, a low wall along the side of this, partly covered with ivy, and partly concealed by shrubs, almost wholly excludes the little traffic there is along the lane, and does not present a hard or very glaring boundary line.

At the western end of the house, a conservatory connects the dining room with what was once a banqueting room, but is now a museum, with statuary attached. The conservatory has three divisions; the two ends being properly the conservatory, with a glass front and roof, and the centre being a small sitting room, fitted with a few elegant little tables and chairs, birdcages, specimens of rare marbles carved into pillars, &c., some charming little statues, vases, and other artistic productions, none of which are large, so that the room is not encumbered by them. There is a good specimen of the Warwick vase, in statuary marble. The roof of this room has an ordinary ceiling, the front only being of glass. Glass divisions can be brought forward, so as entirely to separate this room from the conservatories at either end, if desired. It exhibits a very happy arrangement; for, seated towards the back of this room, with all the comforts of a summer parlour, and without being exposed to the glare of the sun, nearly the whole of the conservatories will be visible, without their actual dimensions being seen, and the tangling festoons of climbers in them add much to the indefiniteness. The song-birds also contribute to the enchantment of the effect.

In the conservatories, there is a paved walk down the centre, and rows of specimen Camellias are planted out in circular plots on either side, the remainder of the floor being covered with slates, painted green.

There is a small kerb-stone on either side of the middle path, and also light pillars for supporting climbers. These last are made a very considerable feature, being likewise trained over the back walls. Fuchsias and other large and elegant flowering plants are placed about among the Camellias on the floor; but all so judiciously arranged as to look furnished without exhibiting any crowding. The general result is an unusually good one, and all is in excellent taste and keeping. The practice of painting the floors green, where they are not to be walked upon, and leaving circular apertures in the pavement for rows of specimen plants, is specially worthy of mention; the former producing a kind of neutral ground tint almost as good as a carpet of moss or Lycopodium, but more in accordance with a building so immediately connected with the mansion, while the series of circular breaks in the pavement carry out the appearance of art which pervades the whole, and prevent the floor from seeming too tame and continuous.

Eastward from the house, beyond the orangery, the garden is backed, on the north side, by a wall, which, with a low covered way in front of it, is used for ornamental climbers. In the border opposite this wall are beds of flowers, edged with slate. The rest of the pleasure grounds, towards the east, are planted with comparatively young trees and shrubs, the whole of which are, however, growing on a grass lawn, and very short scythes are used for mowing among them. On a small mound, composed mainly of brick rubbish, and not having more than a foot of soil on its surface, we were astonished to observe the shrubs quite unaffected with the dryness of the season, and to learn that this brick rubbish retains a great deal of moisture. In this part of the garden there is an Italian trellis-covered walk, embowered with vines. A small tunnel carries a path under the public lane to a boat house on a creek by the side of the river; and there is an ingenious contrivance for letting the boat down an inclined plane into the river, and drawing it up again; his Lordship having a great fondness for aquatic sports.

In the kitchen garden are some remarkable raised borders, from three to four feet above the level of the walks, which are supposed to be the remains of an old vineyard. They are rather useful for early crops. Capital peach and nectarine trees cover the wall behind them, and pears are trained to an elegant espalier wire fence, put up by Messrs. Young and Co., along the front of the border. The walks of the kitchen garden have slate edgings, which are preferable to any kind of plant for the purpose.

At the back of the kitchen garden is a cluster of forcing and other houses and pits, nearly all newly erected, and constructed in the most modern style. There is a vinery, a peach house, and a stove and orchid house built against a wall; and a detached span-roofed house for heaths and greenhouse plants, besides pits for other greenhouse plants, and for pines, &c. The whole of these structures are heated from one boiler. The houses were erected by Messrs. Gray, Ormson, and Brown, and are of wood, glazed with long panes of sheet glass, and fitted up inside chiefly with slate. One of the main reasons assigned for the boiler (which is not a large one) being capable of doing so much work is that it is very carefully set. It is most important to have an experienced man for fixing all the parts of a heating apparatus, as so much of its capacity for working well will depend on the nicety with which such things are done. In the span-roofed heath house, the side lights, instead of lifting up or turning out, or sliding horizontally, slide downwards over the face of the wall, and have cords made of gutta percha, which have hitherto answered.

The contents of the several houses are quite in character with the superiority of their construction. The plants are all well selected, and admirably grown. The orchids are in the best condition and the heaths, azaleas, and other greenhouse plants are first-rate specimens, each plant being cultivated as an individual object, and allowed plenty of space, light, air, pot-room, &c. The dwarf stove climbers, trained to low trellises, are likewise conspicuously good. In a porch to the stove there is a nice little collection of cacti. Many fine seedling pelargoniums, for bedding purposes, have been raised here. The Flower of the Day, with variegated leaves and scarlet flowers, the Cerise Unique, with less variegated leaves, and cherry-coloured blossoms, and several that more or less resemble these, originated with Mr. Kinghorn, the excellent gardener here, and have introduced quite a fresh character into the tribe.

In the vinery Mr. Kinghorn has been practising the system of double cropping, which is done by having an additional row of inner lights to slide along the inside of the front stage, thus making a separate compartment about a yard wide, into which the first vines are put as soon as the crop is cut. As far as it has yet been tested, the plan has proved tolerably successful, and it has, of course, the strong recommendation of making one house do the work of two, which is a peculiar advantage in a small establishment. The pines here are kept in pits, and grown in pots. They appear in the healthiest possible state.

What constitutes the charm of this very interesting place is that everything which is attempted is *well* done. There is an air of extraordinary order and elegance about the whole, which is, as far as permanent enjoyment is concerned, or even in regard to the impression it conveys to a stranger, far more gratifying than a less tasteful or finished assemblage of the most imposing objects in a state of partial neglect or inferior keeping. And as this is a point which even the possessor of the smallest garden may attain, it is the more necessary to press it thus distinctly.

Lord Tankerville's villa, at Walton-on-Thames, is one of those happy examples of architectural treatment which are all the more delightful because they are so extremely scarce. It is in the Italian style, and was designed by Mr. Charles Barry. We know of no instance in which the pictorial effect of the building has been so successfully studied, and its offices and accessories made to play so unobtrusive but important a part in the general composition from the garden front. Unfortunately, the place has been suffered to fall into a very neglected state for the last few years; and, probably, ere this notice appears it will have passed into other hands.

The garden attached to this villa has very little in its situation to recommend it. The country around it is flat and tame for the most part, and the river with a swampy margin. A towing-path also passes between it and the river. It has therefore to depend mainly upon itself, although the river, in some parts, is sufficiently below the level of the garden to render the view of the former pleasing. It likewise takes in a small portion of the wooded hills of the Oatlands estate. But the proximity of the public road (although this was a good deal diverted at no very remote period), and the nearness to Walton Bridge, cause the place to be crowded up with trees on two of its sides. Between the house and the river, especially, the trees so press upon the building, and so narrow the garden, that the effect of both is greatly marred.

Entering by a plain Italian lodge, and passing the stables on the right, a few paces bring us to the entrance porch, which is beneath a belvidere tower. A fine cedar tree, standing close to this tower, with a retiring wing of the building, and a small architectural flower garden behind, form altogether a group such as is seldom seen ; and a few other cedars on the adjoining lawn greatly help the effect. The flower garden is in a corner formed by the retirement of part of the building behind it, and the projection of the tower at one end of it. It is inclosed within a balustraded wall, decorated with vases, and is on a slightly-raised platform, the whole being in excellent keeping with the house.

At the eastern side of the house, the garden stretches away along the top of a bank by the side of the river, being backed by the village of Walton and the kitchen garden on the south. A rather plain wing wall extends from the house to the kitchen garden, inclosing all the offices. From the lawn on this side of the house, however, the roofs and various small towers of the outbuildings, with the house and its scarcely seen tower, and the trees, produce another admirable picture, which is particularly noticeable for the variety of outline and unity of character it presents. The roofs of all the buildings being covered with the broad tiles having raised ridges, expressly made for structures in the Italian style, even the commonest outbuildings possess a certain richness and character, and harmonize well with the principal edifice.

The lawn in the pleasure grounds is rather bare near the house ; but it soon becomes liberally furnished with trees and shrubs, and exhibits many beautiful specimens. The place has been much noted for large exotic plants, some of which are dead, though many yet remain. By the margin of the river, where the place presents a good deal of beauty, there is a large *Rhus cotinus* and a good deciduous cypress, with some bold masses of Portugal laurel, &c. There are many very handsome limes, some large and rare oaks of different sorts, fine hickories and Sophoras, &c. Besides the more detached groups and single trees, among which some beautiful Spanish chestnuts are conspicuous, there is a larger mass of trees, principally limes, forming a lengthened kind of bower, and offering a delightful summer retreat.

On the southern and flatter side of the garden, in a part nearly surrounded by lofty trees, there are good specimens of *Pinus insignis* and *cembra, Buxus balearica, Abies Douglasii*, several thorns, many clusters of various Magnolias, large groups of old Azaleas grown to a great size, Rhododendrons, Kalmias, Andromedas, &c. There is here, also, a small rock garden, for the culture of ferns and alpines; and *Apios tuberosa* grows freely as a climber over a wire trellis near this spot. The whole of this part of the garden is most interesting ; but everything is in a state of great wildness and neglect.

In the kitchen garden thyme is freely employed as an edging, and in the light sandy soil of this place it succeeds well. Grapes were always successfully grown on one of the walls, being ripened by the aid of small bell glasses, which likewise served to keep off insects. Some old plant houses here once contained an excellent collection of both stove and greenhouse plants, together with a great many mesembryanthemums and cacti. There were, in particular, some large palms, which were presented to the Duke of Devonshire nine or ten years ago, and are now growing in the great stove at Chatsworth. They were removed at an immense expense, having been drawn by horses from Walton to Chatsworth. One of the plants (a date palm), when taken up with soil attached, and secured in a packing-case, weighed more than ten tons. They were kept alive and started into growth the first year after removal by being inclosed in a calico tent, which excluded the strong light of the sun, and rendered it easy to maintain a close moist atmosphere around them. This covering was gradually withdrawn as they began to put forth new leaves, and they are now quite healthy and flourishing. ·

Oatlands, which is only a little higher up the river than the place just described, was laid out by Wright, a successor of Kent, who had formerly a great reputation. It possesses many good features, the principal of which are its water and its grotto. The water, which lies in a valley to the north-west of the house, is considered a clever imitation of a river, and might, when in proper preservation, have been mistaken for the Thames. The grotto is an extraordinary one, built by Bushell (a celebrated constructor of these things) for the Duke of York. Its formation is said to have occupied many years. It is of considerable size, and is lined chiefly with shells, spar, and similar materials, so as to have a very artificial character. It is more a curiosity than an object of art; the rules of art demanding that the material employed for these things should be of one general kind, and that they should be such as are found in nature, or might possibly be so. At one period, however, this grotto possessed considerable fame; and there is a tradition that it was once occupied by a sort of congress of kings. In a secluded spot around the grotto is a very singular collection of tombs and memorials to the Duchess of York's dogs. These animals seem to have been great favourites; and there are considerably more than a hundred monumental stones, of various shapes, on which the virtues of the different pets are set forth and their fate mourned, in several languages, and sometimes in the poetical effusions of eminent personages. The park contains much fine timber: but the greater part of the estate is now, we are told, to be carved up into building plots for villas.

Dropmore, the seat of Lady Grenville, is about six miles from Windsor, and a little beyond Burnham. Although it scarcely comes within the range which we profess to include in our descriptions, it ought to be mentioned on account of its well-known Pinetum, which is probably the best and the most interesting in Britain, having been in existence so many years; while its extensive flower gardening decorations are also celebrated.

From the front of the house some fine prospects are obtained through the bold masses of trees on the lawn, the land dropping away suddenly after presenting a sufficient foreground. The views take in Windsor Castle and the hills and woods of Windsor Great Park, with the valley of the Thames spreading out between.

Parallel with the front of the house, the flower gardens extend for a considerable length to the west, and are backed by an architectural wall, and by conservatories, aviaries, &c. Being on a flat surface, a good opportunity is afforded for massing flowers of one colour, and this system is largely adopted. A good deal of variety and richness is produced by the use of vases, sculpture, large china jars, fountains, baskets, &c. There is also a Dutch flower garden, used chiefly for bulbs. On the wall at the back, too, there are many beautiful climbers; and standard and pole roses are freely used in the decoration of this part of the place. Here are likewise some magnificent plants of *Magnolia grandiflora* and *Stuartia virginica.*

The pinetum is planted over a large surface to the west of the house, and, commencing in the more dressed parts of the pleasure grounds, gradually passes into a rougher and more picturesque tract, where a piece of water has been formed, and masses of rock, accompanied with tufts of wild furze, heather, &c., break and diversify the surface. Farther on, the ground is almost entirely clothed with heather, and the woods which confine the whole scene are mostly composed of the commoner species of the pine, fir, and larch tribes. The specimen plants, of which there is a most perfect collection, and many examples of some of the more ornamental species (such as Araucarias, Deodars, &c.), are dotted about on the open glades; and everything like sameness is happily avoided by the judicious intermixture of commoner sorts in groups. A broad walk or drive passes through the whole, revealing all the better specimens and scenes, and being shut up in one part for about one-third of a mile by a grove or avenue of cedars, and in others by passing through dense masses of common pine.

It is impossible to conceive of any better situation and accompaniments for a pinetum than those at Dropmore. The whole tract (which is of considerable extent) is exactly what it should be. There is enough of the roughness and picturesqueness of nature, and the abundance and density of the surrounding pine plantations, to show off the specimens to the greatest advantage, and make us almost fancy ourselves in the more open parts of a pine forest; while there is sufficient attention to culture and keeping not to suffer the wildness of natural luxuriance anywhere to trench upon the plants intended to be displayed, or to take the entire scene out of the domain of art. Consistency and harmony, in short, characterize every part of the district.

Unfortunately, however, the substratum of this ground is a wet gravel, the water lying in it, in parts, at a very little distance from the surface; and as the precaution of draining and of raising the earth for the reception of the plants was not taken in the first instance, many of the older plants, in that portion which is nearest the house, are gradually losing their upper shoots, and their further progress will most likely be checked. This is no doubt owing to the roots having descended into the wet subsoil, and there becoming cankered ; for there is nothing which the majority of the coniferous tribe can less endure than a sour subsoil, in which water lies stagnant. It is well known that they prefer to grow on hill sides, with a sandy soil, and a shaly or rocky substratum. Hence, when they are planted in a flat tract, the ground should always be thoroughly drained, and the soil raised nearly or quite a foot above the surrounding surface.

Many charming specimens of the rarest as well as the most common species are found in this collection. Even those which are of doubtful hardiness are allowed a place, and are annually protected. Perhaps the numerous plants of the *Araucaria imbricata* are among the most extraordinary. To those accustomed only to see the singularly stunted plant at Kew, and the comparatively small bushes throughout the country, the size and luxuriance of those at Dropmore will be truly wonderful. They are towering up with amazing rapidity, making a growth of nearly a yard in height each year. The Araucaria, indeed, doubtless appears more in its true character as a tall-growing tree at Dropmore than anywhere else in Britain. But although it is attaining such a great height—some of the plants being now, we should think, at least 40 ft. high—it still continues well furnished with branches, and has the appearance of a gigantic candelabrum. To the admirer of the pine tribe, this collection will exhibit numberless other species which are almost equally remarkable. We should suppose that the best time to see it in perfection is shortly after the leaves of deciduous trees have fallen, when the year's growth is completed, and the contrast between the various shades of dark green in the pines, and the bareness of the newly-stripped deciduous trees in other parts of the place, is yet fresh and vivid. Mr. Frost is her ladyship's chief gardener.

Knowle Park is the magnificent seat of *Earl Amherst*, at Sevenoaks in Kent, and has come into his lordship's possession by marriage, having formerly been the family residence of the Dukes of Dorset, and once belonging, it is said, to Archbishop Cranmer. Although 24 miles from London, it is such a noble old place that it requires a brief notice here.

Situated in a very charming country, with all the ground softly and beautifully undulated, and enriched with the most splendid wooding, this park embraces some of the best features of the district, and is, for the variety of its undulations, and the magnitude of its trees, equalled by very few others. The beeches are particularly grand; and there are many picturesque old oaks, among which one, which is now dead and partially decayed, is fenced off for preservation, as being of gigantic size both as respects height and girth. A very delightful winding valley, having the top and part of the sides of its slopes picturesquely clothed with old trees, stretches across the park near Sevenoaks, and is crossed by the drive that enters the park in the middle of the town. Some agreeable walks wind among the trees at the top of these slopes, and the public are liberally allowed access to them and to other parts of the park.

The mansion is an exceedingly venerable old pile, for the most part erected in the fifteenth century, though some portions are still more ancient. It is considered as a very fine specimen of the castellated baronial hall, and is in the form of a quadrangle, with a spacious inner court. Regarded pictorially, it presents many attractions, and the rich clothing of ivy with which it is partially adorned greatly heightens its beauty. On the garden front especially, the ivy, by being closely cut in, forms a smooth and luxuriant mantle to the building, without interfering with any of its architectural features, or conveying the idea of wildness and neglect.

To the lover of the picturesque, the private garden, with its ancient terraces, parterres, and sculptured ornaments, its long green alleys broken occasionally by overarching climbers or evergreens, and its numberless ancient specimens of exotic shrubs and low trees (the cypress, juniper, and arbor-vitæ tribe, and the yews, being particularly prominent, and huge Magnolias being also numerous), will afford a rich and unusual treat. Most of the plants having been permitted to take their natural shapes, and some of them to mingle together in groups, the great age of many must of course have contributed to produce the most irregular and picturesque specimens, as well as most artistic combinations. Besides other strange and striking examples, there is an old lime tree on one of the lawns, the branches of which having naturally bent downwards towards the earth, have there struck root, and it is now surrounded with myriads of tufted trees of various ages and sizes, covering altogether an immense surface. The parent plant is, indeed, beginning to decay, and some of its numerous progeny are nearly as large as itself.

Around the same stem a sort of natural bower is formed, from which there are many little winding avenues to the outside, realizing most perfectly the picture of the Banyan, and its

> "Pillar'd shade.
> High overarched, with echoing walks between."

In the woods included within the pleasure grounds, and which formed "the wilderness" of ancient gardens, the ground is allowed to retain its natural variations of surface, and winding walks conduct us through occasional breaks in the larger trees, which are filled with masses of Rhododendrons, Azaleas, &c. From being so much shaded, many of the rhododendrons are drawn up a good deal, and take a more picturesque form in consequence. There is a good small conservatory in the garden, occupied almost wholly with Camellias, which are planted out in beds, and compose some of the best and most luxuriant groups of this tribe which can anywhere be seen. Mr. Don, the brother of the late Messrs. George and David Don, the well-known botanists, has been many years gardener at Knowle, and is most obliging and enthusiastic. A noble old tithe barn, which existed in Cranmer's time, is still to be seen here, and is well worth examining.

Montreal, the former residence of Earl Amherst, and now occupied by his son *Lord Holmesdale*, is at Riverhead, a short distance from Knowle, and is distinguished for its flower gardens and its rockery. It is very pleasantly situated, and has a small river running along its southern boundary. The park is ample, and well wooded, and there are some good plant houses attached to the mansion. When we saw it last, the place was in excellent order, and will repay a visit.

Mrs. Lawrence's gardens at *Ealing Park* have acquired, and justly, a universal reputation, on account of the superb collection of plants which they contain, and the general taste displayed in the arrangement of the place. As they are most generously thrown open to the public for one day in each week during the summer, they demand to be pretty fully described.

The entrance to the park is at the eastern corner, and after passing through the gates, the drive turns to the left, and crosses the open park till it reaches a long piece of artificial water, over which it is carried by a low bridge,—which is in fact a neck of land dividing the lake into two levels,—and soon arrives at the house. There is also a walk from the lodge to the house, just along the belt of plantation which covers the northern boundary. In the lake is a pretty island of weeping willows, which shows well from the house. The drive, walk, water, &c., were planned by Brown; but the southern belt of plantation was afterwards thinned out with great judgment and effect by Repton, who saw that it was concealing the views into the country across the Surrey Hills, and of the Kew Pagoda, gardens, &c., and caused several varied openings in the line of plantation to be made, thereby greatly enlivening and expanding the place.

From the house, which is so unfortunately contrived that the offices are on the south side, and can only be gained by passing the principal entrance door, an opening through an architectural wing wall at the north end brings us at once into the pleasure grounds. This wall is also used to connect the house with a conservatory, which stands on the right as soon as the garden is entered, and is generally filled with Camellias, or other large flowering plants that are not grown as specimens.

At the other end of the house, a short colonnade is thrown out, and supported by low evergreen trees, through which access to what is called the "Italian walk" is given. This is a straight walk, on a descending slope, with pairs of small figures on pedestals at either side of it, and good specimens of Irish yew between these. It terminates in a moderately large circular basin of water, in the centre of which, on a sufficient pedestal, is a figure of Apollo. The walk is kept confined towards the end by large evergreens, which narrow the vista, and restrict the view pretty much to the principal terminating object in the middle of the basin. The figures on the pedestals at the sides are arranged in pairs; on one pedestal Mars and Venus being placed, on another Cupid and Psyche, on a third Castor and Pollux, &c. The general effect is classic and elegant, and consistent with the style of the house.

The lawn view from the front of the house is rich and varied. A great many specimen plants, especially of the coniferous tribe, are scattered about upon the grass, and their lower branches lie down upon it in the most graceful manner. A rustic arch, through which a small fountain is seen, and some fragmentary classic ruins, jut out from the mass of trees and shrubs at different points along the northern boundary, and prevent the abundance of green vegetable objects from degenerating into sameness. Certain cross avenues, however, break up the principal glade more than is desirable. One of these avenues is of *Cupressus macrocarpa*, backed by mixed evergreens. Near the house, among other choice specimens, is a large plant of *Arbutus procera*, which, with its smooth stems, and fine clusters of fruit in autumn, has a striking appearance. *Garrya elliptica* is also large and handsome, and is a most valuable shrub for winter flowering.

When the basin of water is reached, it is found to contain four other figures on pedestals, one of them representing Neptune, another a mermaid, and the remaining two herons. On the east and west sides of this pond, the ground rises into a bank, with large masses of evergreens on the summit. The bank to the east is the highest, and has a splendid cedar of Lebanon upon it, the branches of which are held up by ivy-covered props, so as to allow of its being walked under. Close to this bank is the dairy, a pretty object, and decorated inside with a row of busts on brackets against the upper part of the walls, with flints, shells, &c., on part of the shelves. The door is of stained glass, with wreaths of roses and other flowers.

In the neighbourhood of the dairy, under the large evergreen trees, is an oval arch, formed with masses of fused brick, and supported on either side with a miniature rockery of the same material, clothed with ivy, &c. The design of the aperture is to afford a sudden and confined view towards the park, embracing part of the lake, on the margin of which latter some masses of fused brick have been set up to form an object to this view. Were the scene more definite and contracted, and did it embrace one principal and striking feature, it is probable that this idea of an oval opening, which starts from the level of the ground, and is about the height of a full-grown man, would be very effective, by yielding a kind of telescopic view without the awkwardness and trouble of having to approach so closely to a smaller aperture, or to move about with effort in order to obtain the desired survey. A better example occurs on the other side of the round pond, where, after threading our way amongst large laurels and other evergreens, which group themselves into a natural retreat called the Leicester bower, and turning at length between shaded masses of fused brick, which furnish a shaded home for ferns and alpines, we come all at once to another oval aperture, through which we look out to the pond and its figures, with the grassy bank and noble evergreens beyond. Here there has been more preparation, by a winding and uncertain path, in deep shadow, among imitation rocks, of which the arch forms a part; and the burst of light which we suddenly obtain through the arch, with the limited nature of the view, and the existence of a more definite object in the pond and figures, render this much more satisfactory, and, indeed, decidedly artistic.

We cannot but remark on the felicity with which the oval figure has been chosen for framing these little scenes, and how well the shape and size of the aperture fulfil its intention. Any more irregular opening would have the effect of scattering too much the objects to be revealed, whereas this serves to concentrate and confine them. A circular aperture, again, would produce the same bad result as an irregular one, unless it were quite small, when it would have to be looked through with effort, and the whole scene would be taken in only by degrees. The oval, on the other hand, as here adopted, is in itself a beautiful figure, and directly the eye catches it, all that is wished to be seen through it is exhibited at once. The suddenness with which the view opens upon us is fully half of the charm. Any gradual unfolding of the scene would ruin it.

Following the walk which runs along the boundary of the pleasure grounds, we see how nicely these are separated from the park. A very low hedge is placed in the bottom of a hollow, and its line is broken by a few dwarf evergreens, such as Rhododendrons, scattered here and there irregularly along the inside. Standing on the walk, therefore, or the lawn, we scarcely observe this boundary line, because it is so low and unobtrusive, and does not at all arrest the sight, while it is quite hidden from the other side of the place.

Around some of the plantations at this end of the park, luxuriant masses of the double-blossomed furze form a broken and beautiful fringe, carrying the line of plants well down to the ground, and blending it with the grass, besides making a very brilliant display in the blooming season. Tufts of this furze, or of various brooms, scattered along the margins of park plantations, would often be exceedingly valuable in giving roundness and finish to their outline, and would furnish splendid patches of colour in spring, besides being green and lively through the winter. In this part of the pleasure grounds, the varied openings occasioned by Mr. Repton's operations on the southern belt are especially conspicuous and important, as that belt is so comparatively near.

Two other avenues, besides the one already named, cross the principal lawn of the pleasure grounds. That farthest to the west is composed of Deodar cedars, with a row of Irish yews in front of each line of them, the yews alternating with the cedars. These deodars, of which there are some in other parts of the gardens, are very beautiful specimens, and must, in time, become grand objects. This avenue is terminated by a small temple at the north end, containing a statue of the Dying Gladiator. The temple was much used by Pope when Lord Warwick was proprietor of this place. Another avenue is of *Araucaria imbricata*, the plants being very regular and healthy, and having lines of *Cupressus juniperoides* in front of them.

In addition to these avenues of choice plants, great numbers of rare specimens are placed about the lawn. There is an unusually large and good *Abies Webbiana, Aralia japonica,* a fine Catalpa, many scarce and beautful pines, firs, &c., and some very excellent variegated hollies.

At the western end of the garden, a cedar of Lebanon has been used as the nucleus of a small detached plot, planted to resemble a cemetery of the Crusaders said to be still existing at Jerusalem. Its surface is varied by masses of fused bricks, thrown up into irregular shapes, and formed in one part into a rude and picturesque arch. Groups of the same material are continued from this spot into the pleasure grounds, at the side of a secluded walk which affords an exit from the place towards Brentford. All these masses are partially clothed with ivy, and having generally a rugged outline, it is remarkable how speedily the ivy disguises the meanness of the material, and converts it into a beautiful feature. Irish yews, junipers, savins, weeping willows, &c., constitute the other and appropriate ornaments of the so-called cemetery; which must be looked at solely as a picturesque episode in the garden, and without reference to its avowed purpose.

Nearly adjoining the plot just described is a large circular hollow, surrounded with masses of shrubs and trees, and having a fountain in the centre, which plays over a pile of moss-covered rocks. On the west side of this spot is another fountain, half shrouded by trees, which are mostly weeping willows. Many of the trees here take picturesque forms, and are covered with ivy. The water trickles over masses of stone, clothed with many species of wild plants, and is very pretty in summer, or when the sun is shining. This little scene is quite complete in itself, and being in a corner, and a hollow, much shut in by plantations, it furnishes an agreeable change.

In a survey of these pleasure grounds there is much to satisfy and please. A great deal of variety, and several delightful minor compartments, are secured. In general, too, there is much harmony and good taste shown in the arrangements and the decorations. The leading cause for regret is that the breadth of the lawn has been sacrificed to obtain the cross avenues we have spoken of. These lines of plants cut up the lawn very much, and destroy all appearance of openness or extent. Two of them are likewise altogether without an object; and as the plants in them all grow up, we can only conceive of their becoming still more objectionable. Scarcely any consideration can ever justify the use of lines of plants *across* a lawn that comes into view from the house; and the only show of reason which can be assigned for their use in this case is, that they supply the means of exhibiting some highly beautiful plants to great advantage.

A quiet walk from the western side of the lawn leads through the plantations, beneath an arched trellis embowered with climbers, to the department in which the plant houses are situated. And here the real treasures of the place begin to develop themselves. In regard to the size and rarity of the specimens, the superiority of their cultivation, and the quantity possessed, there is probably no collection in Europe which, in all these respects, can at all rival this.

A walk through the plant houses supplies continual food for wonder and admiration. The conviction is pressed upon us at every step that the power of cultivation " can no further go." And everything is done with a liberality as to space and conveniences which is quite of a piece with the fame of this establishment. The well-known success which attends the exhibition of plants from this place at the great metropolitan shows, will no longer be matter of surprise after the collection is seen. The only occasion for astonishment will be that any other competitor should ever be able to carry off the highest prize.

At the front of the principal group of plant houses is a somewhat square area, arranged as a flower garden, and having little wire temples, as supports for climbing roses, at the corners. Walls covered with climbers inclose it at the sides, and the charming *Clematis montana* is among the most conspicuous plants on these walls. There is a fountain in the centre, and some vases are placed about in parts, while masses of stones at the base of the buildings, and in front of them, receive a variety of pretty trailing and alpine plants. The flower-beds are cut out of the grass, and are each furnished with a single kind of plant, in the usual manner.

The houses, which are composed of a series of span roofs, slightly varying in height, occupy a considerable space, but they do not present one uniform front. The two end compartments, which are supposed to be about 20 ft. wide by 75 ft. long, and each of which is covered by a span roof, are devoted to greenhouse plants. Between these and the centre of the group, there are two short houses, about 15 ft. long, against the back wall, leaving an open gravelled space in the front of them. These small houses are assigned to tall Cacti, large specimen plants, or a mixed collection. The central compartment is about 55 ft. wide, by 75 ft. long, and is roofed by three parallel spans, the middle one being highest. The whole of this portion is kept at stove heat, and it has a glass partition across the middle, separating the stove plants from the orchids. Two other glass partitions in the back part divide it into three unequal spaces, the larger middle portion being given up chiefly to the *Amherstia*, a small aquarium, and some mixed orchids and stove plants, while the side divisions are filled with orchids alone.

The first thing which we notice on entering the plant houses is, that they are raised fully 3 ft. above the ground level, and that therefore they are very dry, and may be made as airy as can be desired. Our next observation is that, although preparing the plants for exhibition is one of the primary objects of consideration here, yet the houses are constructed and the plants arranged so that they can be examined comfortably and displayed well. There is no want of neatness and finish in the buildings; and the stages, paths, &c., are contrived, and the plants disposed, as if everything were intended only to be enjoyed at home. There is no crowding, no inconvenient effort to make the most of the space, no putting the plants where they cannot be fully seen. Everything is planned with great simplicity, and each plant has a sufficient space accorded it to allow it to stand perfectly free, and bring every part of it into view.

A leading feature of the collection here is that the plants grown are all of the most ornamental kind. Although the bulk of the specimens are of rare kinds, and many of them are quite new,—for Mrs. Lawrence spares no expense in obtaining the first available plants of a good new species, and often procures the original specimen,—yet none but the really showy members of each tribe are cultivated, and everything that is not fit for making a fine display is excluded. Hence, there is scarcely a plant in the collection that does not, at some season of the year, perform an important part in maintaining its attractiveness; and all are capable of being so thinly placed about on the stages that each will have ample room to grow and to exhibit itself.

H

To obtain *large* specimens is another great point aimed at here. But this is only sought in so far as it is compatible with extreme *density* of habit, and a complete *mass of bloom*. Plants that look old or ragged are not allowed a place. And the desired result is attained by growing the plants in large pots (only the common pots and no kind of tub being used), and employing rather coarse and lumpy soil, partly mixed with drainage materials. There is also a regular system of pruning and training adopted, from the earliest stage of each plant's growth, so that it is never permitted to become thin or straggling. With many of the species, the shoots of young plants are stopped back several times in each year, and the most careful and constant attention is given to keep each shoot in its right place by sticks and ties. This plan of course imparts to the plants a somewhat formal appearance, and causes some of them to present a little forest of supporting sticks. But as the specimens become old enough to bloom well, they are less rigidly pruned, and begin to require fewer sticks, acquiring altogether a more natural aspect. Indeed, it is pleasing to observe that it is now becoming more the fashion to allow plants to take their natural shapes, with less help from sticks, and only so much pruning as will secure a broad and close mass of flowers.

Provision is likewise made here against the loss of larger specimens, or the having to discard them on account of their size or poorness, by bringing on a succession of plants, in different stages of growth ; young specimens being generally found more healthy, and richer in all the qualities of show plants, except mere size.

For the facility of removal, and also to render each plant more manageable, and prevent the stronger growing ones from injuring the others, everything is here grown in pots, and not planted out. When, therefore, a plant becomes large, or bare, or unhealthy, or in any way undesirable, it can be instantly taken away, without making any gap in the collection. And for the recovery of specimens that may have fallen into bad health, or for retarding the bloom of those which are wanted at a particular time, or for retaining any specimens in bloom that may be required for a special purpose, there are various subordinate houses, pits, and large wooden boxes or frames, in which any of these objects can be quietly carried out. In moving about large specimens, too, a contrivance is here adopted which is very simple and efficacious. It consists in putting an iron hoop, capable of contraction or enlargement according to the size of the pots, round the pot to be moved, just beneath the rim. This hoop is furnished with two strong hooks, one on each side, beneath which two hand spikes made to fit them are placed, and the plant is then carried as if it were on a hand-barrow.

In the greenhouses the most perfect ventilation is provided for by opening all the side lights, so that during the hottest weather the houses may be kept comparatively cool ; and, after the occurrence of great moisture, they may likewise immediately be dried. Beneath the stages, moreover, there are small slides or shutters, for further ventilation ; and these are very useful in winter, as the air they will admit passes over the heating pipes. By their means, likewise, the floor and lower parts of the house can be kept dry. The stages are, for the most part, covered with a thin coating of gravel ; and, to bring the plants as near as possible to the glass, and secure to them a greater amount of air, and guard them against becoming too moist, each of the specimens is generally raised on a large pot, so as to stand from 18 to 30 in. above the stage.

It will of course be impossible, were it even worth attempting, to do more than point out some of the general features of this collection. The two principal greenhouses contain nothing but specimens. The plants in them that are most conspicuous are Boronias, Epacrises, Polygalas, Eriostemons, Pimeleas, Leschenaultias, Croweas, Chironias, Chorozemas, Hoveas, &c., with a few climbing plants trained to low trellises. *Crowea saligna, Boronia crenata* and *serrulata, Chorozema cordata, Pimelea spectabilis,* all the Eriostemons, especially *E. buxifolium* and *intermedium,* and the charming old *Leschenaultia formosa,* are some of the plants here cultivated, which flower abundantly in all stages of their growth, and are of a free and excellent habit. Some 'idea of the size of many of the plants will be conveyed by mentioning that *Pimelea spectabilis* is 27 ft. in circumference, and that, from the edge of the pot over the whole surface of the plant, there is scarcely space enough to allow of the hand being introduced between any of the branches. Nearly every one of the shoots is crowned with a bunch of blossoms in the summer. *Gompholobium polymorphum grandiflorum* is treated as a bush, and makes a beautiful plant in this state.

In the stove the plants are equally good of their kind. A great many handsome climbers are here grown to trellises, and a few of this tribe are also trained up the slender pillars which support the roof. The *Allamanda cathartica, Schotti,* and *grandiflora, Stephanotis floribunda, Convolvulus pentanthus, Hoya imperialis* and *Bedwilli,* several species of *Ipomœa, Echites, Æschynanthus,* and *Combretum, Clerodendron splendens,* &c., are some of the principal dwarf climbers, and are in great perfection. *Medinilla speciosa,* a rare and exceedingly ornamental species, with very large leaves and conspicuous drooping spikes of pink flowers succeeded by showy crimson fruit, is in an excellent state, and blooms for several months.

A glass partition, with a light iron frame (the rest of the houses being of wood), separates the commoner stove from the orchid houses, and from the compartment devoted to the *Amherstia.* Of this last, there is an extraordinary specimen, which is, perhaps, the greatest feature of the whole collection. It is now quite a little tree, although it has only been here four or five years, and has flowered here for the first time in Europe, very few other plants of it existing in England. At the present time (January, 1851) it is again showing a quantity of bloom, which usually expands about April. The leaves, which are pinnated, and are paler in the young state, are of the handsomest and amplest character, forming a head of the most graceful kind. The flowers are vermilion-coloured, and are produced in large drooping racemes, after the manner of a laburnum or *Wistaria.* It is a native of the East Indies, from whence it was obtained through Dr. Wallich; and has reached its present state of perfection here in a surprisingly short period of time.

As it deserves, the plant here receives every attention. It is placed near the back of the house, and grows in a large tub, plunged in a bed of bark. An extra heating pipe passes round the plant, within about two yards of the tub, and an open zinc gutter for containing water is fixed to the top of this pipe. In the front of the plant is a small basin for aquatic plants: and provision is made for spreading over the plant, beneath the glass, an oiled calico screen, which runs on rollers, and which, when used, at once furnishes any required shade, and protects the leaves of the plant from the water that might drop from the roof. A high temperature and a moist atmosphere are preserved.

Besides some interesting aquatics, a number of gold fish are kept in the basin opposite the *Amherstia*, which is, moreover, furnished with a fountain. The back wall of this house is also partly clothed with ferns and orchids, and a few of the more purely tropical stove plants and orchids are placed at the sides of the house; but a considerable open space is wisely preserved in the middle, so as to give more consequence to the *Amherstia*, and cause it to be better seen. The *Barringtonia*, with its noble leaves, seems quite at home in this close stove; and there is a large plant of the curious *Grammatophyllum*, with a very beautiful climbing *Lycopodium*, which has large bluish fronds.

One of the two small orchid houses on either side of that which contains the *Amherstia* is used for Mexican species, and the other for such as require a rather higher temperature. The collection of both these tribes is good, and the plants well grown, but not remarkable. By the side of the paved path, and partly under the stage, there is an open channel or gutter provided for carrying off any water that may be used in syringing the plants, or washing the paths.

Behind the larger group of houses there is a very nice heath house, with a western aspect, and full of the choicest specimens in admirable health. Other and smaller houses are devoted to Pelargoniums, which are placed on stages, to Azaleas, to stove plants requiring bottom heat, and to miscellaneous articles. The Azaleas stand on pots, like the greenhouse specimens, and are most splendid examples of cultivation. As with the greenhouse plants (and also with the heaths) there are successional or younger specimens, which are preparing to supply the place of the larger ones when these wear out or become shabby.

A small stove, which contains a bark bed in addition to the usual heating power, is almost wholly filled with Ixoras of different kinds, plunged in the bark. They are superb plants, and this method of treatment keeps them very luxuriant. *I. javanica*, which is nearly new, has attained a considerable size here, and produces its pale orange flowers most profusely. An extraordinary specimen of *Gardenia Fortuni*, some Rondeletias, &c., are kept in this house likewise; and a wire trellis is beautifully covered with the charming *Dipladenia crassinoda*. Another small stove, with a similar bark bed in the centre, and heated by a tank traversed with hot-water pipes beneath the bark bed, is occupied with various kinds of *Æschynanthus*, Gardenias, and such other plants as flourish best with bottom heat. The very best effects result from this mode of plunging certain kinds of stove plants in a material supplying bottom heat, as they never thrive half so well under any other system of management.

A span-roofed house has lately been built for East Indian orchids, on the north side of the area containing the plant houses. It is heated by hot-water pipes, which pass all round it in the ordinary way, and has no other heating material. The species belonging to the Vanda tribe are chiefly grown here. There are some noble plants of *Aerides* and *Argræcum eburneum*. And the entire contents of the house are so excellent that they are only surpassed by Mr. Rucker's collection. It is a most desirable plan thus to bring this class of orchids together in one house, as well because they can thus be more appropriately treated, as on account of the effect produced by such a combination of exclusively elegant forms.

Calceolarias, Cinerarias, tall Cacti, and many tribes that we need not mention, are cultivated here in the best order in other houses and pits.

Our notice, indeed, can by no means do justice to the place, which contains, even among its minor features and mechanical agents, very much that must interest the general cultivator. For example, there are several large box-like frames, made high enough to contain moderately large specimen plants, and capable of being covered with oiled calico or with glass lights, and ventilated by small slides at the ends, which, with an eastern aspect, are well adapted for receiving plants that have been newly potted, or such as are out of health, or those which may be wanted to be kept from blooming so soon, or to be preserved longer in flower. There are also some very convenient span-roofed pits, the lights of which work on a kind of hook-like hinge at the top, and are fastened down by iron pins in windy weather. There can be little doubt that pits of this description, made about 7 ft. wide and 4 ft. high (or a little higher) in the centre, with the lights to lift up (not slide) from the side, and capable of being taken off altogether if required, are in all respects the cheapest and the most convenient, and the best structures in which to grow those greenhouse plants that may be wanted for decorating a conservatory, drawing-room, or other place where flowers are chiefly demanded.

As a screen to some of the outbuildings in the plant-house department a strong privet hedge is employed, the treatment of which struck us as worth mentioning. The top of it is cut into a series of crescent shapes, the hollow of each crescent having the closely-pruned head of a standard rose just rising above it. A character by no means commonplace, and which may serve as a hint to improve upon, is thus obtained.

The period at which the greatest display of flowers may be seen at this place is during the month of May, when the majority of the house plants are in their highest glory. In June, also, they are almost equally fine ; and in so large an establishment there will, of course, be many plants in flower at all seasons. Mr. May is Mrs. Lawrence's present gardener.

Gunnersbury, the seat of *Baron Rothschild*, is also at Ealing, about half a mile nearer London than Mrs. Lawrence's place. It is a retired and elegant villa, very agreeably situated. The house stands on the top of a sloping bank, which affords an excellent opportunity for having an Italian terrace on the garden front. This terrace is particularly well treated, having a low wall with vases along the front, and being entered upon at one end by an enriched arch, attached to the house and supported with trees, while the other end is finished by a handsome alcove, containing a statue of the Apollo Belvidere.

From the terrace walk there is a pleasant view across a lake in the low ground and the small park to the woods and gentle hills on the Surrey side of the Thames ; everything in this scene being rich and accordant, and the whole being very nicely framed with old trees.

A walk to the westward from the terrace conducts us along the side of the open park, where we soon arrive at a pleasing recess, in which is a marble statue of Eve at the fountain. This is very artistically embowered with ivy, and is so far kept out of sight till it is approached as to convey the idea of being a shaded and sacred nook, into which the living mother of mankind, represented in the figure, might have retired. Two tall and fine cypresses stand by the side of this recess, as if keeping a kind of guard over its sanctity.

A little further from the house there is a nearly circular piece of water, open towards the park on one side, and surrounded with noble trees in other parts. Both the lakes are supplied from a spring on the estate.

This portion of the grounds was arranged by the celebrated Kent. The formality of the outline of the water is now slightly broken by the branches of some of the trees dipping into it. There is a very fine tulip-tree among the other large specimens, and a cluster of excellent cedars. Here, as elsewhere under similar circumstances, it will be noted that a wooden platform, for the purpose of using the boat, is thrust out into the water several yards, and has an exceedingly prominent and disagreeable appearance; which might easily be obviated by deepening the water at any particular point along its margin, and making a small landing-stage to follow precisely the line of the water's edge.

By the side of this piece of water, in the midst of the group of cedars just mentioned, is a classic temple, from the front of which there is a beautiful view over the water, the park, and the country. The interior of this temple appears to be used as a billiard room. It contains at present, however, a most interesting collection of stone figures, illustrative of the "Beggar's Opera," which formerly stood in the open air, but had unfortunately become so injured by exposure that they are now placed here. They are by Thom, the well-known Scotch sculptor of Tam o' Shanter and Souter Johnnie, and are among the greatest *notabilia* of the place. Although executed in sandstone, they are taken from life with the utmost minuteness of detail, the tatters of the garments, the patches (some placed beneath and some upon the older parts of the clothes), the holes and mendings of the shoes, one of which has the sole coming off, and even the very stitches, with their customary want of neatness and concealment, by which the various attempts at preserving some degree of soundness are effected, are all represented with a wonderful fidelity and power. But the expression of some of the countenances is still more striking. In the face of the old soldier, with his wooden arm and leg, who has taken on his only knee the old woman whom he loved in youth, and holds her with his single arm, there is a marvellous expression of resuscitated voluptuousness which is almost more than responded to in the cunning but inviting looks of his ancient companion. The ferocity, too, of the stalwart tinker, who is taking his revenge on the terror-stricken and crushed little fiddler for supposed wrongs done to his wife, is most admirably depicted. There is, indeed, a spirit and a truthfulness about these objects which makes us regret that the unhappy artist did not use less perishable materials, and that he was not more cordially encouraged.

At the north side of the temple containing these figures is a small circular flower garden, surrounded with neat festoons of climbers on a wire frame, and nearly beneath them is a low iron trellis covered with China roses. This flower garden is very nicely furnished with plants in the summer, and the beds are not too crowded. In its neighbourhood there is an immense plant of *Magnolia grandiflora*, which is quite like a tree, and many beautiful specimens of various other low trees. Gunnersbury is rather famed for its large orange-trees, which are kept in an orangery in the lower part of the pleasure grounds.

The kitchen garden here is not remarkable in itself, but is well cultivated, under the charge of Mr. Mills, who is a most experienced kitchen and forcing gardener, and has written several works on different branches of this department, besides being noted in particular for his successful cultivation of cucumbers and pines. On one of the walls of this garden, among a number of middle-aged pear trees, which are in first-rate condition, we observed a tree which, while in full leaf and fruit, had gradually withered away, without any apparent cause. This is one of the strange things which, since the occurrence of the potato disease, are so comparatively frequent among shrubs and smaller plants, but which is seldom seen in fruit trees, where everything would appear conducive to their health.

The glass houses here are somewhat old-fashioned, though they yield excellent crops of grapes, especially a large span-roofed vinery attached to Mr. Mills's residence. A quantity of stove and greenhouse plants are likewise grown very nicely in some of them. We noticed some fine specimens of *Epiphyllum truncatum*, which Mr. Mills contrives to flower twice each year through keeping them always in a warm moist house. We also remarked some young healthy Ixoras in small pots, grown to a single stem, in order to produce one very large head of flowers each. The practice, which is rather common with Hydrangeas and a few similar plants, may be found well worthy of more extensive adoption in small places, where specimens of great size are quite unattainable, for a cultivator with moderate means might thus have the finest examples of various flowers in a small way.

Forced fruits and vegetables not being so much required here as they once were, the forcing department is not so vigorously maintained. Still, when we were there in the autumn of last year, there were melons just ripening off their third crop, cucumbers in various stages of growth, and a great number of very healthy pines. Of the latter fruit Mr. Mills has cut at least one every day for the last two years. The old system of heating by dung linings and plunging in bark beds is that generally adopted here for the pines; and most of the frames are heated by dung also, of which there happens to be a very ample supply. Somewhat less than a dozen pines are now grown in pits on the planting-out system, and these are simply to obtain large fruit. Only one plant occupies the centre of each light in the small frame or pit; but these plants are prodigies of health and vigour. They are growing in peat earth, or in half peat half loam mixed, and the soil is just raised up in roundish hillocks in the middle of the pits, nowhere touching the sides. It is singular that the plan of planting out pines, so much recommended by Mr. Mills, and practised in many large and small provincial gardens, should neither here nor at any other place which we visited near the metropolis, be adopted for more than a few specimens. All the other pines at Gunnersbury, besides those we have referred to, are grown in pots.

Cucumbers are grown here in the ordinary frames, and also in boxes on a shelf at the back of one of the vineries. A kind called the Jewess is Mr. Mills's own favourite. In the open air we observed a new sort of pickling cucumber, which never grows large, and bears very profusely. It is called the Carolina Gherkin.

Mrs. Marryatt's, Wimbledon House, has been elaborately and pictorially described by Loudon, and, like Mrs. Lawrence's, is open once a week to the public in the summer season. At one period, too, Mr. Redding, the gardener, was a very successful exhibitor of plants, and a great many highly ornamental species were first introduced to this place, and originally flowered here. Latterly, however, less attention has been paid to maintaining a high horticultural position; the trees all over the estate have become crowded; plants are very rarely grown for the exhibitions; and scarcely anything is conducted with the same spirit as formerly.

This estate, which comprises about 100 acres, is close to the delightful village of Wimbledon, and embraces some beautiful undulations of surface, charming views across Wimbledon Park, and, in one part, a very rich piece of the river Thames, with much of the valley through which part of the Thames flows, and the hills of Middlesex and Harrow in the distance. Although beautifully placed, however, and presenting some good natural features, the artist who designed it has by no means made the most of it; and now that the trees are becoming crowded, the defects in the plan are more conspicuous.

The house, which is very ample and complete, is rather too near the village, and hence the drive is a little too short for a place of this extent. Were the house farther away from other dwellings, and did we not see it directly we enter the gates, the shortness of the drive would be, as at Kenwood, an advantage. There is a conservatory attached to the house, in which, besides many sculptures and other ornaments, is one of the first plants of *Tacksonia pinnatistipula*, which bloomed here before flowering anywhere else in England, and still covers the roof of the conservatory.

From the garden front of the house there is a good view across the park to a sheet of water in the hollow, and over the trees behind this to a wooded hill beyond. Besides a few effective groups of trees, a charming specimen of an old variegated holly, covered with ivy, stands in the park in front of the house. A walk to the right then carries us through a strip of pleasure ground on the north side of the park, and amongst some very large and varied evergreen oaks, and tufts of hollies, Portugal laurels, rhododendrons, &c. There is, in one part, a small hollow nearly filled with rhododendrons, which are now large and picturesque. There is also a gigantic single plant of the common rhododendron.

At the bottom of the walk just spoken of we arrive at the lake, near the corner of which, on an island, are the remains of a chapel, once much used by the Prince of Condé during the time of his residence here. This island is approached by a bridge, now picturesquely covered with ivy; and from the midst of the other trees which are growing on the island, two or three Lombardy poplars rise, and form, with the other trees, a most beautiful group. Unhappily, they are now decaying at the tops, and will soon have to be removed. A walk to the north-west from this point leads round the boundary of the place, through what is called the wilderness, where there are some fish-ponds. Another piece of water is seen in the hollow below the larger lake. Skirting the lower margin of the principal lake by a green path, backed with trees and evergreens, we first pass an enormous beech tree of the noblest character, and afterwards, near the western end of the lake, come to a fine ivy-clad oak, and the original specimen of *Magnolia acuminata*. It is from a point near the northern end of the lake that the view of the Thames and its valley is to be caught, and this, on a fine day, is one of the most delightful kind. Some of the principal London buildings are also embraced from this spot.

At the south-western end of the lake there is an iron bridge. The walk to the right from this bridge takes us through a thin covert of trees of no particular character, by the side of a narrow winding continuation of the lake, till we merge into another open part of the park, skirting which, with charming scenes across Wimbledon Park, we pass to the grotto. This structure takes the exterior form of a small temple, from the front of which the landscape is very sylvan, varied, and lovely.

On entering the door of this apparent temple, we are astonished to find ourselves in a grotto, built by Bushel, after the manner of that at Oatlands, and lined with similarly unnatural materials. Parts of this grotto, however, where spar only has been employed, and where the surface is broken up into a variety of intricate little cells and recesses, are good. A small aperture at the back, glazed with yellow glass, exhibits the branches and leaves of the plants behind it in a curious colour; and no doubt some really desirable effects might be produced in this way by the employment of a more fitting colour. As a *grotto* this building is, in the main, most unsatisfactory; and the mixing up together of the grotto and the temple is strangely incongruous.

Returning towards the house, we find the flower garden and plant houses on our right, and enter the former through a small gate in the wire fence by which it is inclosed. This flower garden is remarkable for its extent and its variety, as it covers between 3 and 4 acres, and comprises, it seems, nearly 200 beds of different sorts of plants. It also contains a great many interesting specimen plants, and an unusual number of the species which are used in bedding. But it is not laid out with any regularity, nor do the beds or specimens unite well with each other, or form a symmetrical and harmonious whole. The most that can be said of it is, that by the irregularity of the arrangement, the variety of the plants and ornaments, and the beauty and size of many of the specimens, a picturesque and therefore pleasing assemblage is produced.

Whether in a flower garden, which is necessarily an object of art, which generally accompanies a building, and which is intended for the display of the choicest flowers which will at all bear exposure, any departure from the strictest regularity of arrangement is at all allowable, may admit of much debate. In this case, however, where the area is large, and the accompanying plant houses have no architectural pretensions, and the numerous specimen plants are of sufficient size to prevent the eye from ranging over it all at once, some departure from rule is certainly justifiable, if ever it be so; and there can be little danger in asserting that this flower garden is, in summer and autumn, the best part of the place.

There are eight unequal divisions in the flower garden, separated from each other by walks. The plant houses stand at the back of it, but they are not in the centre, and a wall covered with climbers extends from the west end of them to the limits of the garden. A curved walk runs along the front of the houses and wall, leaving a border to both. From the centre of the houses, a walk passes straight down the garden, and another and longer walk crosses this at right angles in the middle of the garden. The remaining walks run up and down the garden in a nearly straight line, except that along the bottom, which is curved and irregular. At the point where the two principal walks cross each other, there is a marble basin and fountain, round which the walks pass. There are also numerous vases by the side of the main walk from the plant houses. Another fountain is placed in the centre of a larger oblong basin, at the lower part of the garden, this being surrounded by small rocks, and used for aquatic plants.

In the middle of another compartment is a large rustic open pavilion or arbour, the outside of which is a series of arches, with a pole in the centre, to the top of which poles from all the upright pillars are fastened. This bower is clothed chiefly with climbing roses, and has a great rustic vase filled with flowers in the centre. An additional open bower for climbers exists on the other side of the garden; and also an arcade or covered way for the same kind of plants along the western boundary of the garden. Wire baskets on the ground, filled with flowers, and having climbers trained over the handles, with vases also containing flowers, are scattered about in other parts, to increase the variety.

H 3

For the most part, the beds are a series of ovals and circles, of different sizes, dotted down promiscuously; though sometimes a row of alternate ovals and small circles runs along each side of a walk, and occasionally the beds are of a slightly different shape, and thrown together in a more regular pattern. In filling the beds, too, with flowers, the general irregularity is preserved; for, except at the margins of the walks, or in any symmetrical pattern, some of them are furnished with tall-growing plants, such as dahlias, &c., and others have the more usual dwarf flowers or those of an intermediate height, but disposed without anything beyond a *general* balance of parts being studied.

Of specimen plants in the flower garden, two trees of the deciduous cypress opposite the plant houses are very conspicuous, and one of them, from having lost its top, has taken a singular spreading habit. A particularly beautiful plant of the *Araucaria imbricata* is, perhaps, the best-furnished specimen around London. It is extremely dense, and every branch, down to the very base, remains quite perfect, although it is growing most vigorously, and is from 15 to 18 ft. high, at least. *Spiræa Lindleyana*, with its large pinnated foliage and bold racemes of flowers, makes an excellent lawn plant here. *Hippophäe rhamnoides*, a beautiful low tree, possessing much character, is in a very fine state. A large mass of ivy forms an interesting lawn accompaniment; as does also a group of Savin, a splendid tuft of *Gaultheria shallon*, some excellent plants of *Andromeda floribunda*, and various groups of Azaleas and other American plants. At the bottom of the garden, indeed, where the shape of the ground is a little more broken and varied, the numerous elegant tribes of American plants are largely grown, and in masses which render them highly effective. By the side of the larger pool of water, there is a good-sized tree of a very peculiar willow, with pendulous branches and curled foliage, forming an elegant object, very suitable for the margins of water. At the edge of this pool we also remarked the uncommon *Arundo donax*, which is a reed-like plant of a striking appearance. A bed of a species of *Lycopodium*, which Mr. Redding calls the American moss, was growing in the lower ground, and had a very curious aspect, imparting some little novelty to a place where the beds are so numerous.

The plant houses, which are heavy, and not well adapted for growing plants, consist of a large and lofty central greenhouse, a stove by the side of it, and a good orchid house. There are two vineries on the east side of the large greenhouse. The orchids, of which there is a considerable number, are mostly good specimens, and in excellent health. The vines had suffered very much from mildew last season.

Leaving the flower garden by the walk that leads to the house, and passing through a rustic arch over the gateway, the path becomes lined with an avenue of middle-aged elms until it reaches an old conservatory or orangery. From hence to the house it has a number of vases and China jars, for supporting flowers in pots, ranged along either side of it during summer. We must not omit to note that a particular breed of cows, which are chiefly black with a white band across the back, is preserved in the park here, and from their peculiar colour, they are rather picturesque.

At *Cheam*, in Surrey, about 12 miles from London, the seat of *Sir Edmund Antrobus, Bart.*, has acquired much celebrity from the admirable plants which are grown there, under the management of Mr. Green, the gardener, who generally secures some of the highest prizes at the great metropolitan exhibitions.

In the place itself there is little to excite attention. A small and very slightly decorated lawn separates the house from a park of limited extent, in which the groups of trees are not conspicuous for age or rarity, but are simply good middle-sized specimens. As the ground falls away from the house into a hollow, and rises again towards the south, some little variety and indefiniteness of view is obtained. But the main characteristic is that of a quiet and secluded home scene.

Between the house and the kitchen garden, a small corner, partially shut in by trees, and backed by the kitchen garden wall, affords space for a little flower garden, in which are grown the ordinary summer flowers, with a variety of Fuchsias, &c., the wall being covered with Tropœolums, Maurandyas, and many fugitive as well as permanent climbers. A walk and shrubbery border is continued round the kitchen garden, and the border contains two very handsome specimens of *Cupressus torulosus*, which are 15 ft. or more in height, and very dense. It loses none of its elegance by having grown to this large size, and is, from the uncommonness of its character and appearance, a peculiarly desirable object either for lawns or shrubberies.

Entering the kitchen garden, which is of limited extent, we see a few common-looking houses against the back wall, and when told that these and two or three pits by their side contain all the extraordinary plants which are sent to the exhibitions, and are likewise used for growing grapes, &c., we feel that this is indeed the pursuit of cultivation "under difficulties." The only house in the place that seems at all fit for growing plants in is a low pit-like structure, which is comparatively new, and is used for stove plants. There is a path at the back part of this house, and the rest of the space is occupied by a raised pit, filled with bark, in which the pots are plunged. It is heated by hot water, and occupied by Ixoras, the species of *Æschynanthus*, climbers trained to low trellises, Allamandas, *Lisianthus Russellianus*, &c., all in the richest health. *Allamanda grandiflora* is here grafted on the old *A. cathartica*, and grows and flowers more strongly in consequence. Mr. Green is remarkably successful in the culture of *Lisianthus Russellianus*, which, though usually considered a shy plant, flourishes here in great beauty, and single specimens bear hundreds of flowers in the summer. Its principal requirement is to be kept dry in the winter, and grown rapidly afterwards.

Besides the stove plants in the house just alluded to, and of which there is a very select and well-chosen stock, a mixed collection of equally choice and good greenhouse plants is grown here. But it is in Azaleas, and the larger kinds of Cacti and Heaths, that the place is particularly rich. And these are grown in the most inconvenient houses, being merely old-fashioned vineries, planted against the back wall of the garden, and having an ordinary lean-to roof. By dint of great contrivance, and the use of various kinds of stages, the space in these houses is all employed, and the plants are brought up tolerably near the glass. But from the roof being lofty, and the paths very narrow and of irregular heights, the houses are neither adapted for comfort nor display. And yet the Azaleas and Cacti are such as can scarcely be equalled in any other place, whatever may be the facilities it possesses.

Of Azaleas, all the best show kinds are grown, and there are glorious specimens of each sort, which are literally sheeted over with bloom in the month of May. In Cacti, Mr. Green has found the greatest advantage result from grafting the weaker and thin-stemmed varieties on the strong-growing ones. *Cereus speciosissimus* is extensively used as a stock for the various kinds of Epiphylla, and answers most perfectly. Even the very strong *C. hexagonus* has been employed as a stock in one or two instances. *Epiphyllum speciosum, truncatum, Ackermannii, Ackermannii grandiflora*, and others, are all grafted on the *Cereus* before named. Some are, however, grown on their own roots, for variety. There are magnificent plants of most of these, and of *Cereus speciosissimus, Mallisonii*, &c., with several hybrids. The best kind now grown, in fact, is a hybrid between *C. speciosissimus* and *E. Ackermannii grandiflora*, having flowers of the size of the latter variety, with the exquisite blue centre of the older species. There is likewise a promising newly-imported *Epiphyllum*, with broad and deeply notched leaves, which has not yet flowered. *Cereus Egertonii*, with the habit of *C. Mallisonii*, and having a purple centre to its flowers, is considered superior to the older variety.

From the space being so limited, the Azaleas, Cacti, &c., are mostly put out of doors, under the partial shade of a north wall, during the latter part of summer; and this, no doubt, renders them more fit for standing through the winter in a comparatively crowded state, while it also tends to ripen their annual growth, and to strengthen their disposition to flower. A better screen, however, than a north wall has been tried by Mr. Green, and given great satisfaction. It consists in planting a row of scarlet runners across the open garden, and placing the plants behind them. These are found to shelter the plants sufficiently, while they yet allow them some light, and they admit of the plants getting plenty of air without producing currents.

In some frames and pits Pelargoniums and Calceolarias are well cultivated. Of the latter tribe Mr. Green has long been a successful breeder, and has raised many good seedlings. A new cucumber pit, well contrived, and heated by hot water, contained, last autumn, a set of young plants, which were to be trained up to trellises near the glass, and were intended to last all the present year. The system of growing cucumbers to trellises is now, we perceive, in very general use around London.

As an illustration of what skill and application will effect with the most imperfect appliances, the plants at this place, were they not so thoroughly good in themselves, would be emphatically worth seeing. But their more absolute merits of course increase their attractiveness.

The gardens of *A. Palmer, Esq.*, at Cheam, are only a short distance from those of Sir E. Antrobus, on the other side of the village. The two places possess much the same character, and similar classes of plants are cultivated in them, especially Cacti and Azaleas. With both these latter tribes the collection is well furnished; and although the houses are more commodious, and the plants less numerous, than at Sir E. Antrobus's, Mr. Falconer, the gardener, turns them out a good deal at the end of the summer and during the early autumn. A new seedling *Azalea* has been raised here by Mr. Falconer, and called Bianca. It has perfectly white flowers, which are large and of a good shape, being much superior in every respect to the old *A. indica alba*.

One of the houses here has lately been fresh glazed with rough plate glass, the panes in the upper lights being joined at the ends by being cut very square, and not at all overlapped. It is not yet ascertained whether this mode of glazing will keep out wet; and it is exceedingly probable that, from the almost necessary imperfection of the joints, it will occasion drip. It certainly looks neat, and saves just a small quantity of glass.

In the stove, some old plants of *Renanthera coccinea* are made to bloom freely every year, by hanging them up near the glass, and keeping them almost dry, during the latter part of the summer. Treated in this way, the plants themselves look a little yellow, but their showy flowers more than repay the diminished verdure of their appearance.

Much attention is given by Mr. Palmer to growing and preserving the different kinds of fruit, and the apples, pears, &c., are all good, and are stored with great care. Some of the older kinds of apples are also to be found here in their genuine state. Down the middle walk of the kitchen garden, various plums are grown upon a wooden trellis, which is arched over it. The plan answers very well, and saves space, besides making the walk into a sort of bower.

Nonesuch, the seat of *W. F. G. Farmer, Esq.,* nearly adjoins Mr. Palmer's estate, but is a more extensive domain, with an ample park, and good pleasure grounds. The property has for many years been noted as having supplied the site of one of Queen Elizabeth's palaces, which had fine old terrace gardens attached to it. Scarcely a relic of these now, however, remains, and the present house is quite on the other side of the estate. A noble elm tree in the park, not far from the supposed site of the former palace gardens, still bears the name of Queen Elizabeth's elm, and is a beautiful specimen.

Towards the end of the eighteenth century, the gardens at Nonesuch were altered to the modern style by Whately, the author of "Observations on Modern Gardening," whose brother then owned the property. At a subsequent period the house and gardens were entirely removed, and now occupy a position near Cheam. They have been most extensively renovated and improved, within the last seven or eight years, by the conversion of the old kitchen garden into pleasure grounds, and the formation of a new kitchen garden on the east side of the approach from Cheam.

Entering the estate from the village of Cheam, there is an avenue of Scotch firs leading from a main road to the house, by the side of the garden wall. This avenue is a rare and beautiful object, as the trees have become old, and many of them are very picturesque.

On the south side of the house there is a charming piece of lawn, on which a grand old cedar spreads its branches over a large surface, while many venerable trees inclose a bold and pleasing hollow. Beyond the more immediate precincts of the house, a series of flower gardens, with patches of open lawn and masses of low shrubs and specimen plants, cover the site of much of the former kitchen garden, and are terminated by a raised terrace bank, along the front of a nice group of plant houses. Outside this terrace a pinetum has been formed, in which many of the plants are making a rapid growth, and will soon begin to acquire a good character.

Within the flower garden a long wire arch, covered with climbing roses, is a conspicuous feature, and large quantities of standard and climbing roses are scattered about. Around a basin of water there are some excellent specimens of *Cupressus pendula* and other plants ; and on the adjoining lawn is a singular plant of the Deodar cedar, with very dense weeping branches. The weeping holly, and a great number of rare ornamental plants, are dotted about the place, and will in time impart to it a highly exotic air.

In the beauty and fineness of the grass on the lawns, the rich and appropriate furniture of the flower-beds, the healthiness of all the groups and specimens, and the peculiar neatness and finish of everything, this place is a very striking example of the effects of culture and good keeping, and does honour to Mr. Carson, the gardener, under whom all the recent changes have been effected.

The plant houses, like the rest of the place, are neat, elegant, and appropriate; and comprise a stove, a greenhouse, and an orchid house, glazed in the best manner, and heated with hot water, by Mr. Weeks of Chelsea. They contain a first-rate selection of plants, which are in the highest order; every plant being a specimen, and each specimen an ornamental species. Nothing could be more beautiful or more gratifying than this very compact collection, the excellence of which is only very partially declared by the many prizes which Mr. Carson obtains at the great London exhibitions. The orchids, especially, are unusually good, and are arranged very tastefully. A recess in the orchid house, over an open cistern filled with water, is devoted to ferns, which are attached to the wall, and are most characteristic and elegant. The backs of the houses, with the accompanying conveniences, are nicely screened from view by a mass of large evergreens; and a small contiguous frame ground is also inclosed by shrubs, so as not at all to intrude on the pleasure grounds.

In the new kitchen garden everything is executed with equal judgment and taste. The forcing houses and their contents are all excellent. Cucumbers are trained on trellises, one set of plants bearing a whole year. A collection of splendid Azaleas is kept here, except during the flowering season. They are never placed out of doors in summer and autumn, and consequently look very green and fresh through the late autumn and winter months.

Cambridge House is the residence of *H. Bevan, Esq.*, at Twickenham, just above Richmond Bridge. It is well placed for taking in a near view of Richmond Hill, with its scattered villas and broad masses of wood, while the garden front is not much overlooked from any public road. The pleasure grounds are not large, comprising chiefly a walk and narrow lawn along the front of the house to the kitchen garden, and having a number of specimen plants and a few flower-beds placed on the lawn. But they lie well open to the park, from which they are only separated by a light fence, and which has thus all the effect of a large lawn. Many fine elms adorn the place in different parts.

Attached to the house is a good conservatory, in which, besides the usual decorations of plants in pots and climbers trained to the roof, there are many elegant ornaments, such as richly-carved brackets attached to the wall, for receiving conspicuous and spreading specimens, handsome marble basket-like vases, supported on the heads of beautiful marble figures and filled with graceful plants, and other sculptured marble figures. An air of great richness and variety is imparted by these objects, which nearly always have a good appearance in a conservatory attached to a mansion.

At a little distance from the house, there is a large and lofty greenhouse, or orangery, for orange-trees and other tall greenhouse plants. The roof is covered with vines, which answer well for a late crop. There is another show greenhouse, in which, among some good specimens of ordinary species, we noticed a number of seedling Pelargoniums, of bedding-out kinds, and of the scarlet-flowered variegated sorts, and the cherry-coloured varieties raised at Lord Kilmorey's. Several of them are distinct, and will be useful in varying the appearance of flower-beds.

A neat gateway, of open iron work, leads from the pleasure grounds to the kitchen garden, where there are some excellent ranges of glass, in which grapes, peaches, pines, &c., are well forced, and in a lengthened succession. This department is a good deal attended to, and everything appears to be managed neatly and successfully. The houses are heated by hot water, and the pits, of which there are several ranges for pines, melons, cucumbers, &c., derive their heat from dung linings. In order to prevent the latter from looking untidy, or becoming a nuisance, and to save the heat from escaping, they are all covered with wooden shutters, which fasten down closely over them, and keep them entirely out of sight.

In one of the larger houses there is a nice collection of stove plants, including most of the more fashionable and showy kinds, with a variety of low climbers grown to trellises. Earthenware troughs are placed over the heating pipes in this house, for containing water to produce evaporation. A row of capital hollyhocks was growing in a border of the kitchen garden when we visited the place last October; and this is one of the few gardens near London in which we observed any care bestowed on that very handsome and valuable flower. Its usefulness for planting among low shrubs, or towards the front of new ornamental plantations, to break the outline, is by no means appreciated as it should be. Mr. Pennycook is Mr. Bevan's gardener.

Pain's Hill, the seat of *Mrs. Cooper*, at Cobham in Surrey, about three miles further from London than Claremont, is a place which contains such splendid features, and has been so much referred to in different works as a grand specimen of modern landscape gardening, that we judged it worthy of a special pilgrimage, and were not at all disappointed. It was laid out by the Hon. Charles Hamilton, son of the Earl of Abercorn, and is said to have been formed from an old common or waste.

The house stands on the summit of a steep slope, at the bottom of which runs the river Mole, and a bold stone bridge, which carries the Portsmouth road over the river, forms a conspicuous and effective object from the house. As viewed from this bridge, too, the house itself has a very imposing appearance, its handsome portico, erected by Mr. Decimus Burton for a former proprietor, rising to the full height of the building, and being supported by massive pillars. It is also well furnished with large trees on either side, while the slope of the park in front is open enough to show all its beauty and breadth, yet being sufficiently studded with specimen plants to preserve it from plainness. A large *Mespilus canadensis* was, when we saw it in the autumn, and when it had acquired all its mellow red and yellow tints, a remarkably good feature on this park slope.

After passing from Cobham Bridge under a neat suspension bridge which connects one part of the park with a more northern portion (the ground on either side of the Portsmouth road being 15 or 16 ft. above the level of the road itself), we ascend a hill, at the top of which is the entrance to the place. Directly we get within the gates, we receive evidence that the hand of taste has been at work upon it a century back; for some superb thorn trees of several kinds, and various species of pine, are placed about the park, which opens out with great indefiniteness and beauty towards the south-west.

Attached to the house is a lofty conservatory, well stocked with plants; and from the garden front the view of Cobham Bridge is obtained. In order to shut out the village from the house, a large island has been formed in the river, and covered with trees which effectually conceal all the neighbouring buildings. Only one small cottage-like villa is seen at the end of a glade of grass on the other side of the river, and this appears to belong to the estate, as we believe it actually does. The pleasure grounds and flower garden lie principally on the north side of the house. Here there are many magnificent cedars of Lebanon, of different habits and characters, besides beautiful specimens of several of the pine and fir tribe.

The flower garden is a nearly circular plot, raised towards the centre, and situated in the front of some old plant houses, being almost wholly surrounded by shrubs and trees. It contains a great many standard and climbing roses, with several beds of roses alone in the centre. By the side of it is a light open wire temple, covered with climbers, standing over a round basin of water. In clear sunny weather the reflection of the climbers in the water is often exceedingly beautiful. A neat wire trellis was clothed with *Tropæolum speciosum*, a rather uncommon and extremely showy red-flowered species, which bears seed most abundantly. Some very fine Shaddocks are growing in an old orangery at the back of the flower garden.

What renders this place so famous is the planting of the park, and the arrangement of the lake and its accompaniments. All this has been well described by Whately in his work on "Modern Gardening," published towards the end of the last century. But the trees have now received all the beauty and character which age can impart, and the manner in which the place was neglected by late proprietors has given an air of picturesqueness to many parts which is quite in accordance with the genius of the spot.

The lake, which occupies about 40 acres of ground, and is wonderfully varied by islands and windings, lies in the bottom of a narrow valley, which is somewhat higher than the river Mole, while the ground rises from it with a beautiful sweep, on the north, east, and west sides, a close plantation, forming the boundary of the estate, bordering it on the south. The slope of the park, and all the upper ground of it, is delightfully studded with trees, in the disposal of which great judgment has been displayed. There are several noble groups of the common acacia and of firs, cedars also occasionally appearing.

Striking across the park nearly south-westward from the house, and skirting the lake in the hollow, where a plain wooden bridge crosses an arm of it, we ascend the hill at the end of the park, and from a summer-house on the site of what was once a Turkish tent, we look down on a glorious piece of home landscape, including part of the lake, a portion of the park, the house, a Gothic temple on an opposite eminence in the park, and masses of the most magnificent and varied woods. Near this point is a temple dedicated to Bacchus, with an enriched pediment, on which are represented some Bacchic festivals. There is a prospect tower not far from this temple, towards the end of the property, commanding views of the whole estate and country, and said to take in St. Paul's Cathedral at London in clear weather. The trees have, however, grown so large and dense that the views from the tower are not nearly so good as they once were.

A close plantation covers the steep bank which descends from the side of the park to the valley of the Mole, and at the bottom of this hanging wood, which is composed almost entirely of firs in some parts, a water-wheel, not far from the head of the lake, pumps water from the river to supply the lake and the house. The valley in this part is wild and picturesque, and there is a beautiful hemlock spruce near the water-wheel.

At the head of the lake some noble plane trees are placed about, and a green path then passes along the southern margin of the lake, with a plantation to define it on the right. The slightly irregular width of this grass path, and the varied fringe of shrubs and trees on the one side, with occasional specimen trees at the edge of the water, is in excellent taste. Some of the water-side trees here, and in other parts, are the cut-leaved alder, which has acquired a great size and uncommon beauty. A small island near this end of the lake is clothed entirely with common alders, and has a most pleasing effect, the branches dipping into the water on all sides, and the shape of the island being nearly round. The Mausoleum, an old ruined arch with fragments of ancient tombs and altars, forms an interesting side scene, in a recess near the lake. There is a superb scarlet oak close to this spot.

A rustic bridge, made of acacia wood, and exceedingly simple in its form, crosses a part of the lake to another island. This bridge, without any appearance of art, is one of the best of its kind which could be constructed, and is infinitely more in character with the rest of the scene than the dressed wooden ones which lead to the grotto island a little further on ; for, as a general rule, no description of small bridge harmonizes well with scenery that resembles nature but some kind of rustic one.

The grotto island is the largest and most varied of all the islands which adorn the lake. A fine tulip tree overhangs the water just after the island is entered upon. There are several most splendid cedars upon it also, two of which are by far the largest which are to be found anywhere near London. A common oak tree here, as we learn by an accompanying inscription, was planted by Lord Carhampton in April, 1817, in honour of the Duke of Wellington's victories. It is now a middle-sized and flourishing tree. A Weymouth pine, which is generally a mean-looking tree, is here seen in a very picturesque state. At the edge of the water, too, is an unusually large and ancient savin ; and a common alder, with nearly twenty stems, is extremely striking.

On this large island the grotto is the principal feature, as it is one of the greatest attractions of the place. It is, indeed, one of the very few creations of its class which can at all be commended ; for in it there is nothing to offend, but everything to astonish and delight. Age has unquestionably done much to sober it down and blend it with the accompanying scenery, while the ivy and other wild plants with which much of its exterior is mantled, contribute to impart to it a still greater accordance with nature. It is situated on the margin of the lake, and is composed externally of masses of a dun-coloured perforated stone, which is also used for lining the lower part of the interior. The roof and upper parts of the inside are, however, formed with whitish spar and stalactite, the spar being arranged into shapes resembling large irregular stalactite. An immense deal of variety is attained, both outside and inside, in the disposal of the different parts, rude masses of rock being scattered about the exterior, so as to carry out and prolong the character into the surrounding ground, while a number of very irregular openings inside reveal the water, the island itself, or the park, in a great many beautiful aspects. A small cascade is made to pour itself down some rocks in the interior, and wind about till it discharges itself into the lake.

Altogether, this grotto is almost the only one worthy of the name which can be met with in England.

Another dressed wooden bridge, which is the more inappropriate from being near the grotto, leads us again to the side of the lake, and along its northern edge, passing many noble trees, to a ruin, part of which is mantled with a superb mass of ivy, while a large and luxuriant tuft of pyracanth spreads over some fragments at its base. We then strike through a close wood to the Gothic temple before alluded to, where there is another fine view of the lake, the woods, the prospect tower with its neat spire rising above them, and the park. The cedars and other trees on the margin of the lake and the slope of the park are well shown from this point. Proceeding to an opening which has been made in the woods to afford a distant prospect into the country, we find several large cork trees standing out in the glade by themselves. A walk across the park to the east then conducts to the kitchen garden, which is by the side of the river Mole, and is only to be noticed as being on or near the site of an old vineyard which once existed here. The vines in the forcing houses, although quite young, had undergone a serious visitation of mildew last autumn. Mr. Collison is the gardener.

Pain's Hill will occupy at least three or four hours to walk round it even hurriedly. It is, in many parts, far too much encumbered with trees, and would be greatly improved by judicious thinning, and by openings to admit views of the neighbouring country. But, for its specimen trees, its groups in the park, the beauty of its undulated ground, the charming diversity of scene which its lake presents, and for its admirable grotto, it is a place which will bear much examination and study, and may doubtless be inspected again and again with increasing pleasure.

The gardens of *Sigismund Rucker, Esq.*, at Wandsworth, though small, exhibit some interesting features, and contain a very fine collection of exotic plants, especially orchids. Of the latter tribe the plants here are probably unequalled in this country, and they invariably obtain some of the best prizes at the great exhibitions. The collection of heaths, too, is of the highest excellence, though these are gradually being dispersed, as opportunities arise, that more undivided attention may be given to the orchids.

The place is situated on West Hill, and the house lies rather near to the road. There is little view beyond it. A small conservatory is attached to the house, and contains, among the usual floral ornaments, several elegant sculptured figures, China vases, &c. The lawn, which is exceedingly neat, and very tastefully arranged, is decorated with numerous masses of rhododendrons, azaleas, roses, and occasional beds of summer flowers, while there are many specimen plants of the Deodar cedar, *Araucaria, Abies Douglasii*, various pines, some excellent standard Rhododendrons, a beautiful patch of *Juniperus sabina tamariscifolia*, &c. Of the roses, the hybrid perpetual varieties are chiefly grown, and as these come into bloom after the rhododendrons and azaleas, and remain flowering till late in the season, the place is kept continually gay.

The plant houses are placed in a small kitchen garden at the bottom of the pleasure grounds. With one exception, they are all low span-roofed structures, with a stage or pit in the centre, paths paved with slate, and narrow slate stages at the sides. The orchid houses have no upright side sashes; but a house devoted to heaths, where more light and ventilation are required, is furnished with side lights, all of which are capable of being opened. Hot-water pipes pass round the houses, under the side stages, but not down the centre, and the entrance is at one end only. The heating apparatus is Mr. Shewen's, being a modification of Rogers's conical boiler. In the orchid houses, which are shaded during summer, and ventilated chiefly by opening the doors, light inner doors are provided, the upper part being composed of fine gauze; so that when the outer ones are open, these may be closed, to prevent the entrance of insects.

The whole of the houses are remarkable for their extremely neat and orderly appearance, being kept particularly clean, and well white-washed, and duly painted. Indeed, this part of the garden, like the pleasure grounds, is conspicuous for the highest keeping, everything being as cleanly and orderly as it would be in a drawing-room. And this is, of course, one of the most attractive characteristics of the place.

In the excellence of the orchids here, there is a striking evidence given of the advantage of attending mainly to one tribe of plants. This one thing, done well, gives a celebrity and an interest to the place, which nothing but the very largest and richest general collection could other-wise impart. There are three houses appropriated to the orchids. One contains only the Vanda tribe and those which require the highest tem-perature. Another is used for the Mexican species, and there are many beautiful ferns along with these. The third, which is an old lean-to house, against the back wall of the garden, is filled with Cattleyas, Den-drobiums, and such of the Oncidiums and allied genera as want an inter-mediate temperature. The first of these groups is incomparably the richest, as well in beautiful forms as in fine specimens; the plants of *Aerides*, *Saccolabiums*, Vandas, &c., being most superb. There are several pitcher plants here also.

May, June, and July are the principal flowering periods with the orchids; but there is always a number of them in bloom at every season; and so rich is the collection here, and so well is it sustained, that there is seldom a period at which some new or very rare species is not in flower. It should be observed, however, that the having new or uncommon species is by no means the leading object aimed at here. Every species that has not some really ornamental character is at once discarded as soon as it is proved; and hence only the showiest and best members of the tribe are really cultivated.

A small span-roofed stove contains many pretty species of *Æschynan-thus*, several Hoyas, of which *H. bella* is new and extremely beautiful, some Allamandas, Dipladenias, &c. Some fine Camellias are grown in an-other house, near which is a nice aviary. The heaths are kept in a house by themselves, and placed out of doors in the autumn. A few pits and frames complete the stock of smaller plants. Hedges of Arbor-vitæ ex-tend along the sides of the walk where the houses are placed, and screen the intermediate parts between the houses, and the fire-pits, &c., from observation. Mr. Mylam has been many years gardener here.

Burntwood Grange, the residence of *H. Grisewood, Esq.*, between Wandsworth Common and Garratt Lane, is a small place recently laid out and planted by Messrs. Rollisson, of Tooting, and the house enlarged and remodelled, and a conservatory added to it, by Messrs. Trollope, of Parliament Street, London. The conservatory, which is in the Gothic style, like the house, we have thought so excellent, that we have ob-tained permission to give the annexed illustrations of it. Its merits are, that it unites and harmonises well with the house, of which it forms a constituent part, and not a mere adjunct; while there is a novelty and

EXTERIOR OF CONSERVATORY, BURNTWOOD GRANGE.

INTERIOR OF CONSERVATORY.

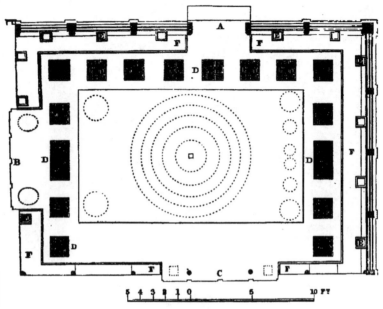

PLAN OF CONSERVATORY.

richness in the interior of the roof, and a simplicity in the arrangement of the plants, which also recommend it to notice. At a period when buildings of this kind are yet generally such commonplace things, mostly without any style at all, and just tacked on to the house at any point where they may be wanted, with little regard to their harmonising with the design of the principal elevation, a conservatory like this is a pleasant and worthy deviation from the ordinary practice.

Our engravings exhibit the elevation, with part of the house attached, a view of the interior, showing the form of the roof, and a ground plan in which the stages, borders, paths, &c., are delineated. From the first of these it will be seen that the conservatory occupies a corner of the building, where the main wall retires, and is therefore essentially a part of the general structure, not standing out beyond either the front or the end of the house; while the lowness of the roof, as compared with that of the house itself, rather tends to heighten the character of a Gothic building like this. The ground plan will indicate that it is connected with both the drawing-room (B) and billiard-room (C), standing at the end of the former and in front of the latter, so that it can be enjoyed from both. (A) is the entrance from the garden. In the arrangement of the interior, too, regard has been had to the character of art which a conservatory attached to a drawing-room should maintain. Hence, the path is paved with mosaic tiles, the gratings for admitting hot air (D) being of brass, and a neat kerb-stone being placed around the sides of the path. The centre portion is paved with good flag-stones, and there is a light iron stage, of an oval shape, in the middle, while very handsome porcelain vases, filled with flowers, occupy the corners,

DAIRY, BURNTWOOD GRANGE.

and also the corners of the path, as shown on the plan. Between
the path and the walls there is a narrow border (F), covered with
Lycopodiums, Heliotropes, and various low-growing plants, which make
a neat fringe to the whole. Climbers are trained to the roof, and a
chandelier is suspended from the centre. The main feature in the ground
plan is that the space is not at all crowded, and everything employed is
good and tasteful.

Another sketch which we insert represents a pretty dairy at the end of
the house, which is appropriately fitted up, together with a series of
terraces, with steps and vases, which occupy this part of the garden. At
the top of these terraces is a nice span-roofed stove, filled with good
plants, and having some novel and ornamental baskets of pottery ware
suspended from the roof for receiving orchids, &c. Near this stove is a
long flower garden, well filled with various summer plants. The lawns
in front of the house are bordered with handsome evergreen shrubs, and
there are particularly fine specimens of *Andromeda floribunda*, with a
beautiful Deodar cedar. The kitchen garden is well arranged, and contains some first-rate forcing houses and pits. The entire place is kept in
the most perfect order by Mr. Hoskins, the gardener.

William Leaf, Esq., has a delightful place at Streatham, in Surrey which, though originally comprising the poorest elements, has, by the spirited diversion of the road in front of it, and of a public footpath which crossed the middle of what is now the lawn, been made into a thoroughly excellent villa garden. We believe it was laid out by the late Mr. Loudon.

The house is in the Italian style, and a semicircular projection, supported on pillars and surmounted by a dome, is thrown out from the front of the upper stories, while a terrace walk extends along the principal or garden front. Near the end of the terrace is a conservatory, with a curvilinear iron roof, and having the specimens planted out in beds. The Acacias, Polygalas, and some other plants in it are extremely fine.

In the garden and on the lawn there is a number of rare and ornamental shrubs. A high bank has been thrown up, and happily clothed with pines and other trees at the lower part of the garden, to exclude the walls, &c., of a neighbouring estate. In the middle of a small pool of water an island is entirely covered with the common dogwood, which, spreading down its branches to the water, forms an interesting object at all seasons, but especially when its leaves change colour in the autumn, and while the red bark of its shoots is so conspicuous during winter.

From one side of the lower part of the lawn, the ground in an adjoining field dips suddenly, while the scene opens out upon a very richly wooded valley, and expands towards the hill of Wimbledon, with its charming park; a more extensive valley spreading away to the left of that hill till the horizon is nearly lost in mist. Nothing of this kind could be more beautiful than the tufted heads of the many venerable elms and oaks over which the eye here roams, and which are sufficiently beneath the level of the garden to offer no obstruction to the more distant view. This scene is, of its kind, without a parallel in the neighbourhood of London, and is commanded both from the house and lawn, the latter being well connected with the field by a sunk fence. In no place have we ever witnessed more fully the value of that species of fence in leading the eye imperceptibly over the garden boundary; or the advantage of an elevated site in overlooking all that is good in a wooded landscape without revealing any lines of hedge or other divisions.

From another part of the grounds a prospect is obtained, between some ancient elms, of the greater part of London, with much of the valley of the Thames westward, and all the beautiful low hills on the northwest and west sides of the metropolis.

In the kitchen garden there are extensive forcing houses, pits, &c., which are constructed and managed in the first style, Mr. Leaf having been most liberal in his expenditure in this department, as throughout the whole place, to render everything as perfect as possible. A good many greenhouse and stove plants are grown in some of the houses. On the south side of the house, a very inartificial small opening has been made through the branches of some old trees, to let in a beautiful landscape towards Croydon and the hills beyond. This is so cleverly done that it does not at all bare the windows of the house to the public gaze; while the view of the porch-like front of the house, with its dome, obtained through the opening from Streatham Common, is very striking and effective. Mr. Butcher is the present gardener here.

The delightful garden of *John Warner, Esq.*, is situated about a mile from the Broxbourne Station on the Eastern Counties Railway, and 17 miles from London. It has been under the superintendence of Mr.

Williams for nearly 30 years. On the lawn near the house are some very fine specimens of the fern-leaved beech, weeping elm, deodar cedar, *Daphne pontica*, and many other very ornamental trees and shrubs.

An excellent view of this lawn is obtained from a raised terrace of some length at the upper end ; and from this terrace a closely-shaded walk descends in a winding direction to a lake, which is crossed by a rustic bridge. Here the spectator is astonished by an admirable imitation of broken rocks, formed entirely of bricks and cement, which have all the appearance of having been worn by the current of a stream. Almost adjoining these is a rustic building, in full accordance with them. Apart from this is a garden partly devoted to dahlias, and adjoining the lawn on one side of it is a border of roses, consisting of dwarfs and standards, among which are many of the new and leading varieties. In the middle of this garden, and entangled into one mass, is a large column of roses, chiefly the *R. sempervirens*, the effect of which is decidedly good when in bloom.

The scene is here again varied by the introduction of a Gothic arch in ruins, and entirely covered with ivy, the whole structure resembling the remains of some ancient building in a state of decay. Near this spot there is also a waterfall, supplied from a neighbouring brook; and by the side of it is a rustic seat, covered with roses, ivy, and honeysuckles, from which we pass on to the rose garden. This is formed on a mound of earth, four feet high, and is divided into four beds of equal size, composing a circle. There are twelve Gothic arches with iron standards about seven feet high and six feet apart, which form the outer circle, and from these several rods are thrown towards the centre, where they meet, and are joined to an upright central one, thus making a sort of tent-like canopy. There are four arches for ingress and egress.

At a short distance from the rose garden is a pinetum of some extent, tastefully laid out and planted, and containing many interesting specimens in a young stage, which seem to be in a very thriving condition. The soil is of a loamy texture, and appears to suit them admirably.

After leaving the pinetum, we come to a small garden in connection with the bath house, in the front of which is a very pretty fountain ; and along the bank of the lake a figure of Neptune is seen reclining on a rock, which towers from the surface of the water, a fountain dispersing its streams over and around it. There is likewise a small island, planted chiefly with weeping ash, willows, &c.

On approaching the house, we enter a small flower garden, tastefully arranged, by the side of a conservatory. It has a north-west aspect, and is on a gradual descent. A terrace walk extends along the side facing the south, at the bottom end of which are several glass structures for the growth of exotics. One of them is a large span-roofed house, devoted to the culture of orchids ; and among these are some splendid specimens. The north end of the house has a dark roof, under which are some very large ferns, growing among masses of rock-like cement, and having a wild and natural appearance. We owe this account to Mr. J. Keir, an excellent gardener at Cheshunt, who has also kindly furnished us with a subsequent notice of Messrs. Paul's nursery at Cheshunt.

The small town-garden of *N. Ward, Esq.*, at Clapham Rise, is, though a mere narrow strip of land, interesting for its examples of the glass case which Mr. Ward invented for London cultivators, and which has obtained so much notoriety under the name of the Wardian case. A number of these are ranged along a wall on one side of the garden, and are filled with ferns, &c., in the best health. They are peculiarly adapted for ferns, mosses, and small orchids, the elegant forms and bright green colour of which they exhibit to much advantage.

But Mr. Ward has also a small stove, somewhere about 18 ft. by 12, which he treats as a Wardian case, and the interior of which is arranged with great taste. An irregular open area is preserved from the door to about the centre of the building, this space being covered with iron grating for the admission of heat from below. Around the sides of this irregular area masses of rockwork, of varying height and character, are placed, and among these are planted out ferns, lycopodiums, mosses, dwarf palms, Cannas, Caladiums, Achimenes, orchids, &c., the roof being clothed with passion-flowers. The whole is most beautifully executed, and exhibits a very natural and pleasing arrangement, possessing a great deal of character.

This house, which has a span roof, is kept quite close, like a Wardian case, only being opened when required to be entered, and well shaded in sunny weather. Mr. Ward considers that this plan of treatment saves much trouble in watering, giving air, &c., and it certainly has the recommendation of succeeding well with him, and being very tastefully adopted. There can be no doubt that, as regards the mere arrangement of the interior of plant houses, this is a movement in the right direction.

Although we have taken notes of many other private gardens, and some of them are entitled to a high rank, yet they are either remote from London or not readily got at, and as the line must be drawn somewhere, we pass on to another class, which will demand less of our space.

The Zoological Gardens*, in the *Regent's Park*, do not contain much that requires notice in a gardening point of view, but demand a passing glance. They are entered from the road which surrounds the Regent's Park on the north-west side, and lie on both sides of that road, the two parts being appropriately connected by a short tunnel. Being situated within the actual boundary of the Regent's Park, they have the advantage of looking upon its large area of greensward on the south side.

A straight principal walk passes through the garden at an oblique angle from the main entrance, and by a flight of steps over the roof of one of the larger menageries, this roof being balustraded at the sides, and forming a large terrace platform, from which much of the garden and the park may be viewed. The sides of the walk leading to this terrace are bordered by lines of standard roses, and a series of small flower-beds, backed by shrubs.

The rest of the garden is laid out in the most irregular manner possible, so as to obtain a great number and variety of walks. Most of the shrubs and plants are healthy and flourishing, and some of them are handsome. On a raised bank at the south side of the garden, where the grass is carried up to the base of the shrubs which clothe its summit, a number of strong-growing herbaceous plants are scattered about in front of the shrubs and among them, and, growing out of the grass, they contribute to break and soften off the outline of the shrubs. In another part there are one or two pleasing islands, clothed with a thicket of dogwood, privet, &c., in the midst of pools used for water-fowl; and besides being in themselves picturesque, on account of the denseness of their clothing, these islands form an excellent cover for the birds to retire into.

In one part of the garden, where some evergreen shrubs and specimens

* The notice of these gardens is inserted here, having been accidentally omitted in its proper place.

had been newly planted last winter, these were somewhat unnecessarily protected by having a quantity of straw loosely shaken over them. Some very large specimens of weeping ash have their branches fastened flatly to a trellis which forms a kind of covering to a place in which a number of birds are kept, and though they have a very artificial appearance, they create a good shelter.

Several of the structures appropriated to different animals are picturesque, and pleasing examples of the rustic style. The new aviaries, too, appear well arranged and excellent, and when partially clothed with climbers, as seems to be intended, they will be yet more suitable and beautiful. Everything in the way of buildings is, in short, substantial and respectable; and the gardens are kept as neatly and well as the large number of visitors will allow them to be. There is a particular air of cleanliness and comfort about all the houses used for birds and animals. The inclosures for birds, &c., are surrounded mostly by a wire fence, with a row of close wires curved boldly outwards at about two feet from the ground, to prevent any small wild animals or vermin from entering the inclosure.

Passing through the tunnel, that portion of the garden north of the park road is on the slope of a bank, with a canal at the bottom, and constitutes a pleasant and shady summer walk. The new museum, the giraffes, the huge hippopotamus, &c., are in this direction. There are some handsome thorns in a few of the inclosures. We cannot speak of the collection of animals, &c., in this place, though this is undoubtedly very perfect, and all are in the best condition.

NURSERIES, FLORISTS' GARDENS, &c.—The characteristic of the London nurseries, and that which mainly distinguishes them from provincial establishments of this sort, is that they abound in indoor exotics. With a few exceptions, such as the great Exeter nurseries, for example, exotic plants that require protection or artificial heat are but sparingly and imperfectly grown in the provinces, as compared with London; and, on the other hand, provincial nurseries are, from having a better atmosphere, and often from a superior method of treatment, the best marts for hardy trees and shrubs. In general, there is far too much use made of the knife in the London nurseries, and ornamental plants are budded or grafted on stocks that are too tall, so that hardy plants obtained from them will often be many years before they become bushy, and some of them will never do so. This is a defect which is, however, in part remedied in some establishments, and which will, we hope, soon be entirely done away with; as nothing can be more objectionable than the pruning up of trees, that are intended for ornament, to bare tall stems.

The nursery of *Messrs. Loddiges*, at *Hackney*, is one of the oldest and most celebrated of the London gardens of its class, although it is now, from the expiration of the lease of part of the ground, and the encroachments of a rapidly-enlarging population, becoming somewhat crippled, and is in process of transformation. The objects for which it has been most famed are its palms, orchids, camellias, and arboretum. The latter was long regarded as the most complete in the country, and contained many rare specimens, the whole of the plants being arranged alphabetically by the sides of an almost labyrinthine series of paths. But the atmosphere having become so deteriorated by smoke, and the ground being wanted for other purposes, this most perfect collection, which has been the foundation of most others of the kind throughout the country, will, we believe, have gradually to be relinquished.

Of palms, the collection yet remains entire, and is one of the finest that is known, having been enriched at various times by presents of rare specimens from several European sovereigns. The palm house has a lofty keel-shaped roof, with two low lean-to structures at the sides, the whole being open on the inside. The plants are all kept in tubs, for the convenience of lowering and removing them, and there are very high doors at one end of the house for the latter of these purposes. Several specimens have, however, broken through the roof, and had to be checked. So thickly are the plants placed, and so large have they become, that the interior of the house has now quite the character of a tropical forest or jungle, the broad leaves of some of the palms often excluding what is behind them, and giving a great indefiniteness to the scene. Many years ago this house was peopled with canaries and other birds, which ranged at full liberty within it, and must have given a great charm to it; but they were found to injure the ferns so much that they had to be removed.

At the northern side of the palm house, in a very appropriate position, is a beautiful collection of stove ferns, among which are many rare and curious plants, while the whole group presents numerous delightful features. Orchids, especially the *Stanhopeas*, are likewise suspended in many parts of the house. Being so thoroughly filled with large-foliaged palms, the house requires scarcely any ventilation, and only receives that which can be obtained from the doors. It was formerly traversed by small perforated water-pipes in various parts, by filling which with water, and keeping on the supply, the whole house was effectually watered and syringed.

Tacked on to the western end of the palm house, is a very long span-roofed structure devoted to orchids. Messrs. Loddiges have probably an unrivalled collection of these, in point of numbers, and many of the individual specimens are very fine. The orchid house has an ordinary flat stage at the sides, and a lower one, for large plants, in the centre; but a great proportion of the plants are suspended. It is kept at a high temperature, and is pretty thickly shaded in summer, no ventilation being allowed except at the end door. Of course there is a great deal of moisture preserved, to compensate for the amount of heat, which is often extreme on a sunny summer's day. The plants are all labelled with strips of zinc, the numbers on which refer to a catalogue which was issued by Messrs. Loddiges, and in one copy of which, obtained about 1840, there are more than a thousand species enumerated. There are always a number of species belonging to this exquisite tribe in flower; and whenever we have visited the place, there has generally been some new species in bloom. In October last, we observed in this house some very rare and handsome ferns, newly imported.

There is a long span-roofed house for Mexican orchids on the east side of the somewhat square area round which the plant houses are ranged. This house is of course kept at a lower temperature, and, consequently, in a dryer state. A very fine specimen of the Elephant's Foot (*Testudo elephantipes*) stands at the north end of this house.

A new house for orchids has also been built on the south side of the place, and contains the pick of the collection. It is a low span-roofed structure, with fixed bars, not lights, and glazed with Hartley's rough plate-glass. It has small ventilators at the ends, and requires a good deal of shading. The mode of heating is by one of Shewen's boilers, which is placed beneath the house, at one end, and a flue surrounds the

I 2

boiler, further to economize the heat. Messrs. Loddiges have many of these boilers in different parts of their nursery, and all of them are acting most satisfactorily. We understand that the new orchid house is the first of a series of span-roofed structures which are to be erected along that side of the garden.

In the interior of this orchid house the plants are placed on slate stages at the sides, and raised on pots or wooden frames in the centre. There are many first-rate specimens here, and all in the highest health.

The terrestrial orchids, and such plants as cannas, curcumas, young palms, with a great variety of stove plants, are kept in a warm close house to the west of the palm stove. The cactaceous tribe are in an adjoining house. And to the west of these again, there is another stove, heated on the tank system, in which slate was tried as a material for forming the tank which contains the hot water, but has been found incapable of bearing sufficient heat, and splits up so much under these conditions that wood has been substituted for it, and succeeds very well. The tank is now chiefly made of planks about an inch thick.

Passing through the range of houses which is continued from the eastern end of the palm stove, and reaching the south side of the area, we enter the greenhouses, where there are some beautiful araucarias, many greenhouse ferns, and a number of very handsome lilies during summer. It is here that the first of the camellias begin to occur, and these are continued, almost exclusively, until the path diverges to the right and left into the large camellia house. This is an extensive structure, with a wall down the greater part of the centre, and two curvilinear roofs, of iron and glass, one fronting the south and the other the north. That facing the north is much the highest, and this division of the house is also broader. Most of the plants are in pots, but a few are planted out. Some of the specimens are very large and fine, though many of the best have been recently sold. So large and dense are several of the plants, that birds build their nests in them. Altogether, there is an immense collection of these plants, which are well grown, and of every variety as to size. When in flower, about the end of March or the beginning of April, they make a most gorgeous display; and Messrs. Loddiges are very liberal in allowing respectable parties to see them.

In the remaining greenhouses, and in the numberless pits and frames contained within the area already mentioned, a stock of almost all the better greenhouse plants is kept. And though no part of the place is remarkable for high keeping, it deservedly possesses a world-wide reputation for its palms, orchids, and camellias.

The nursery of *Messrs. Low and Co.*, at *Clapton*, is little more than two miles from Messrs. Loddiges, and may be visited at the same time. Here, from the system adopted of rapidly clearing off the stock, there is seldom any large specimen plants to be seen. But a very considerable stock of the most popular greenhouse plants is reared and kept in the best order ; and from the enterprise of Mr. Low, great numbers of new plants are sure to be found in his nursery, at almost every season of the year.

The stock of the hardier and more showy heaths, and of those plants which peculiarly suit the London markets, was particularly good when we called here last autumn. Both in the greenhouses and in long ranges of excellent pits, there was an extraordinary quantity of plants of this description, in the most beautiful health and keeping. In the pits a bed of large clinkers is made at the bottom, and small cinders, on which the pots rest, are placed over these.

Several peculiarities in the construction of plant houses occur here, and are worthy of note. The principal heath house has ventilators, in the shape of sliding shutters, both in the back and front walls, by which it can be aired in wet weather, without allowing the rain to enter. In a stove, where rare and delicate plants are kept, several small frames and lights are placed, in which any very tender or newly-potted or un-healthy plants may be put, and supplied with a suitable atmosphere of their own, or preserved from drip, or occasionally shaded, or otherwise peculiarly treated. The same arrangement is made in a house where a multitude of rare things are grafted; the newly-grafted plants being kept in these little frames till the scion has thoroughly taken hold of the stock. The plan is also adopted in the propagating house, and does away with the necessity for using bell-glasses. To one of the stoves, moreover, there is a kind of porch, which is used as a potting shed, so that the plants to be potted have never to be taken into the open air, or carried to a distance.

Besides the immense stock of greenhouse plants above referred to, we observed a large quantity of camellias, a collection of stove ferns containing above 240 varieties, a great number of the charming *Daphne indica rosea*, a considerable collection of herbaceous plants, and several thousands of the common arbutus in pots, in an excellent state. The new seedling Himalayan rhododendrons, also, looked better here than at almost any other place where we saw them, being kept in a cool house, and not placed in a stove.

Of scarce or novel plants, besides a great many of which we made no record, we noticed a lot of seedlings collected by Drummond in the neighbourhood of Lucky Bay, and between that and Swan River. There are six or seven Daviesias, and many other interesting and promising plants among them. *Thuja chilensis* is a plant very much like an *Araucaria* in habit. *Weigela Micandorfiana*, from Siberia, is said to have yellow flowers. *Gaultheria organensis* is a climbing species. *Viburnum suspensum* is not much unlike a Laurustinus, and believed to be hardy. In the stoves, the variegated Arum, and the variegated Screw Pine, are singular and interesting. *Allamanda neriifolia*, from the Jardin des Plantes at Paris, is described as having yellow flowers with red stripes. *Franciscea eximia* is a handsome species, and *Achimenes longiflora alba* is very beautiful, and flowers with the facility common to the genus. The rare *Amherstia* is also here, and a collection of Smith's yellow rhododendrons.

Our space will not permit us, with reference to either this or any other nursery, to describe the houses and their contents individually. We can only further remark, that everything about this nursery is in that orderly and neat state which the energetic and bustling mode of business pursued by its principal would lead us to anticipate. One of Mr. Low's sons has been a collector of plants in Borneo and other tropical countries, and has sent home many valuable things, which are of course to be found in this establishment.

Messrs. Rollisson's Nursery, at *Tooting*, is about seven miles from London, on the Surrey side, and has been long noted for heath-growing. It has latterly, also, acquired a large collection of orchids, and contains a very good assortment of general greenhouse and stove plants, besides having an excellent stock of ornamental shrubs and trees, especially the American plants. The latter are grown in various plots, apart from the main nursery.

All the more modern plant houses in this nursery are span-roofed, the heath house being one of the best specimens of its class. Houses of this shape are found much more commodious, more easily constructed, and more suitable for plants ; while their internal arrangement is so very simple. In the heath house the path surrounds a broad central stage, while there is a narrower stage at each side. There are side lights to this house, down to the level of the side stages, and all those lights are made to open, so that the house can be rendered very airy. In the old orchid house, which is now a general stove, the arrangement of the paths is similar, only there is a raised pit down the centre, and an open tank in the middle of the house, and the heating apparatus is within the house, at one end, but is approached and tended from the outside. There are no side lights to this house, and the lights of the roof appear to be mostly fixed. The new orchid house is very similar.

The older houses are much loftier, and are built against a south wall. They are filled chiefly with general greenhouse plants, and one of them is devoted to camellias. Another comparatively new house is used for rarer stove plants and climbers. One of the greenhouses, too, is entirely filled with plants of *Rhododendron javanicum*, of which Messrs. Rollisson possess a great stock, as it was introduced, we believe, by their collector, Mr. Henshall, who has also sent home a number of other excellent plants, and was to go from Java to the Moluccas. This rhododendron appears to thrive very well in a greenhouse, and flowers while in a very dwarf state. The flowers are orange coloured, and are generally produced in August.

The heaths in this establishment still maintain their excellence, and are placed out of doors during the autumn months. The orchids are also good, and there is a large quantity of them, while the stock is continually being augmented. Many novelties will likewise be found here, both among greenhouse and stove plants, particularly the latter. Several small houses in a court at the back of the principal garden contain some of the most scarce and valuable plants, and the propagating part of the business is here carried on. Here, too, against the walls of the various buildings, and in sheltered corners, some of the less hardy climbers are grown. The new species of *Ceanothus* have been kept against one of these walls for the last year or two without protection. Some of the best and newest herbaceous plants, annuals, bedding plants, &c., are grown in the open garden fronting the principal houses.

At the end of the large new orchid house, a very complete collection of Pitcher Plants is kept ; and as some of them are quite novel, and all of them are exceedingly interesting, we insert a popular description of the various sorts with which Messrs. Rollisson have obligingly favoured us. The plants are grown at the hottest end of the house, as they are excessively fond of heat and moisture.

Nepenthes distillatoria, the common Pitcher Plant, was first introduced about the year 1789, and is by far the most generally cultivated. It is a native of China and the Indies, and is readily distinguished by its pitchers, which are usually from 8 inches to a foot long, of a pale green when young, afterwards of a reddish brown, especially near the mouth of the pitcher. The lid is of a circular form, and is furnished with a small spur * at the back. The leaves are usually about 18 inches in length and 3 inches wide, and smooth on the edges. Before the pitchers open, they are one-third filled with a transparent fluid, by which ants, cockroaches, and other insects are attracted and drowned. Independently of the curious character of the plant, it deserves culture as an insect trap.

N. lævis is the smallest of the genus, as regards both the plant and pitchers. The leaves are 7 or 8 inches in length, and 1½ inch wide, smooth and glossy, entire on the margin, and tapering to a narrow point. The pitchers are from 2 to 3 inches long, of nearly the same form

* This spur is common to all the Nepenthes.

as *N. distillatoria*, pale green when young, afterwards veined with red. They are furnished with two narrow fimbriated wings. This species may be distinguished at first sight, even without the pitchers; for the leaves, independently of being so narrow and pointed, are deeply channelled. It is from the East Indies.

N. phyllamphora. The leaves of this plant are furnished with small teeth on the margin of each, by which character it may always be distinguished from all others in cultivation. The whole plant is of a much paler green than any of the others. The leaves vary from 1 foot to 18 inches in length, and are from 3 to 4 inches wide. The pitchers are of a pale green, entirely destitute of marks, about 6 inches in length, and similar in form to those of *N. distillatoria*, the stem being smooth. It is a native of the East Indies.

N. Raffesiana is very robust in habit. The stem is thick, and covered with a buff-coloured mealy substance; the leaves are very strong, being from the stem to the pitcher 3 feet in length, undulated, and 5 inches across at the widest part. The pitchers are very beautiful, and are 10 inches in length, pale green, and richly mottled and spotted inside and out with a glossy reddish brown. The lid is also similarly marked. When young, the plants produce pitchers widest at the *lower part*, and furnished with two fringed wings; but as the plant advances, the tendrils become spiral, and the pitchers are produced without wings and widest at the *upper part*. When laden with its richly-coloured pitchers the appearance of the plant is truly noble. It is said to be from Singapore.

N. albo-marginata is of dwarf habit compared with others of the same family. The leaves are 18 inches long, smooth and glossy on the upper surface and rough underneath, and about 1½ inch wide. It may be distinguished by a beautiful white band round the outside of the mouth of the pitcher. The pitcher is pale green inside, and on the outside it is streaked with red, and 4 inches long. This is also from the East Indies.

N. species, Java. This plant is new to the country, and supposed to be the one described by Dr. Blume under the name of *Nepenthes gymnamphora.* It was sent from Java by Mr. Henshall, the collector to the Tooting Nursery, about two years since, along with another species mentioned below. The leaves at present on the plant are 7 inches long and 1½ inch wide, tapering, surface smooth, margin minutely serrated. The pitchers are 3½ inches long, contracted on the upper half, of a light green outside, and the inside beautifully spotted with red. The mouth of the pitcher reaches down to one-third of the length of the same, a peculiarity not to be found in any other Nepenthes; and although the pitchers at present on the plant are small, there is no doubt of its being a very beautiful species, for the pitchers gathered in its native locality and dried previous to their being sent home, are of large dimensions, of a purplish hue inside, and may now be seen in the Museum at Kew Gardens.

N. species, Java. Like the preceding in form and size, but the pitchers are entirely destitute of spots or markings of any kind; being pale green inside and out.

N. Hookeriana. In its general aspect this plant resembles *N. Raffesiana.* The leaves are 21 inches long and 4 inches across, margin entire, and the surface smooth. The pitchers are 4 inches long, of a pale green, spotted and marked with red inside and out, gradually widening upwards, and invariably destitute of wings. The inside is furnished with a rim half an inch wide from the mouth downwards, which is sparingly striped with red. The lid is nearly erect, and, compared with *N. Raffesiana*, the mouth is more horizontal.

N. ampullacea. The stem and leaves of this plant are hoary, and the pitchers widely different from all others. They are usually about 3 inches in length, and 1½ inch wide. The mouth of the pitcher is *horizontal*, which is not the case with any other Nepenthes. The operculum, or lid, is not half large enough to cover the mouth of the pitcher, being 1 inch long and only a quarter of an inch wide. In form the pitcher is elliptical, of a green colour in young plants, but when more mature they are spotted with red. The linear lid is alone sufficient to distinguish this species. It is from the East Indies.

N. sanguinea. The pitchers are of a beautiful red, but young plants will produce pitchers with only a few red spots and streaks. The leaves are thickly set on the stem, 16 inches long, and very smooth and glossy. The pitchers are 6 inches in length, a little contracted on the upper half, and furnished with two membranous fimbriated wings. The operculum is ovate. The plant, when sufficiently mature to produce its red pitchers, is strikingly beautiful. It is from Mount Ophir.

N. Raffesiana—var. This is in all respects, save in the colour of the pitchers, like *Raffesiana*, but the pitchers are so intensely spotted and mottled, that they look as if the ground colour was red, with a few green spots upon it. As the plant constantly produces pitchers exhibiting this peculiarity, it may be considered a permanent variety.

The beautiful *Cephalotus follicularis*, which is like a miniature pitcher plant, and the singular but more common *Dionœa muscipula*, accompany the pitcher plants already described, and make the collection of this tribe complete.

The *Exotic Nursery, King's Road, Chelsea*, was founded in 1808 by *Mr. Knight*, who, having purchased the land it occupies, has almost annually built upon it fresh plant houses, and raised it to its present acknowledged eminence. In 1845 Mr. Knight associated with him his nephew, Mr. Perry, and in their joint names the business is now conducted.

It is very appropriately called the "Exotic Nursery," being particularly rich in plants that require shelter, and not, until very lately, including the culture of the commoner trees, but only of the more ornamental and curious hardy plants. A new and handsome entrance has lately been made at the upper side of the nursery, on the Fulham Road, and by this, or by the older one in the King's Road, the place may be approached. The plant houses lie nearer the latter of these entrances, and, in fact, a glazed passage conducts from the door to the old conservatory, where there are some very large plants of *Rhododendron arboreum*, which occasionally flower in great profusion.

Passing through the conservatory, we enter a court surrounded with plant houses, and in this open space the bulk of the greenhouse plants are very tastefully arranged during summer, on a flooring of cinders. The plants are grouped together in masses, according to a fixed and regular plan, with passages between the groups; and much variety is attained by the aid of taller plants, conifers, standards, &c. Some standard bay-trees, with roundish heads, are particularly observable, and, are considered a good substitute for orange-trees in Italian gardening. They simply require protection from very severe frost in winter.

On the stages in front of the houses at the north side of the square, several ornamental oblong flat vases are placed, for containing aquatics. The pretty little *Nymphæa pygmæa* is grown in some of them. A small stove, further on, has its roof entirely covered with *Stephanotis flori-bunda*. This is a low span-roofed house, and has a bark bed in it, besides being heated by hot water. In a lofty orange house, the pretty little Otaheite orange is extensively grown, and is nearly always in bloom. The collection contains a great many Indian and hardy Azaleas, some of which are seedlings. A larger stove, in two compartments, comprises many singular and beautiful variegated plants; and as these are now much sought after, we have obtained from Messrs. Knight and Perry the following list of the stove varieties which they cultivate:—

Phrynum zebrina.	Tillandsia acaulis sonata.
Tillandsia sonata.	Croton pictum.
Dichorizandra discolor nans.	„ angustifolium.
„ variegata.	„ latifolium.
„ rubra striata.	Dracæna terminalis.
Duranta Beaumardii.	Echites picta (climber).
Maranta zebrina.	Eranthemum leuconervum.
„ bicolor.	Hoya variegata.
„ rosea-lineata.	Vriesia speciosa.
„ alba-lineata.	Aspidistus variegata.
Tillandsia campanulata.	Jasminum gracilis variegatum (climber).

Many of these plants are extremely beautiful, and all are worthy of being grown, as they tend so very much to enliven a collection in winter.

The propagating house is very complete in this establishment, and is freely shown to visitors. It has a northern aspect, and is filled with small raised frames, the lights of which are hung on hinges at the top. In these frames the cutting pots are plunged in fine coal ashes. A potting and compost shed, and a house for young stock, are all under the same roof.

A new Aquarium has recently been built here, partly to accommodate the *Victoria regia*, and partly to show how the now popular tribe of aquatics may be managed. This is the first nursery establishment in which anything of the kind has been attempted; and there is scarcely a private garden at present in which a house so complete, and a collection so comprehensive, exist. We are much indebted to Messrs. Knight and Perry for being able to supply an interior view and section of this Aquarium, as well as to give a description of it, and add a list of the plants grown in it.

This building was constructed by Messrs. Gray and Ornson, and is rather more than 37 ft. long by 30 ft. wide. It is composed of two span roofs, supported by iron columns, and incloses a slate tank, 30 ft.

INTERIOR VIEW OF THE AQUARIUM.

long and 22 ft. 9 in. wide, with the centre part intended for soil 3 ft. deep, and the sides 18 in. A commodious path surrounds the tank on two sides and at the entrance end, while the furthest or eastern end of the tank is at the extremity of the house, thereby affording the means of giving up about 5 ft. at the eastern end of the tank to the Nelumbiums, Papyrus, and other tall-growing aquatics. The square of the tank (that is, 22 ft. 9 in. each way) is devoted to the *Victoria regia*, with the exception of the corners, which are occupied by *Nymphæa stellata, rubra, cœrulea*, and *sanguinea*. The noble *N. dentata* finds a place at the east end, under the *centre* of the house, which, perhaps, is barely high enough for the Nelumbiums. At intervals of 7 ft. along the sides and west end of the tank are placed little vases containing *Nymphæa pygmæa*, and the roof is relieved by pendent vases for orchids or other plants that delight in such a situation. At the west or entrance end of the house is a narrow platform occupied by a succession of oblong tanks for the culture of *Aponogeton juncifolium, Pistis stratiotes*, and other curious little water plants requiring a high temperature.

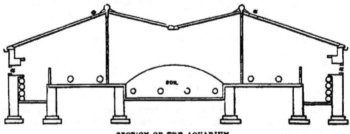

SECTION OF THE AQUARIUM.

The atmosphere of the house is warmed by four 4-inch pipes, extending the whole length on both sides; and the water by eight 4-inch pipes, four of which traverse the deep, and four the shallow part of the tank. Ventilation is secured by six apertures (*a, a,* in the section), covered with sliding slates, in the wall on each side of the house, by twelve ventilators placed in the highest part of the two ridges of the roof, and by two larger ventilators at each end of the house.

It having been judged by competent authority that motion in the water where the *Victoria* grows is a desideratum, it is imparted here, but in a novel way. The supply of water is brought from a distant reservoir, into which it is pumped by manual power, and is not abundant : it has therefore to be economized. It is introduced into the house by a large leaden pipe, which, narrowing itself at the orifice, discharges the water into a copper vessel, containing about a quart, so fixed on an axis that when it is full, the increased weight at the lip of the vessel causes it to turn over and cast its contents into the tank, which, being about 20 in. beneath, receives so great an agitation on the surface of the water as to put the whole in movement. The vessel regains its equilibrium by a weight attached to the base, and then receives a fresh supply, to be again discharged when the vessel is full, and so proceeding till the water in the reservoir is exhausted. At some future period this little device may be clothed in a more elegant form.

The slate tank is set on a bed of concrete ; and the soil for the *Victoria* is composed chiefly of Wanstead loam, with a little leaf mould, and a good portion of silver-sand.

Altogether, this Aquarium is a very complete and interesting structure ; and that our account of it may be in no respect deficient, we insert a list of the water plants which it contains :—

Victoria regia.	Nymphæa sanguinea.
Nelumbium album.	Thalia dealbata.
,, luteum.	Limnocharis Humboldtii.
,, speciosum.	,, Plumierii.
,, Count of Thun.	Pistis stratiotes.
,, caspicum.	Pontederia crassipes.
Euryala ferox.	,, cordata.
Nymphæa dentata.	Caladium bicolor.
,, stellata.	,, pictum.
,, rubra.	,, esculentum.
,, cœrulea.	Ceratopteris thalictroides.
,, pygmæa.	Aponogeton juncifolium.
,, odorata.	Papyrus antiquorum.
,, ,, minor.	

In the outdoor department this nursery is particularly well furnished with plants of the coniferous tribe. There is a most extensive and complete collection of the better kinds, all grown in pots, and embracing plants of various sizes. Messrs. Knight and Perry have, indeed, published a very useful synopsis of the coniferous plants grown in their establishment.

All the more ornamental American plants are also extensively grown here. The rarer azaleas and rhododendrons are especially abundant and good. We observed, also, a very fine specimen of that peculiarly handsome plant, the *Andromeda arborea.* Messrs. Knight and Perry have likewise a new autumn-flowering laburnum, which we saw blooming profusely in October last, and which will be a curious and interesting addition to the shrubbery. The trained fruit-trees are likewise good at this nursery, and are first trained to stakes, in the open quarters, then to a very low wall, and ultimately to a higher wall, to prepare them for sale.

In order to afford the gardeners entering this establishment an opportunity for improving themselves, and to render those who are recom-

mended to places more fit for undertaking their varied duties, what is
called the "study" has been most liberally constructed here, and fitted
up at great expense, being furnished with appropriate books, drawing
instruments, chemical apparatus, &c., to which those who work in the
nursery have free access after working hours.

About three years ago Messrs. Knight and Perry greatly enlarged
their outdoor space by the purchase of a large piece of land at Battersea, called the Brooklands Nursery, in which they now grow a very excellent collection of the best hardy ornamental trees and shrubs. This
branch nursery occupies about twelve acres, and is laid out in square or
oblong plots of a given size, so that the contents of every one of these
plots is easily ascertained for working purposes. Two borders filled with
beautiful specimen trees extend down the centre ; and among the plants
grown here there will be found many very rare, curious, and handsome
low trees, fitted for lawns or gardens. All the better sorts of plants are
labelled. Part of this nursery is appropriated to fruit trees, and another part to an American garden ; while a place is provided for growing
all the more pleasing hardy aquatics. Near the entrance, where a hedge
was wanted as a screen, this has been supplied at once by using the
black Italian poplar.

Messrs. Henderson's nursery, at *Pine Apple Place, Edgware Road,* is
one which has long been noted for the neat and careful cultivation of
heaths and general greenhouse plants, and for supplying all kinds of
forced and other plants *in flower* to those who, living in London, have no
means of growing them for themselves. It was also formerly a good deal
occupied in the rearing of vines ; but this part of the business is now,
we believe, very little attended to.

Within the last ten years, in fact, this nursery has undergone a very
great change, and assumed a much higher position. The number of
plant houses has greatly increased ; a collection of orchids has been
added ; all kinds of stove plants are now extensively cultivated ; the
preparation of mere flowering plants for the London drawing-rooms is
less regarded, and all the more general objects of the best London
nurseries are largely studied and provided for.

The orchids (which, with the rest of the indoor plants, are under the
management of Mr. Appleby) are now grown in what was formerly the
camellia house, at the back of Messrs. Henderson's residence. They are in
excellent health, and comprise several rare species. The old orchid
house, the warmth from the heating pipes of which is partly admitted
through perforated zinc fixed in the stages, is filled with stove plants,
and contains many beautiful lycopodiums, ferns, &c., with the lovely
Stephanotis floribunda covering the roof. This house has a kind of large
porch just within the entrance, which can, when necessary, be used for
potting, &c., and does away with the necessity for carrying the plants
into the open air. It is partially filled with plants, but only so as to
leave space enough for any desired operations.

Another span-roofed stove has a sort of ante-chamber, separated from
the rest of the house by a wall with doors ; and around this area all
the more showy plants that happen to be in flower, or the rarer species, are
arranged on stages, or on the floor if they happen to be large. The remainder of the house has a raised pit in the centre, with flat stages at
the sides, and paths between the pit and the stages. Some of the best
stove climbers are planted out in parts of the pit, near the sides, and
trained up the light pillars which support the roof, and in festoons along

the side of the pit. The Allamandas and kindred plants here grow very luxuriantly, and flower in great abundance. In reference to the stove plants in this house, and the plants throughout the entire place, it may be mentioned that only the really good sorts appear to be grown, and that many of the more ornamental older species are freely cultivated.

In a house at the south side of this principal stove, which is entered from the back, a good deal of the propagating work of the nursery is carried on, and very rare or new plants are generally kept. There is commonly a number of highly interesting objects in this house, and we here noticed the variegated *Primula sinensis*, variegated Oleander, &c. *Medinilla speciosa*, a fine new species, and *Gesnera Murkii*, a very pretty dwarf kind, were flowering in the stoves last autumn.

The greenhouses to the right-hand side of the entrance are generally filled with flowering plants at all seasons of the year, and the supply is kept up by forcing in other houses and pits. A span-roofed greenhouse on the right of these is a neat and useful structure, devoted to general greenhouse stock, the peculiarity of which in this establishment is that it is always well grown, and kept in the best order. A few pretty bulbs or other flowering plants are mostly placed here and there on the stages of this house, to give a little life and variety. When we were there in the autumn, it was thus decorated with some very excellent and splendid varieties of the Guernsey lily.

A house used almost entirely for Pelargoniums, in which the best fancy and other kinds are cultivated, stands just beyond the present orchid house. Higher up the nursery, there is a capital span-roofed house for specimen greenhouse plants, in which there are some beautiful heaths, and a variety of other greenhouse species, of large size, and very nicely cultivated. The roof of this house is covered with *Mandevilla suaveolens*, which flowers nearly all the summer and autumn. This specimen house stands high, and all the side lights open so that it can be most perfectly ventilated. Another greenhouse at the back of it is filled with myriads of smaller plants, in the best condition. There are many other houses, used for greenhouse plants or for forcing, and a great number of pits and frames, in which the younger heaths and greenhouse plants are principally grown.

In the beds and borders of this nursery, a multitude of the most showy herbaceous plants is cultivated. Everything novel or beautiful in the way of double-flowered varieties, or such as have variegated foliage or striped blossoms, or which are truly worth growing, is generally to be found here; there is, besides, a good collection of alpines and plants suited for growing on rockeries, kept in pots. The hardy shrub and ornamental tree department is not extensive, but a few fine climbers exist on one of the walls.

The nursery of *Messrs. Lee*, of *Hammersmith*, is one of the oldest in the neighbourhood of London, and the founder of it raised it to great fame and prosperity during the latter part of the last century. From taking thus quite a leading position, it fell, of late years, far behind establishments of even inferior magnitude; at least, so far as indoor plants are concerned. It is now, however, again rallying, and appears to be conducted with more spirit, and to embrace more of the newer and favourite plants.

The greenhouses here are very extensive; but they are lofty lean-to erections, probably almost as old as the nursery itself, and but indifferently fitted for the culture of plants. There is, however, a good stock of many species; and some of the older inhabitants of our greenhouses may, perhaps, be more readily met with at this nursery than elsewhere. A smaller house is now used for stove plants, among which are several of the larger tropical species; while another house is appropriated to stove plants and orchids, of the latter of which tribes there are only a few kinds. One house which we entered was filled with young vines, and another contained a large stock of Messrs. Lee's new bedding-out Pelargonium Flower of the World, as well as some other rather similar seedlings, and a few better-known varieties.

A very full collection of Fuchsias occupied another house. The best kind in this house was *F. ignea*, a variety raised by Messrs. Veitch of Exeter. The flowers are very large, with the colours (crimson sepals and purple corolla) bright and strong, and the sepals reflexed. It is a plant of an excellent habit. Other good varieties were *striata* (Veitch); Don Giovanni, with a fine open corolla; Grand Master, similarly fine; and Prince of Orange, with pale and large flowers.

The most interesting house in this nursery is that used for propagating purposes. This house has in it several little span-roofed frames, for receiving the more delicate plants; these frames having sliding lights with wooden catches, so as to be capable of being opened for air, and being furnished with a hole in the side through which smoke may be introduced without opening the lights, in case the plants should ever require fumigating. In this house we observed the *Cæsium arboreum*, a beautiful and strong-growing plant, like a climbing Lycopodium; *C. Schotti*, also pretty; *Lycopodium apoda*, a very dense-growing and delightful species; and *Andropogon schœnanthus*, the Lemon-scented Grass. A very pleasing group of dwarf variegated stove plants occupies one end of the house. Among these are *Thunbergia Dodsii*, *Eranthemum variabile*, the variegated Screw Pine, variegated Tillandsias and Marantas, *Justicia zebrina*, *Croton variegatum*, *Hoya variegata*, *Hæmadictyon nutans*, *Dieffenbackia seguinum pictum*, and *Aspidistra lurida variegata*, besides the *Anæctochilus setaceus* and other allied plants.

In a corner of the nursery there is a collection of the elegant dwarf Chrysanthemums which are called Lilliputians, and which only grow about 9 in. or a foot high, and are consequently very suitable for small places or for low stages in a greenhouse. The following twelve kinds were described to us as being the best.

Pompone d'Or.	Pompone Le naine Bébe.
,, Bijou.	,, La Laponne.
,, Bizard.	,, Petit Poucet.
,, Chapeau.	,, Sydonie.
,, Julie Langlade.	,, Tom Ponce.
,, La Lilliputienne.	,, Toulousaine.

The open nursery contains a large quantity of standard roses, some very handsome specimen magnolias, hollies, &c., borders down the centre filled with rare and excellent conifers, and the usual stock of trees, shrubs, and fruit trees. The *Phormium tenax*, which has attained a considerable size, is growing in the border near the house; and there is a fine *Magnolia grandiflora* on the dwelling house itself.

Messrs. Whitley and Osborn have a nursery at *Fulham*, which is well known as a repository of ornamental shrubs and trees, most of the hardy kinds of these being nicely grown and carefully named; the nomenclature adopted being that of Loudon in his "Arboretum Britannicum." Fruit trees are also well cultivated, and named with equal care.

There is here to be seen the original specimen of the Fulham oak, which is a magnificent tree, and has attained a great size. Beneath its shade, and close to the very trunk, where nothing else will live, a mass of the *Aucuba japonica* is flourishing most luxuriantly. In another part of the garden is a very fine and picturesque old plant of *Laurus sassafras*, besides a noble cork tree, some immense weeping elms, a particularly large golden-edged holly, an excellent cedar, purple beech, and many other mature specimens. The curious *Colletia horrida* is also here in a thriving state. Many plants of *Wistaria sinensis*, of great bulk, are scattered about the nursery, and treated as bushes, being grown to about 10 or 12 ft. in height, and then prevented from spreading further by pruning.

The coniferous tribe is particularly well illustrated in this nursery, and includes all the beautiful Junipers, Cypresses, Thujas, &c., cultivated in pots, so as to be readily removable. The American plants are also abundant and healthy. Among the large stock of ornamental trees, we observed a number of good plants, grafted standard high, of the somewhat uncommon but highly beautiful *Robinia inermis*, which is so well suited for planting in avenues in formal gardens, or for specimens on lawns. The plant houses are not extensive here, hardy plants being the chief things cultivated ; and of these there is likewise a considerable number of herbaceous species.

At *Vauxhall* the nursery of *Messrs. Chandler* is celebrated for its camellias, of which there is a large quantity, well grown, and of various heights. When in full bloom, during March and April, they create a superb display. They are cultivated both in houses and pits, the development of flowers being hastened or retarded according as the plants are or are not placed out of doors during the summer. When they are kept in the house all the season—as they were last summer—they bloom a fortnight or three weeks sooner, and the leaves assume a much brighter green tint during autumn and winter. The plants are slightly shaded in summer (the houses having a southerly aspect) by the inside of the glass being whitewashed. The stocks are raised for grafting, and the process of grafting is carried on, in pits and frames. A few of the common kinds are planted out in the open borders, and against a north wall ; but, although they have stood uninjured for many years, their flowers are almost annually spoiled by early frosts.

On the same wall as the camellias are many remarkable plants of the *Magnolia conspicua*, which are exceedingly beautiful when laden with their large white flowers in early spring. A large *Wistaria* in the open ground is treated as a kind of low tree, and makes an interesting and showy object. Rows of climbing roses in the borders are kept cut down to within about 4 ft. of the ground, so as to form bushes ; and in this state they are very pleasing where formal plants are required, though not, of course, so elegant or picturesque as when treated more naturally. The hardy shrubs are in a healthy condition here, and well grown.

A span-roofed and other greenhouses near the entrance are used for show plants when in flower, and these are filled, in autumn, with a collection of Chinese Chrysanthemums, of which Messrs. Chandler have a large quantity. These plants are not here cultivated to a great size, as they would require so much space to accomplish that ; but there is a great variety of them grown, and all the best known sorts are kept. In one of the greenhouses, too, a nice little collection of the smaller cactaceous plants is preserved.

Mr. Glendinning's nursery, at *Turnham Green*, has long been in existence as the *Chiswick Nursery*, and it is said that heaths were cultivated here almost earlier than in any of the metropolitan establishments of. this kind. Since it came into possession of the present proprietor, this nursery has greatly risen in character, and is still constantly improving. New houses have been erected, a wider range of plant culture has been taken, and a considerable interest is made to attach to it on account of the spirit and enterprise with which new plants are procured, and the successful manner in which they are flowered.

The collection of stove and greenhouse plants in this place is now decidedly good, and includes many novelties. The plants are grown in houses devoid of any pretension, and in narrow pits, some of the newer of which last are span-roofed. A long pit of this description was put up last year, and is two yards wide, with a fixed ridge along the centre. The latter is supported by having the rafters tied together, at every third light, by narrow bars of iron, placed rather more than a foot below the ridge. The whole is neat, light, and inexpensive, and the lights at the sides are all made to slide, and to take off. Ventilation can be given by iron gratings, with a sliding shutter in the front and back wall, when the lights are not wanted to be open.

In the stoves here we noticed *Æschynanthus zebrina*, and *Lobbiana*, *Hoya campanulata*, *bella*, and *imperialis*, *Cyrtoceras reflexa*, *Ixora odorata*, with large leaves and long pale flowers, *Gardenia Fortuni*, *Allamanda grandiflora*, and many other novel plants flowering profusely. A large plant of the somewhat uncommon *Statice arborea* was in one of the greenhouses. Many of the greenhouse plants are cultivated as specimens, and are in a very creditable state. There is, moreover, a house appropriated wholly to heaths, all of which are in beautiful health, which is said to be mainly due to their being watered with rain-water.

The pine and fir tribe receive much attention here, and there is a good stock of all the best of the conifers. The beautiful *Cupressus macrocarpa* (which is sweet-scented), *C. Goveniana*, and *C. funebris*, were especially conspicuous; and there is a cedar like the Deodar, only of a stiffer habit, which goes under the name of the Mount Atlas Cedar.

Messrs. Paul and Son, of *Cheshunt*, have the nearest nursery to London that is much celebrated for the culture of the rose, and their garden is noted for its very select stock of this queen of flowers. It is situated about 14 miles from London, and near the Waltham Cross station of the Cambridge line of the Eastern Counties Railway, being about the middle of the High Street of Cheshunt.

The nursery covers an area of about 40 acres, of which six acres are devoted to roses. The soil is a light, sandy, and poor loam, and the aspect south-east. A considerable portion of the six acres is used for standards, from three to five feet in height, and what are called dwarf standards. The stocks for budding are planted in the winter and spring months in beds, the rows in these being two feet apart, and the plants nine inches from each other in the rows, the tallest plants being kept in the centre or at the back of the beds. At the time of budding, which takes place the following summer, the greatest care is exercised in keeping the different sections separate, and the plants remain in the beds until the autumn of the ensuing year.

As much of the success attending the cultivation of the rose depends on the mode of pruning adopted, it is here distinctly borne in mind that hard and close pruning for strong-growing kinds tends to the production of too much wood, without flowers; while the opposite of this is the case with the weaker-growing sorts. The pruning is regulated accordingly.

The climbing roses are trained here to larch poles 10 or 12 ft. in height, and allowed to hang down from these in a weeping or natural form. They are arranged in straight lines, and when in bloom some of them are truly magnificent ; but there appears to have been a great oversight, at the time they were planted, by arranging them along each side of a very narrow walk. There are some excellent specimens of standards, that were planted about ten years ago, on either side of a broad gravel walk which forms the principal entrance to the nursery. They are chiefly about 4 ft. in height, and are very lovely when in flower. The method of pruning these has been to keep the centre shoots well thinned out.

Adjoining the above is a rosarium that has been planted in compartments. It consists of standards and dwarf standards, the tallest of which are in the centre of the beds. They comprise all the leading varieties, and present a very useful mass for the purchaser to select from. Contiguous to these is a small arboretum, planted two years ago, and containing, especially, some choice Pinuses.

Besides the general stock of standard roses, many thousands are grown in small pots, so that at every period of the year orders can be executed to any extent. These potted plants are arranged in beds about 4 ft. wide, and plunged in any light material to protect their roots from the heat in summer and the cold in winter. The more tender kinds of China and odorata roses are kept in shallow pits.

A great many roses are also grown in large pots, for the purpose of exhibiting at the Horticultural and other local societies' shows, where the leading prizes are often obtained. The mode of training these is to keep the branches as close as possible to the front of the pot, and to let them rise at the back, which is found much better for showing their blossoms than when they are trained in a flat or conical form. In order to promote a free growth, copious waterings of liquid manure are given. Indeed, high manuring is at all times recommended, and the best time for applying it is November.

None of the dwarf roses are here grown in masses of one kind, except in so far as each sort is kept distinct in the compartments, which produces a similar effect. The month of June is considered the best time for viewing the summer-flowering varieties, and from August to November for the autumn-blooming kinds.

Beside roses, fruit trees, forest trees, shrubs, herbaceous plants, dahlias, hollyhocks, &c., are pretty largely cultivated, as well as many of the best coniferous plants. There are likewise a few plant houses and pits.

One of the most striking gardening features within a moderate distance of London is the American plants in the nurseries near Bagshot. The older of these establishments belong to Messrs. John and Hosea Waterer, that of the former gentleman being at Bagshot, and the latter at Knapp Hill, not far from the Woking Station of the South-Western Railway. Both of them are, we believe, very much alike in regard to the nature and quality of the plants cultivated. We shall only, therefore, notice one of them, as this will serve for a general description of the other.

The nursery of *Mr. H. Waterer*, at *Knapp Hill*, is situated in a low, flat district, with a soil which, in many parts, consists of pure heath-mould to the depth of 10 or 12 ft. It is therefore peculiarly suitable for rhododendrons and the kindred genera, which flourish upon it with a facility and luxuriance that is most wonderful, as compared with the state in which they are ordinarily seen. Rhododendrons, in great variety, all the best azaleas (including many seedlings), kalmias, ledums, and a multitude of pretty dwarf evergreens which are comparatively little known, are here grown in large quantities, and attain a great size; so that, during the time of flowering (which is about the beginning of June), this nursery presents one of the most gorgeous spectacles which it is possible to conceive.

The practice of growing rhododendrons as standards, varying in height from 3 to 5 ft., is also here carried out very extensively, and with the greatest success; many of the specimens being exceedingly handsome. The charming *Kalmia latifolia* grows here in the highest vigour, and frequently attains the height of six or more feet, flowering in astonishing profusion. From the nature of the soil, too, plants move from here with large balls of earth, and in the greatest safety. Indeed, for many years past, the Messrs. Waterer have been accustomed to hold an exhibition of their American plants, while in flower, in the neighbourhood of London; the specimens being moved from the ground to the place of exhibition just as they were coming into bloom, and returned to the nursery after they had ceased flowering, without deriving injury from the change.

The soil of this nursery seems also very suitable for lilies and some other bulbous plants, and the coniferous tribe flourishes extremely well upon it. Indeed, Mr. Waterer has a fine collection of conifers, and likewise a capital stock of all sorts of evergreen shrubs and low trees.

During the month of June a visit to this and the Bagshot nursery would furnish one of the greatest floral treats of the season.

Messrs. Standish and Noble have a nursery near *Bagshot*, which is rich both in American plants and conifers, and lies at the distance of 6 miles from the Farnborough station of the South-Western Railway, and 4 miles from the Blackwater station of the Reading and Reigate Railway. This nursery occupies 25 acres of land, of which glass forms no feature, the principal aim being to grow every kind of ornamental tree and shrub, especially evergreens. Each new arrival is subjected to the ordeal of an ordinary winter; when, if it is found wanting in hardiness of constitution, it is discarded as a hardy ornamental plant.

Particular attention has here been paid to the raising of hybrid rhododendrons; the object kept in view being to procure richly-coloured and fine-flowering varieties, of sufficient lateness in blooming to escape the spring frosts so prevalent in this climate. Amongst the newer hybrids, *Towardii* is the most conspicuous. A very peculiar and beautiful hybrid is named Mrs. Loudon, and, unlike any other rhododendron, the flowers are spotted on all the segments. But perhaps the most remarkable rhododendrons occur in an exceedingly dwarf race, which has been originated by repeated crossings with very closely-allied varieties, or by what is technically termed breeding "in and in." So dwarf are they, and so speedily do they arrive at a blooming state, that plants not more than 9 in. in height, and only of three years' growth from the seed bed, bloom abundantly. From the profusion of blossom which they yield, their dwarf habit, and compact growth, Mr. Standish thinks it is not too much to say that they might with propriety be used in masses for filling the formal beds of a parterre.

Besides large quantities of dwarf worked varieties, many standards, on stems from 3 to 5 ft. in height, are here grown; and there is an im-

mense number of seedlings, of every variety of character and parentage.
Of the Sikhim Himalayan rhododendrons, introduced by Dr. Hooker, there
are nearly 100,000 seedling plants.

In addition to all the best hardy ornamental plants usually met with
in nurseries, Messrs. Standish and Noble possess many very recent introductions, of which they have the only specimens, or, by being the sole
importers, hold the entire stock. Foremost among these stands the
Cupressus funebris, promising to be one of the most elegant of hardy
trees. Of this they have about 15,000 plants, varying in height from 3 in.
to 2 ft., and all seedlings. They have imported one plant which is 4 ft.
6 in. high, and by the next exhibition season it will reach 6 ft. in height,
when an idea may be formed of its beauty.

They have also the rare and distinct *Abies Jesoensis*, one of the most
beautiful of its class; *Cephalotaxus Fortuni*, a new Larix with very large
foliage; and the arborescent *Juniperus sphærica*; as well as three new
species of Arbor-vitæ, *Cupressus elegans*, *C. macrocarpa*, and the very
unique *C. Goveniana*. The last-named plant possesses as beautiful a green
colour as almost any other evergreen, and preserves it through the winter
quite unchanged. Of *Cryptomeria japonica* they have bedded out
20,000 seedling plants of various sizes, from 6 in. in height to 6 ft.; and
they have also some nice plants of the dwarfer variety, *C. japonica
nana*.

From the north of China, Messrs. Standish and Noble have imported
above 400 plants of new varieties of Tree Pæony, in 21 kinds, varying in
colour from white to pink, salmon-coloured, red, plum-coloured, and deep
purple. A great portion of them will flower in the present spring, about
the first or second week in May. They have likewise the beautiful *Rho-
doleia Championi*, supposed to be hardy, six new azaleas, one of which
has flowers marked like a carnation, with purple stripes on a white
ground, while another is an evergreen, with large thick leaves, and
flowers which are also large and deep red. As it is a native of the north
of China, there is little doubt as to its hardiness. All the new azaleas
are likely to bloom in May.

Amongst camellias, these gentlemen have a great acquisition in six
plants of a species with yellow flowers. They have further imported
seedling plants of *Quercus inversa* and *Q. sclerophylla*, both evergreen,
and the latter a remarkable plant. Five new hardy species of *Viburnum*
are likely to bloom in May. And there are here several new hollies,
quite distinct, with *Berberis japonica*, a very strong-growing shrub, and
a noble evergreen. Other new plants likewise exist in this nursery, and
more are now expected.

Having heard a good deal of the simplicity and cheapness of the
structure in which rhododendrons are grafted at this nursery, it may be
well that we here describe it. The soil is excavated to a convenient
depth and width, and the earth thrown out forms the side walls. Upon
this is placed a plate of wood for the support of the rafters, which are
formed of unplaned deal, of light substance, and covered with a water-
proof calico. After the rhododendrons are removed in autumn, such
structures become useful and excellent hybernatories for many plants
that require only slight protection. Ventilation is provided by an aperture being left, the whole length of the roof, at the top, on one side, and
which is covered when not employed by boards attached by hinges to the
extreme ridge, the whole having a span roof. A door is fitted to one end,
and entrance is gained by two or three descending steps. The propa-

ating pit is very similarly constructed, only it is of course glazed and heated. The material used for plunging the cutting pots in is a mixture of cinder ashes and saw-dust, which is found to answer perfectly for this purpose.

Mr. *Smith* has a nursery at *Norbiton*, in Surrey, which has long been favourably known for the seedling azaleas sent out from it, but has of late years come more into note in consequence of the numerous yellow rhododendrons which have here been raised. The colour of these rhododendrons, which varies very considerably, is of course obtained from the yellow Chinese azalea being employed as one of the parents; but although Mr. Smith has been very successful in combining the size and form of the flowers and the mode of flowering in rhododendrons with some of the colour of the yellow azalea, he has not yet been able entirely to secure the excellent habit and foliage of the rhododendron in any of the new varieties. Hence, the latter have, for the most part, a poor and straggling habit, and are only interesting when they are in flower. While the blossoms are expanded, however, some of the new kinds are particularly striking.

Mr. Smith has now about 50 different kinds of the yellow rhododendrons, varying in habit, and having shades of colour from a pale lemon to a light brownish hue. A hybrid of *R. ponticum* is said to be the other parent of these besides the azalea; but the perfection of the form in their flowers seems to ally them more to *R. campanulatum* or *catawbiense*. A good collection of other rhododendrons, and a very large quantity of the various kinds of greenhouse azaleas, are the main things cultivated here. The month of May is the best time to see the yellow rhododendrons and the azaleas in flower.

We remarked that Mr. Smith uses a copper watering-pot, which does not require any painting, and which lasts for an incredibly long period, with proper care. We saw one which had been employed for more than 30 years, and did not appear at all worse for wear.

At *Lea Bridge*, near Leytonstone, there is a very rising nursery conducted by *Messrs. Frazer*, who generally succeed in carrying off some of the highest prizes at the great metropolitan exhibitions. The grounds are extensive, and well filled with the best hardy shrubs; while the houses and pits, which are numerous, are furnished with the most popular plants of the day. This nursery is particularly worthy of note for bringing forward specimen plants for the exhibitions. There large houses are now (in the spring of 1851) well stocked with fine bushes of azaleas, epacrises, ericas, and all those handsome greenhouse species which form the foundation of the great shows at Chiswick and Regent's Park.

The environs of London abound in minor nurseries, particularly about Brompton, Chelsea, &c., some of which are good of their class; but they are so exceedingly numerous that it is impossible to notice them satisfactorily; and we can only pretend to describe the few which, from their size, or the peculiarity of their contents, appear to be the most prominent.

Mr. *Gaines, of Battersea*, is an extensive florist as well as nurseryman, and possesses an immense quantity of indoor accommodation for plants. Pelargoniums are very largely cultivated, and several houses are almost entirely occupied with them. The show-house is a span-roofed structure, rather broader than such houses are commonly made, with a raised shelving stage in the centre, and a large shelved stage at the north end for the fancy sorts. In the months of May and June, this house contains' above 400 distinct varieties of pelargonium, all blooming at the same time. The effect is, of course, a very splendid one. Among novel or peculiar kinds, we noticed the *odorata variegata*, which is remarkably sweet-scented, of a very dense habit, with white flowers; the *cerise unique*, which is a new cherry-coloured bedding kind, with a good leaf; the Hero of Surrey, which Mr. Gaines considers one of the best fancy sorts ; Rollisson's Unique, a good scarlet variety ; Mount Hecla, with a variegated leaf, having a broad white border, and compact heads of scarlet flowers ; and Tournament, the centre of the leaf of which is a very pale green, and the flower scarlet. These are principally summer plants, for beds and borders.

A great many greenhouse azaleas are grown here, as well as the best rhododendrons ; and Mr. Gaines has some excellent and little-known seedlings of the former. In the outside beds, too, there was a first-rate collection of flower-garden plants, including several new and handsome verbenas, and a brilliant scarlet lobelia, with very large flowers, called Victoria. Dahlias are also a very great feature here, and are admirably cultivated. A new dwarf sort was blooming last autumn, which promised to be very useful for growing in beds, as it is singularly low in its habit, has dark leaves, and cherry-coloured flowers, of a good size and form. It is named Prince Arthur. Some of the varieties with striped flowers are very attractive and noble, especially one known as Rachel. Numerous beautiful coniferous plants are also fostered, and among them we saw the *Cupressus funebris*.

In the greenhouses there is a large quantity of plants, fitted for furnishing London houses or parties, and also many specimens. Crassulas, ericas, *Cytisus racemosus*, &c., constituted the staple of the former kinds, while there was a very large *Epacris miniata* among the latter. Cinerarias and calceolarias receive a good deal of attention here, especially the calceolarias, which are beautifully grown. There are likewise a great many fuchsias.

In almost all the plant houses, or at the end of them, there is an open tank for rain water, lined with Roman cement. These tanks are constructed simply of brick, and coated inside with cement, and they never get out of order. About 40 of them are scattered about the nursery, attached to the different houses, the rain water being found invaluable for plants.

Mr. Gaines uses a very simple and effectual boiler for heating some of his houses, constructed by Mr. Spiller, engineer, of Battersea. It is of a somewhat conical shape, open in the centre, supplied with fuel from the top, and having small flue pipes running up through the body of the boiler. It is made of wrought iron.

The garden of *Mr. Groom*, at *Clapham Rise*, is more peculiarly a florist's establishment, and is very rich in all kinds of bulbous plants. Mr. Groom has, especially, long been celebrated as a tulip grower ; and, about the second week in May, the tulips are a great attraction. The bed under canvas is 120 ft. long, and contains 2000 bulbs. The general collection of tulips comprises about 250,000.

Besides tulips, Mr. Groom grows from 1200 to 1500 auriculas, which flower in April ; anemones, which blossom in May and June ; above 50,000 ranunculuses, which are in perfection in the early part of June ; a great many hybrid seedling lilies, blooming in June ; carnations and picotees, which flower in July ; above 90 sorts of gladiolus, blossoming in July and August; the true *Lilium japonicum*, in flower about June; and the varieties of *Lilium lancifolium*, which flower from the end of August to the middle of October. By a little forcing they may be had in bloom from May to October. There is an immense stock of these last, which are admirably grown in the open air.

In addition to these, this nursery contains more than 500 plants of Amaryllises, besides seedlings, blooming at various periods, together with the following, among numerous other beautiful bulbous plants :—

Calochortus luteus.	Phœdranassa obtusa.
,, venustus.	,, chloracea.
,, barbatus.	Rigidella immaculata.
Cyclobothra alba.	Coburgia miniata.
Calliprora flava.	Hymenocallis Harrisiana.
Brodiæa grandiflora.	Caliphraria Hartwegiana.
Tritonia aurea.	Cyclamens of various sorts.

With such a combination of pleasing objects, all of which are very carefully grown, and everything kept in the neatest order, this garden must necessarily be a very interesting one at almost any period from the beginning of May till October. The Japan lilies are, of themselves, a source of the greatest attraction for several months.

Mr. Cattleugh's garden, at *Chelsea*, has been generally considered a first-rate place for florists' flowers. Pelargoniums, calceolarias, and cinerarias constitute the chief features of this class; and there are some large greenhouses in which they are grown. But from part of the nursery being required for building purposes, and from Mr. Cattleugh appearing to give more of his attention to general greenhouse and stove plants and fruit, the florists' flowers do not seem to be so much regarded, and the whole nursery looks out of order. We only saw, as worthy of remark, a good stock of strawberry plants prepared for forcing, and a large quantity of the pretty *Weigela rosea*. Some plants of *Stephanotis floribunda*, *Aphelandra cristata*, and other stove species, were well grown and in good condition.

Mr. Beck's, at *Isleworth*, is a small well-kept place, remarkable for the large numbers of seedling pelargoniums that are raised in it every year, and from among which some of the best and most fashionable varieties now in cultivation have been selected. It also contains a small but excellent selection of orchids. These are grown in the very best manner, under the management of Mr. Dobson, and some of the plants are large. *Dendrobium nobile* obtained the first prize as a specimen at the London Horticultural Society's exhibition last year.

Here may also be seen the best ways of applying *slate* for garden uses. In lieu of the common garden-pots it is employed here extensively and successfully in the shape of tubs, and also for rafters and plates for pits and frames. As an edging for flower-beds its application here is worthy of record. Some object to this kind of edging that it is formal and plain; but that drawback has been obviated in this instance by dividing the part raised above the ground into a series of little semicircles, or scallops, of 3 in. in breadth, leaving a square space of 2 in. between each curve. Where the line is straight, a long piece of slate is used, and cut in the manner thus described; but for curves, smaller pieces have to be employed, and fixed in some firm bedding of masonry.

Slate is also used here for plant stages in the greenhouse, with several advantages, arising from its neat appearance, great durability, and being easily cleaned. A very neat moulding is made to the edges, which imparts quite an ornamental character. Where not subject to blows from any hard instrument, it is in some respects to be preferred to wood, for many garden purposes. The green Devonshire slate is used in several instances, and in respect to colour is preferable to the Welsh. Mr. Beck raises from 800 to 1000 seedling pelargoniums every year.

Of *Market Gardens*, in which extensive forcing is carried on, that of the late *Mr. Wilmot*, at *Isleworth*, is one of the most extraordinary. The number of houses filled with vines and pines is truly marvellous. Pines are here cut every day in the year. They are almost entirely Queens, and are grown in houses which all greatly resemble each other, being slightly sunk in the ground, narrow, low, with that part of the roof which is over the path at the back sloping towards the back wall, and quite opaque, being formed of wood coated with tar. They are heated by hot water, and have a pit in them which is filled with fermenting bark, in which the pots are plunged. All the pines are grown in pots.

The vineries are very similar in shape to the pine houses, and the vines were planted without any preparation of soil for them. Those for the later crops are placed outside the houses. Grapes are cut here all the year round, the Black Hamburgh constituting the staple of cultivation, and West's St. Peter's being grown for the later crops. Within the last year or two several houses have been planted with young vines of the Pope and Mill Hill grapes, from which Mr. Wilmot had great expectations. Two crops of grapes are obtained out of some of the houses. Only the vines used for later crops appear to have been attacked at all by mildew.

This garden contains about 100 acres of land; and Mr. Wilmot was accustomed to say that he grew everything upon it, from a potato to a pine-apple. Of a very excellent French bean, called Wilmot's Early Forcing Bean, he grew an immense quantity.

The garden of *Messrs. Chapman*, at *Vauxhall*, is rather celebrated for grape-growing, which is conducted in a great number of houses, and with signal success. There are other good forcing gardens at Vauxhall, in the neighbourhood of this.

Our object and space do not permit us to say more of the market gardening around London, or to describe that branch of it which is carried on in the open air. We will only remark that it has, in the districts near Fulham, Battersea, Hammersmith, Deptford, and more remote parts, attained a perfection which renders it a beautiful as well as interesting sight to examine the regularity and richness of the crops, the rapid system of clearing and fresh-cropping, and the mode of preparing and packing the produce for market. Perhaps in no one department is English gardening carried to a higher excellence, or managed with more method and skill, than is to be witnessed in the market gardens which supply the metropolis.

THE END.

G. Woodfall and Son, Printers, Angel Court, Skinner Street, London.

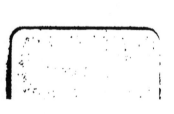

Lightning Source UK Ltd.
Milton Keynes UK
UKHW020659220221
379183UK00010B/828